Eli Ginzberg

Festschriften Series by Transaction

Joseph L. Blau
History, Religion, and American Democracy
Maurice Wohlgelernter, ed.

Herbert Blumer
Human Nature and Collective Behavior
Tamotsu Shibutani, ed.

Werner J. Cahnman
Ethnicity, Identity, and History
Joseph B. Maier and
Chaim I. Waxman, eds.

Rose Laub Coser
Social Roles and Social Institutions
Judith R. Blau and
Norman Goodman, eds.

Gray Dorsey
Law, Culture, and Values
Sava Alexander Vojcanin, ed.

Abraham Edel
Ethics, Science, and Democracy
Irving Louis Horowitz and
H. Standish Thayer, eds.

James W. Fesler
The Costs of Federalism
Robert T. Golembiewski and
Aaron Wildavsky, eds.

Raymond Firth
Leadership and Change in the Western Pacific
Richard E. Feinberg, ed.

Eli Ginzberg
The Economist as a Public Intellectual
Irving Louis Horowitz, ed.

John Hicks
John Hicks: His Contribution to Economic Theory
K. Puttaswamaiah, ed.

George C. Homans
Behavioral Theory in Sociology
Robert L. Hamblin and
John H. Kunkel, eds.

Irving Louis Horowitz
The Democratic Imagination
Ray C. Rist, ed.

Ian Kidd
The Passionate Intellect
Lewis Ayres, ed.

Georg Lukacs
Georg Lukacs: Theory, Culture, and Politics
Judith Marcus and
Zoltan Tarr, eds.

Joseph B. Maier
Surviving the Twentieth Century
Judith Marcus, ed.

Robert K. Merton
Robert K. Merton and Contemporary Sociology
Carlo Mongardini and
Simonetta Tabboni, eds.

Hans J. Morgenthau
Truth and Tragedy
Kenneth Thompson and
Robert J. Myers, eds.

George L. Mosse
Political Symbolism in Modern Europe
Seymour Drescher, David Sabean,
and Allan Sharlin, eds.

Gwynne Nettler
Critique and Explanation
Timothy F. Hartnagel and
Robert A. Silverman

Karl Popper
Critical Approaches to Science and Philosophy
Mario Bunge, ed.

Earl Raab
American Pluralism and the Jewish Community
Seymour Martin Lipset, ed.

Paul Samuelson
Paul Samuelson and the Foundations of Modern Economics
K. Puttaswamaiah, ed.

Pitirim Sorokin
Sorokin and Civilization
Joseph B. Ford, Michel P. Richard,
and Palmer C. Talbutt, eds.

Aaron Wildavsky
Budgeting, Policy, and Politics
Naomi Caiden and Joseph White, eds.

Hans L. Zetterberg
Sociological Endeavor
Emil Uddhammar and
Richard Swedberg, eds.

Eli Ginzberg

The Economist as a Public Intellectual

Irving Louis Horowitz
editor

Routledge
Taylor & Francis Group

LONDON AND NEW YORK

First published 2002 by Transaction Publishers

2 Park Square, Milton Park, Abingdon, Oxfordshire OX14 4RN
711 Third Avenue, New York, NY 10017

Routledge is an imprint of the Taylor & Francis Group, an informa business

First issued in paperback 2017

Copyright © 2002 Taylor & Francis

Library of Congress Catalog Number: 2001053518

Library of Congress Cataloging-in-Publication Data

Eli Ginzberg : the economist as a public intellectual / Irving Louis Horowitz, editor.
   p. cm.
A festschrift in honor of Ginzberg by world scholars.
Includes bibliographical references.
ISBN: 0-7658-0132-9 (cloth : alk. paper)
   1. Ginzberg, Eli, 1911- 2. Economics—United States. 3. Intellectuals—United States. 4. Manpower policy—United States. 5. Medical policy—Economic aspects—United States. 6. United States—Economic policy. 7. Economists—United States—Biography. I. Title: Economist as a public intellectual. II. Ginzberg, Eli, 1911- III. Horowitz, Irving Louis.

HB119.G56 E45 2002
330'.092—dc21   2001053518
[B]

ISBN 13: 978-0-7658-0132-6 (hbk)
ISBN 13: 978-1-138-50946-7 (pbk)

Contents

PART III: The Scholarship of Eli Ginzberg

Introduction

The world of Eli Ginzberg can readily be thought of as a triptych—a career in three parts. In his early years, Ginzberg's work was dedicated to understanding the history of economics, from Adam Smith to Wesley Clair Mitchell, and placing that understanding in what might well be thought of as economic ethnography. Ginzberg's earlier efforts took him on travels from Wales in the United Kingdom to California in the United States. His poignant account of Welsh miners in an era of economic depression and technological change is a landmark work. His memories of a cross-country trip during the first year of the New Deal provide insights and evaluations that can scarcely be captured in present-day writings.

The second period, which commenced with Eisenhower's election as president in 1953, corresponds to Ginzberg's increasing involvement in the practice of economics, in issues related to manpower allocation, employment shifts, gender and racial changes in the workforce, and a growing concern for child welfare and education. His work entailed growing interest in the role of federal, state, and city governments, and he focused on the question of how the public sector impacts all basic social issues. Ginzberg linked the economics of budgeting to the sociology of stratification. His work sufficiently transcended political ideology that seven American presidents sought and received his advice and participation. One might say that Ginzberg was the father of labor and work allocation studies, and thus he is central to the rise of applied economics both before and after the Second World War.

After receiving well-deserved encomiums and congratulations for intellectual work and policy research well done, Ginzberg went on to spend the next thirty years of his life carving out a position as a preeminent economist of social welfare, health services, and hospital administration. It is this latter portion of his life that is the dominant—but not exclusive—subject of *Eli Ginzberg: The Economist as a Public Intellectual.* What is apparent in his work of this period, as well as in that of others, is the growing interaction of all the social sciences—pure and applied—to develop a sense of the whole. The estimable contributors to this *Festschrift,* drawn from a wide network of scholarly backgrounds, have come together to provide a portrait of a figure who spans the twentieth century, and yet points the way to changes in the twenty-first century.

Within the triptych is a unified and singular person. Eli Ginzberg from the start possessed a strong sense of social justice and economic equality grounded in a Judaic-Christian tradition. The spirit of public welfare, philanthropic giving, and a commitment to social justice beyond economic equity all play a part in Ginzberg's work. All of these aspects come together in the writings of a person who has transcended parochial beliefs and given substantive content to the often-cloudy phrase *public intellectual.*

The notion of a public intellectual has been ridiculed by op-ed geniuses who see themselves as the clarion callers of the people, and even more by academic figures who feel that going beyond the parameters of research findings constitutes an illicit extension of their qualifications. This is not the place to argue the fact-value dualism, or what constitutes the proper role of the professional economist or sociologist in the larger society. What does need saying is simple enough: there are serious and overriding issues of public concern in any given epoch. These engage a special cluster of unusually talented and courageous scholars for whom such issues demand the infusion of reason into a context of passion. Economists, like other social scientists, have had their share of contributors to policy-laden issues. Some of them indeed are well represented in this volume. None has a higher claim to being a public intellectual than Eli Ginzberg.

The task of a *festschrift* is difficult enough when celebrating talents who reach the ripe age of sixty-five or seventy. But in properly honoring someone who has gone beyond his ninetieth birthday, and who has had multiple career tracks in which he has made unique contributions, such a task becomes close to insurmountable. Since most of the contributors to this volume are considerably younger in years than Eli, they have a far stronger sense of his contribution to the area of health welfare and service than to his earlier work in human resources, economic sociology, and anthropology. In addition, any sense of the world as it was, say, in the New Deal period—

or for that matter during the Great Society—is mired in obscurity and ambiguity. So the participants in this volume can each contribute a sliver of insight into Eli's life, with the hope that the overall effect is to illumine the larger whole.

It is my belief that the volume succeeds in this goal. It does so because the person behind these multiple achievements is correctly perceived as a single individual. The overall thrust of Ginzberg's work is remarkably well captured precisely by intense examination of the specific parts singled out for scrutiny. In addition, several essays make a valiant, and largely successful, effort to treat Ginzberg whole—as a theoretical unity with practical parts. This is not to say that all the bases, or parts, are fully covered. Ginzberg's work in relation to racial and minority rights, his own strong religious convictions, and his place in the pantheon of Columbia University "greats" are really not amply covered. But then again, these blank spots will allow the editor of some further *festschrift* to complete the picture. For one volume, I think the picture is sufficiently complete as to provide a compelling picture of the person being honored.

One very significant element in a *festschrift* is the importance of the contributors as scholars in their own right. The contributors to this volume are master figures in the history of the social and economic sciences—people who merit special recognition in the form of *festschriften.* As a consequence, the essays herein offered are not paeans of praise or adulation, but often-sharp commentaries of a critical nature. If the highest form of friendship is criticism, then this volume is an ample demonstration of just such regard. Without demeaning or dismissive attitudes toward the person who is the subject of this volume, each contributor, to a greater or lesser extent, uses the essay as a forum to present his own contributions as illumined by Ginzberg—and no less, the shortcomings in his work, real or imaginary, that might lead to a different set of results. The areas of medicine, health policy, and the social status of health workers are vast, and growing more complex over time. In this, perhaps the highest compliment of all can be paid to the present volume: it can be read without a presupposition of foreknowledge of one person's contribution—but as a collective portrait illuminating an area of deep concern.

It has been my good fortune to know Eli reasonably well—at least in his third career period. It has also been my good fortune to have supervised a *Festschriften* series for Transaction that now includes twenty-four volumes of tribute. Eli fits easily in this list, and perhaps even deserves a special place of honor within it. Throughout the long process of gestation and creation, he has been a tower of support—with a proper sense of when to help and when to let the course of events takes its own turn. The volume concludes with five of Eli's recent essays in lieu of a response. He was given that opportunity, but chose instead—I would say wisely—not to respond to individual points but offer a sense of what a man of ninety can still contribute to the great debates of the time. The secret of Eli—which reveals itself to those of his friends who have known him over time—is not his age but his youth. That twinkle in his eyes translates into a sense of intellectual adventure that still very much guides his research and his writings. As a result, while the contributors offer comment and tribute to the past efforts of this protean figure in the history of applied social research, he himself shows what it means to remain at least one lively step ahead of his interpreters.

Let me conclude with an acknowledgment to the contributors to this effort. Each and every contribution was uniquely written for this occasion. The authors were asked to focus directly on the impact or implications of the ideas of Eli Ginzberg on their own work, and invariably did so. Each individual was asked to write in a manner accessible to an educated (but not necessarily specialist) readership. The results speak for themselves. As in all such endeavors, there were delays in completion, compounded by the usual rewrites and updates. So it is hardly surprising that the work appears one year after the actual event of Eli Ginzberg's ninetieth birthday. But we collectively agreed at the celebration of that occasion that this may be a blessed omen—with but twenty-nine years left to go in order for him to reach the age of the supreme Hebrew prophet, Moses.

Irving Louis Horowitz
November 10, 2001

Part I

Personal Memories

1

Eli Ginzberg: Listener and Scribbler

Rashi Fein

Eli Ginzberg's contributions to economics as well as to the formulation of economic policy proposals in various applied areas are many. Given his wide range of interests, his taste for "scribbling," and his long and continuing span of professional activity, it would most assuredly be impossible to select a single essay or volume that all readers would agree best represents the quintessential Ginzberg. There simply are too many worthy books and essays that would compete for that distinction. Yet, though there may be no single quintessential Ginzberg publication, it seems to me there is a quintessential Ginzberg. It is found in virtually everything he has written.[1]

The common thread through Eli Ginzberg's writings, the thread one knows one will find when one examines his earliest as well as his most recent publications, is methodological in nature. That methodology is the unifying force that distinguishes his writings, which would enable a knowledgeable reader to pick up a volume or read an article and immediately know that its author was Ginzberg. To my mind, his methodological approach has been his strength and may well be his most important contribution to economics and to economic policy. Given his important influences on human resource policy and the many contributions he has made to our understanding of the performance of the health sector, the statement that his most important influences may be methodological appears most surprising. Nevertheless, I would argue that might well be the case for two important reasons. The first is that the particular methodology and perspective he has utilized has, to a significant degree, been

Rashi Fein is professor of the economics of medicine emeritus at Harvard Medical School.

kept alive by his efforts over a span of over half a century. In itself that is no mean feat. Its importance leads to the second reason: having been sustained, the methodology remains alive and can be utilized by others. That methodological contribution, therefore, is the subject of this essay.

I begin by quoting from three tributes to Professor Ginzberg. They are found in the *Festschrift* edited by Ivar Berg and published in Eli Ginzberg's honor in 1972, *Human Resources and Economic Welfare: Essays in Honor of Eli Ginzberg*[2]. In that volume, Father Theodore M. Hesburgh, then the President of the University of Notre Dame, wrote: "For Eli Ginzberg the involvement in change began almost thirty years ago, in 1942, with his book *Grass on the Slag Heaps: The Story of the Welsh Miners*. Only a rare eye and sensitive soul would have been cognizant of the plight of the Welsh miners caught in a morass of poverty between the two wars since it, seemingly, had no effect on his own life. Ah, but it did, as in actuality it affected all men, just as the plight of America's deprived today has its impact on our total society."

In the second tribute, Robert M. MacIver, then the Lieber Professor Emeritus at the New School for Social Research, wrote: "His research interests were not restricted to cold facts but extended to the more humane problems of the oppressed and downtrodden. . . I was a trustee of the National Manpower Council of which he [Eli Ginzberg] was then director. . . As a member of the board . . . I had an excellent opportunity to see Eli in action. Very unobtrusively he listened and observed, noting not only the proposals of the Board, but also the warmth, indifference, or degree of enthusiasm of the responses of the various members. . . Every year, often in early spring, he would visit some countries far afield and when he returned with a store of information, he would report on it to our government and he would visit us and tell us the story. His observations were always keen and Eli never lacked the capacity to tell the tale with sprightly conviction and zest."

In the final tribute in the volume, George P. Schultz, then the Secretary of the Treasury of the United States, wrote: "For the past thirty years, Eli Ginzberg has been uniquely associated with the origins of many of the most important developments in the manpower field— both in government and in the academic world. His role has been that of an innovator and stimulator of ideas. . . But let me turn to another side of the man—to Eli the Counselor. . . I appreciated his important role of Counselor . . . when I became the Secretary of Labor. In that office I spent many an hour listening to and participating in the discussions of the National Manpower Advisory Committee chaired by Professor Ginzberg. My most vivid memories of this Committee's work are not the long discussions but rather the remarkable letters which he would send to me and the Secretary of Health, Education, and Welfare summarizing the Committee's recommendations and observations. These letters should be studied as models of precision, tact, and wisdom. His unusual ability to synthesize and summarize the deliberations of committees made up of people of quite different backgrounds was constantly demonstrated through the NMAC letters. He was able to 'feel' a consensus without soliciting votes and bring forth agreement of Committee members on some of the more difficult problems of our society. . . As a cabinet official, I studied these letters with care, knowing full well that I was reading more than the deliberations of a committee, that I was in the fortunate position of hearing from a wise counselor who had read extensively, studied long, observed carefully, and could deal with practical issues."

I digress for a moment to note that the letters Secretary Schultz refers to were published.[3] I note further that I have encouraged every former student who has had the opportunity and responsibility to serve as a member or as the chair of a standing advisory committee to read that volume. Among other things, one learns that much can be accomplished if one has and pursues a long-term goal (an agenda) and has a strategy (a procedural plan) that addresses that agenda even while responding to the needs of those who sought advice. Indeed, if one reads carefully and with an eye both to style and substance, one might well conclude that collection of letters might take its place as the quintessential Ginzberg!

If one were to make a list of keywords and phrases found in the tributes cited, one would discover that they include: "listened," "observed," "feel a consensus," "observe carefully." Eli Ginzberg's most basic personal characteristic is described as "a keen eye and a sensitive soul." His approach and behavior is certainly captured in Professor MacIver's phrase: "he would visit some countries far afield and . . . [he] *returned with a store of information* . . . [my emphasis]" At a time when many, if not most, economists did their research without leaving their offices (except, perhaps, to go to the library), Eli Ginzberg was "in the field." Instead of studying the data others had gathered—presumably to describe various aspects of the world which they thought interesting and/or revealing—Ginzberg adopted the "novel" approach of going out into that world, making his own observations (including gathering his own data) that might illuminate the questions he felt should be asked, and listening to and synthesizing the answers. Furthermore, and most importantly to Professor Ginzberg, data did not necessarily mean quantification. Attitudes, values, traditions, history, human aspirations and foibles, all these were also were data. The world he examined could not be captured alone in numbers. Qualitative research stood on a par with quantitative and the word "data" applied to both the qualitative and the quantitative.

At an American Economic Convention some many years ago, perhaps in the early 1950s, a young Paul Samuelson debated Fritz Machlup on the use of mathematics in economics. In today's world, the notion that the issue was debatable seems startling. Those without a sense of the history of the discipline of economics may not appreciate the intensity of the debate and the forms it took, e.g. would mathematics be accepted as meeting part of the requirement that Ph.D. candidates had to exhibit proficiency in two foreign languages? It may seem odd, and the more so when one considers that even Machlup, who argued that mathematics was important but had a limited use in economics, seldom came into the classroom without his compass and dividers and used geometry (after all, a branch of mathematics) to enlighten his students about Joan Robinson's views on imperfect competition. As I recall, in the rebuttal arguments Samuelson turned to Machlup and pointed out that Machlup should not be so disturbed about mathematics, that it was no more than a "language," but a very special and powerful one whose utility and strength derived from its precision. It was a language that did not permit vagueness, expressions like "sort of," or contradictions. Mathematics was only a language, a very precise language, but it could only say what otherwise might appear in words. My recollection is that an urbane Machlup turned to Samuelson and asked: "A language? Like English, but more precise? Paul, how does one say [and now a dramatic pause] 'I love you' in mathematics?"

I do not know whether Eli Ginzberg attended that AEA convention and, if he did, whether he heard the exchange that I report. But

Ginzberg's printed record does more than suggest that Machlup's comment would have struck a responsive cord. I offer evidence to support that conclusion. In May 1962, with support from the U.S. Public Health Service and the National Institutes of Health, the Bureau of Public Health Economics of the School of Public Health, as well as the Department of Economics of the University of Michigan, sponsored and hosted the first "Conference on the Economics of Health and Medical Care."[4] This was a significant event in the area of academic study called "medical care" and an important development in the history of what became the field of health economics. Conference papers and comments were presented by a most distinguished group of "general" economists. In part, this reflected the fact that there were very, very few economists who were known as health or medical economists or individuals whose exclusive, or even primary, area of interest was the health care system. In part, of course, the attendance by what might have been called "mainstream" economists reflected the fact that most economists were generalists and, by definition, mainstream. The profession had not yet entered today's highly fractionated world of specialization and sub-specialization.

Not surprisingly, Ginzberg attended the Conference. He delivered the first paper in the introductory session on "The Role of the Economist in the Health Services Industry." As he put it, the paper was presented "to provide guidance to the panelists." Its title (compare Machlup's comment on mathematics) was "Medical Economics—More than Curves and Computers." The paper was prescient for it was delivered well before the development of the ubiquitous desktop personal computer. In 1962, "computer" meant a mainframe device to which very few economists had even limited access. Nevertheless, Professor Ginzberg saw what was coming and in his paper he revealed his skepticism about the future of medical economics and, as well, his recipe for a successful effort.

On the former, Ginzberg, aware of the developing interest in medical economics, suggests the danger that the field "[may go] the way of academic economics [with] advances in economic methodology, not in health programming. For the current interest may result in many intricate manipulations of variables with the aid of calculus and the computer which may not significantly advance the understanding of...the economics of health. The likelihood of such an untoward outcome is increased in direct proportion to the *lack of knowledge of economists concerning the structure and functioning of the relevant institutions* [my emphasis].” The paper goes on to provide numerous illustrations of the health sector's special characteristics and of the behavior of key actors (read: “physicians”) who, in large measure, determine how the sector functions. These characteristics and behaviors, often at variance with the sorts of models that economists bring to their analyses, lead to a series of questions that Eli Ginzberg felt economists should address. It does not come as a surprise to find that most of the questions remain valid analytical issues and describe problems the American health care system has not yet “solved.”

In concluding the brief, but packed, paper, Professor Ginzberg summed up his point of view: “The best mix for medical economics would include 1 part of economic concepts to ten parts of institutional knowledge to 20 parts of social judgment.” That recipe should not mislead us. I rather suspect that in allocating about three percent to “economic concepts,” he equated that term with “curves and computers” and fancy mathematical analyses. In the context of his paper, the term was shorthand for the dangers medical economics faced. Nevertheless, the fact is that Ginzberg's analytical thought patterns were (and remain) those of someone whose professional growth took place within the world of economic concepts and ideas. Those concepts accounted for far more than three percent of his insights and his success.

I recall returning to Johns Hopkins University a few years after I began teaching at the University of North Carolina (Chapel Hill). I met with the chairman of my Ph.D. committee and told him how troubled I was: I had not used any of the tools I had learned during my years of graduate study in economics. I had not drawn a single price discrimination curve! More than that, some non-economists had read my dissertation, which reported on interviews with general practitioner physicians regarding their choice of practice locations, and understood it! I was troubled that all this offered evidence that somehow I no longer was an economist. In responding to my concern my chairman attempted to reassure me by arguing that economics involved patterns of thought and ways of looking at a problem. The fact that people understood my questions and their significance did not mean that they, in other disciplines, would have asked the same questions. What made one an economist was not the frequency with which one drew a price discrimination curve (and by, extension, used a computer), but the nature of the questions one asked and the way one approached and thought about a problem.

That answer applies to Eli Ginzberg's comment about "economic concepts." Whether he likes it or not, he is an economist. He may suggest we need only one part economic concepts, but that is simply because his use of economic concepts is so deeply ingrained that he may be unaware that they are ever present. Ginzberg's use of economic concepts reminds one of Molière's *Le Bourgeois Gentilhomme*: "Good Heavens! For more than forty years I have been speaking prose without knowing it." If, indeed—perhaps, especially if—medical economics is more than curves and computers, it requires more than one part economic concepts. Of course, Professor Ginzberg's publications provide ample evidence that he knows and uses sociology, political science, psychology, and history—that is, other social sciences and humanities—but the framework for his observations and analyses is that of economics. An earlier and richer economics (economics as social science and intellectual pursuit rather than economics as applied mathematics) to be sure, but economics nonetheless.

Ginzberg's recipe includes "institutional knowledge and social judgment," the very characteristics that the three tributes I cited earlier refer to (albeit their authors use different words). Institutional knowledge is gained by observation, by obtaining answers to questions (questions that, in Professor Ginzberg's case, derive from his education as an economist), and by listening. Social judgment, I believe, is his way of describing and emphasizing his sense of the political reality, of the need to take account of institutional frictions and sources of opposition, of what is and what is not possible. On that, as on all matters of judgment, scholars and those involved in the public or private political world (the university, the modern corporation, the different levels of government) will differ. Inevitably, the various assessments will reflect different time horizons and degrees of patience.

Ginzberg seeks change, but believing that change occurs in a slow and measured way, he has an abundant supply of patience. That, surely, is the reason he writes policy analyses and proposals rather than manifestos. His policy prescriptions reflect his priorities; they also reflect his sense of the doable. While he has described himself as "the skeptical economist,"[5] I would suggest if one wants to probe beyond his relationship to his home discipline of economics, that a broader appropriate title might well be "the caring moderate."[6] The "moderate" describes his judgments that changes that occur too rapidly increase the probability of untoward side effects, that were we to take more time these side effects could be mitigated and, thus, the changes would be more effective. Even change—perhaps particularly change—should come in moderation. The "caring" takes account of his concern for others, most especially those who have been and remain left out, who do not have the opportunity to reach their full potential. It is no accident that he has been associated with the "conservation of human resources" all these years and that that activity has paid special attention to the condition and to the needs of African-Americans. While, taken literally, his recipe suggests that social concern is not a necessary ingredient in creating a successful medical economist—the recipe prescribed "social judgment" rather than "social concern" —it most assuredly is a necessary ingredient in the mix that makes up Ginzberg the man and that is reflected in his various books and articles. Father Hesburgh's comments about *Grass on the Slag Heap* refer to social concern. As others see him, social concern is an important ingredient in the kind of medical economics Professor Ginzberg practices. Furthermore, I believe that though Ginzberg did not prescribe it for others, he meant to do so, for he would consider it an important ingredient in assuring relevance, in itself a necessary ingredient in successful medical economics.

The institutional approach that characterizes Professor Ginzberg's work has been evident from the very beginnings of his professional career. It was visible in his first published volume: *Grass on the Slag Heaps: The Story of the Welsh Coal Miners*[7] (note the use of the word "story" —surprising for its daring—by an economist). Perhaps, earlier, he was drawn to his doctoral dissertation topic, *The House of Adam Smith*[8] (the first book-length study of *The Wealth of Nations*), by the fact that, among many other things, Adam Smith was a most careful observer and recorder of the world around him. Certainly Ginzberg's future methodological trajectory was evident upon completion of his doctoral dissertation when he accepted the William Bayard Cutting Traveling Fellowship that, in 1933-34, took him across the United States and permitted him to interview senior executives of forty of the largest American corporations. I stress that his task was to interview executives rather than to examine company annual reports. It is true, of course that the use of the interview technique and the view that we could learn from answers to interview questions was not uniquely his. It had a long tradition in economics and was part of the institutional economics approach practiced primarily by labor economists. What is unique (or, in any case, rare) is that Ginzberg did not discard the institutional approach or the exercise of social judgment even as "mainstream" economists came to scorn "institutionalism" as insufficiently rigorous (more like journalism at worst or sociology at best[9]) and to dismiss judgment as non-objective and to place too high a value on "relevance" rather than on advancement of the discipline of economics.

The latter point merits additional elaboration. It is not an accident that the three tributes cited earlier all stressed Ginzberg's contributions to committees and commissions. Indeed, the comments derive from intersection between the authors and Professor Ginzberg in those venues. Of course, an examination of his rich and long bibliography reveals important contributions to our understanding outside of commission and committee reports. Nevertheless, it is important to understand that, as he himself has stated: " From the end of World War II until the end of 1981 I led a double life between teaching and doing research at Columbia and being steadily involved in consulting work for the federal government including in particular the Department of Defense and the U.S. Army; the Labor Department where I served 13 Secretaries of Labor; the Department of State under whose auspices I visited about 40 foreign countries to study and assess their manpower policies; and still other agencies of the federal government such as the General Accounting Office."[10] It is difficult to imagine that there was any single other economist outside of government who was more involved with the federal government than he. Nor is it likely that there was any other individual from any discipline or sector who wrote, consulted, or testified on as many diverse issues. In some sense his various writings read like committee reports (on occasion, a committee of one). Indeed, they were reports to the reader and were organized in that way: they stated the problem and described its significance, analyzed its characteristics, suggested what might occur in the absence of action, presented a menu of proposed actions, and offered a research agenda that would add to our understanding and knowledge. His publications certainly reflected the fact that he spent time in Washington and at Columbia.

Nevertheless, the important point to recognize is that the world of Columbia and the world of Washington, in fact, were not worlds apart. In terms of the nature of his work and interests, Professor Ginzberg did not lead "a double life" at all. The world of Washington informed his work at Columbia and the world of Columbia research was carried with him to Washington. There simply is no question that the work done in each venue was enriched by the work carried on in the other. It is certainly the case that without the research activities that he and his collaborators were engaged in at the Eisenhower Center for the Conservation of Human Resources his contributions in Washington would have been far less informed, persuasive, or influential. It is also the case, however, that without experiences gained in Washington, the selection of issues to be examined back in New York would have been far less nuanced, rich, or important.

The corollary point that should be made explicitly is that, consciously or unconsciously, Ginzberg selected the audience to whom he would address his work. In general that audience was the informed individual who might apply the information and concepts provided. I do not mean to downgrade the interest with which professional economists might read his work. Nor do I mean to downgrade how much specialists in human resources or health care or education or discrimination studies (to mention only a few of the many areas that his work addressed) might learn from his articles or books. I mean, instead, to emphasize the applied nature of his efforts and the fact that he did not place a premium on contributing breakthroughs in methodology or in general economic theory. Given the audience he wanted to address and to influence, it made sense to publish in the journals that practitioners might read (e.g., "The Journal of the American Medical Association") rather than the journals whose primary audience was likely to be comprised of fellow economists (e.g., "The American Economic Review").

I cannot leave that subject without taking note of a special characteristic of his work. Few of his colleagues (indeed, no other name comes to mind) have been as prolific in examining substantive applied areas of human activity, constructing a list of questions that, if investigated, would illuminate these various activities and add to our knowledge and understanding, and thus, provide the profession with a "research agenda." These research agendas, often appearing as reports and essays, sometimes the concluding section of a more general report, and sometimes reflected in the works he organized—the essays he commissioned and edited—have provided a theoretical structure to the fields he addressed. They helped inform policy and have helped build fields of scholarly inquiry.

So, too, it has been with the field we call medical or health economics, a field that in no small measure was built by Professor Ginzberg. Perhaps he will choose to write a book on the history of medical economics. If so, it is a pity that the logical title, *Present at the Creation*, has been preempted by Dean Acheson[11]. Ginzberg's first book in the medical economics area was published in 1948[12] (it goes without saying that his most recent book in that field—I write in 2001—appeared in 2001[13]). Indeed, he was present at the creation. There were very, very few medical economists in 1948. Those who defined themselves that way most often worked for the Social Security System or the Federal Security Agency, the precursor to the Department of Health, Education, and Welfare. They gathered data on health expenditures—numbers preceded by the economic common denominator, the dollar sign, but did little analytic work of an economic nature. Furthermore, it is doubtful that any chairs of economics departments came to the annual American Economic Association convention looking to add a medical economist to their faculty roster, and that remained true for many years after 1948.

That situation has changed markedly. In part, of course, the growth in the number of medical economists reflects the growth in health services research, a direct result of the rapid expansion in the size of the health sector and in the proportion of the GDP accounted for by national health expenditures. In part, the expansion of medical economics reflects the contribution of a number of mainstream economists whose interest in the area has served to legitimize it to the profession at large. Of course, a very substantial role was played by Eli Ginzberg through the (by my count) thirty-three books and monographs in the health field he wrote or edited. The breadth of their subject matter underlines their significance. They range from examinations of health care in New York City and in other urban communities to system-wide questions that affect the nation. Similarly, they examine different kinds of health care services: from nursing to hospital care; from physician services to home health care. Nor does this exhaust the breadth of topics. They also include an examination of various target populations: young people and children at risk, AIDS patients, and health care for the poor. Ginzberg has also examined issues in biomedical research, medical education, and the role of academic health centers. Thus his contributions built a field, not a niche product.

We are misled if we conclude that the various titles reveal only the wide interests of the author. They illuminate the difference between the health policy work of Ginzberg, a medical economist, and the work classified as health services research, the current fashion among many (though, of course, not all) who call themselves health or medical economists. Of course, health services research is "where the money is." That is what the federal government, in particular, supports through grants and contracts and is what many young scholars believe health policy is about. There is a world of difference, however, between the significance of the questions asked and the methodologies used in those studies and the issues raised and methodologies pursued by Ginzberg. Without exception, in examining important questions, his books offer insights and provide a framework for the reader. That is inherent in the methodology. The important epidemiologist, Alex Langmuir, who founded the Epidemic Intelligence Service as part of the (now called) Centers for Disease Control and Prevention (CDC), believed in "shoe-leather epidemiology." The term described the philosophy or methodology: get out into the field, gather the data, absorb the smell and character of the community or place where you find the problem you are investigating. Ginzberg's methodology is that of "shoe-leather economics."

I conclude with one last vignette that I believe illuminates the importance of the "listening" part of his methodological approach. I recall a meeting, chaired by Professor Ginzberg, of the Board of the Manpower Demonstration Research Corporation (MDRC). I attended because the subject of the meeting was a paper that I had written, as I recall it, about needed research that the MDRC might want to undertake. The discussion was vigorous and wide-ranging. As the hour approached for the meeting to end, Ginzberg, in his role as chairman said: "Let me tell you what I've heard." I leaned over and expressed astonishment at the notion that he could summarize what struck me as a discussion in which there were as many points of view as there were participants. As I recall it, he accepted my comment as a challenge and said something like: "Just watch." I did, and learned that there is listening and there is listening. Where I, and, I suspect, some of my colleagues had heard discord, he picked out the agreements and heard harmony. Where I heard a rambling discussion, he heard a recurrent theme. Where I heard a series of disconnected statements, he heard continuity. His summary suggested that what for me was a stimulating and interesting day, for him was a day from which, by listening carefully, he had been able to extract and distill agreement about next steps for the organization. I concluded that I did not know whether he did or did not enjoy music, but that if he did it was because he knew how to listen and to hear that which many of us miss. I concluded that, if he had devoted himself to musical criticism, we would all have enjoyed reading the program notes and reviews he would have written.

The title of this short essay is "Eli Ginzberg: Listener and Scribbler." In truth, the best source on this subject, the one that best explains how he developed the methodology and why he believes in it, is found (not surprisingly) in his own book, The Skeptical Economist. I suggest it is the case that to be a skeptical economist one must first be a realistic political economist, one who respects history, social and moral philosophy, and the various other disciplines that contributed to the development of the discipline that came to be known as "political economy." While that term has virtually disappeared, there still remain those who, in fact, practice political economy, who understand the importance of institutions, and who gain their knowledge of how particular institutions function by asking relevant questions and listening to the answers. They are the "keepers of the flame." Among those who retain the conviction that economics is a social science and whose contributions reflect that belief, Eli Ginzberg ranks high.

Notes

1. I would write "everything," but use the qualifier "virtually" because honesty would compel all of us to admit that we have not read everything Eli Ginzberg has produced.
2. Berg, Ivar (ed.), *Human Resources and Economic Welfare: Essays in Honor of Eli Ginzberg*, New York: Columbia University Press, 1962.
3. National Manpower Advisory Committee, Eli Ginzberg, Chairman, *Manpower Advice for Government: Letters to the Secretaries of Labor and of Health, Education, and Welfare 1962-1971*, Washington, D.C., U.S. Department of Labor, 1972.

4.   *The Economics of Health Care: Proceedings of the Conference on the Economics of Health and Medical Care, May 10-12, 1962*, Ann Arbor: The University of Michigan, 1964.

5.   Ginzberg, Eli, *The Skeptical Economist*, Boulder CO, Westview Press, 1987.

6.   I recognize that this phrase comes close to another one in current use, "compassionate conservative." While the latter would be appropriate, it has been appropriated. Now that it is part of the political vernacular, it might conjure up images that would be troubling to some and praised by others. In neither case would the phrase be viewed as neutral and descriptive rather than evaluative.

7.   Ginzberg, Eli, *Grass on the Slag Heap: The Story of the Welsh Miners*, New York: Harper and Brothers, 1942.

8.   Ginzberg, Eli, *The House of Adam Smith*, New York: Columbia University Press, 1934.

9.   Among some economists this order is reversed.

10.   Correspondence by Eli Ginzberg, prepared at the request of Irving Horowitz, March 22, 2000.

11.   Acheson, Dean, *Present at the Creation,* New York: W. W. Norton & Co., 1987.

12.   The Committee on the Function of Nursing, Ginzberg, Eli, Chairman, *A Program for the Nursing Profession*: New York, Macmillan Company, 1948.

13.   Ginzberg, Eli, et al., *The Health Marketplace: New York City 1990-2010*, New Brunswick, N.J.: Transaction Publishers, 2001.

2

The New Era as Seen by a Young Man

Robert M. Solow

One risk that comes with a very long and very productive career is the likelihood that even fairly attentive readers may eventually forget that writer's earlier work, or not even know that it exists. It is a safe guess that most of the contributors to this volume think of Eli Ginzberg mainly as a contributor to the literature on the distribution of healthcare, or as a participant in the public discussion on the labor-force participation of women and minorities and other aspects of manpower policy. Some will know that the precocious Ginzberg's first book—published when he was twenty-two—was a study of Adam Smith and his immediate predecessors and successors in political economy.

At just about that time he was awarded a travelling fellowship, and used it to go about the country interviewing high officers of a number of major corporations—mostly, but not entirely, manufacturing companies, as would have been natural for the period. One of the products of that enterprise was a book entitled *The Illusion of Economic Stability*, published in 1939, when the (still-precocious) author was twenty-eight, and the depression of the 1930s was barely at an end. As my tribute to my old friend on this occasion, I propose to discuss this book. It is not at all like archetypical Ginzberg either in content or in style, but I think it does have some intellectual or attitudinal affinities to the later and more familiar work of its author.

It was not this sort of continuity, however, that led me to *The Illusion of Economic Stability*, but rather a different kind of historical artifact. We now tend to think of the long boom of the 1920s as

Robert M. Solow is Foundation Scholar at the Russell Sage Foundation in New York City.

the prologue to, or even the origin of, the crash of 1929 and the depression of the 1930s. Of course, the business-executive protagonists and, with very few outliers, the standard contemporary commentators on the scene did not see it that way. The phrase that was coined at the time to encapsulate the long prosperity was "The New Era." Now *that* rings a bell. It would have taken only a stray neuron fired a millisecond earlier to have invented instead an alternative slogan—like "The New Economy" just for instance. That is the parallel between the 1920s and the 1990s that interests me.

Needless to say—as one normally says of something that needs to be said—the mostly manufacturing-based, and still non-trivially agricultural, economy of the 1920s has little texture in common with the much richer, technologically more advanced, and mostly service-based economy of the 1990s. The particular common response that I want to discuss is the belief that somehow the rules and generalizations had changed, that the future would be utterly unlike the past, that the new era (economy) was *sui generis*.

Here I want to be clear about my own take on the meta-question. The young Ginzberg is plainly cynical about all that careless talk of The New Era. He can suppress the occasional sarcasm only with difficulty, and sometimes not at all. (Remember that he was writing in 1939 after two downturns and ten years of depression.) It is not so clear whether his preferred view is that (a) the basic truths of economic theory are, if not eternal, at least enduring, and unlikely to make a convenient exception for the new era, or that (b) any talk of enduring abstract truth is its own illusion, and mildly analytical description is as deep as it gets. On that second view, the New Era talk was a fatuous error, but might conceivably have turned out to be valid. On the first, it was intrinsically implausible from the word *Go*.

Unlike the young—or the old—Ginzberg, I am a model-builder by inclination and training. I like to quote the Oxford philosopher John Austin who said something like: "One would be tempted to call oversimplification the occupational disease of philosophers if it were not their occupation." So too for economic theorists. But I believe rather strongly that the "right" model for an occasion depends on the context—the institutional context, of course—but also on the current mix of beliefs, attitudes, norms, and "theories" that inhabits the minds of businessmen, bankers, consumers, and savers. In this way, I end up not so far from the young Ginzberg, though not exactly in the same place.

A subsidiary analogy between the 1920s and the 1990s is the significance of the stock market boom that characterized each period. *The Illusion of Economic Stability* does not dwell in a serious way on finance-theoretic insights into the bull market of the 1920s, and I do not want to make any refined analogy with the 1990s. But I do want to comment in due course on the young Ginzberg's observation that he had witnessed an episode of what he could fairly have called "irrational exuberance," if that phrase had occurred to him.

Speaking of phrases, I want to comment very briefly on the style and tone of the book. The prose is tighter and more aphoristic than later Ginzberg, and the tone is more detached, even sardonic. I do not know where this came from, if it came from anywhere in particular. Young Ginzberg certainly did not imbibe it from mentors like A. F. Burns and J. M. Clark, although some of his ideas about business cycles do come from them, as will be seen. I hear a little Thorstein Veblen in the prose, and indeed Veblen is cited more than once. The style is not the man, really, so no inference is to be drawn. But the observation is worth making.

If an illusion of economic stability suffused the 1920s, summed up in the phrase about The New Era, what was its origin? The first 28 or 29 percent of the twentieth century were, on the whole, pretty good years, especially contrasted with the two major depressions of the 1870s and 1890s. It is true that there had been a very sharp and painful recession just after the first World War; but, as Ginzberg points out, that could be categorized as war-related and therefore extrinsic, and therefore not part of the inescapable normal shape of things.

True enough, as Ginzberg says, but he then goes on to offer a less obvious and more interesting suggestion. During the early 1920s the "scientific management" movement hatched the notion that seasonal unemployment and the parallel excess capacity could be smoothed away by regular production for stock. Notice that this was a firm-by-firm proposition, not a macroeconomic stabilization scheme, although stability at the firm level would imply aggregate stability. To be able to use inventories to buffer production from seasonal shifts in demand, firms would have to offer price incentives or other rewards to buyers who would commit to long-term purchase agreements. Alternatively, they could integrate forward, absorb retail outlets, and again pursue price variation to smooth production.

Apparently these efforts met with some success. Young Ginzberg notes that *that* may have been an illusion, induced by the generally buoyant macroeconomic trend. Even so, one can see how business executives might have told their interlocutor that they had in fact found the key to stability of sales, profit and employment.

Another possible contributor to this mind-set was the "doctrine of high wages." That pat phrase set off a vague echo in my head, but it is a doctrine that has not survived. It was live at the time, according to young Dr. Ginzberg. He reports that sticky nominal wages and falling prices after the slump of 1920-21 left real wages fairly high. This state of affairs proved compatible with prosperity, despite earlier calls from the business community for rolling back wartime wage gains.

The natural explanation was that American manufacturing had achieved high productivity gains and unprecedented efficiency. Foreigners came to observe and admire. A virtuous-circle argument then went on to claim that high wages were actually necessary for a high productivity economy, because they created the mass market that was needed to buy the resulting flood of goods and allow the exploitation of scale economies. It appears that more than a few employers bought into this idea.

In actuality, nominal and real wages rose only very slowly after 1924. The doctrine of high wages rested neither on theory nor on practice, but on faith. The young and already cynical Ginzberg commented that "... more important than the facts were the encomia showered upon the doctrine by labor and capital alike. Criticism can seldom withstand enthusiasm, for enthusiasm is always strongly motivated." That does not sound like the diplomatic sage we celebrate today. The young Dr. Ginzberg apparently had a sharp tongue in his head. Besides, it has to be admitted that there was an ample supply of tempting targets. The same could be said about similar effusions today. Maybe there is something about periods of prosperity that encourages "enthusiasm." If you like to look for parallels between The New Era and The New Economy, this might be one.

If the young Ginzberg already knew that perpetual economic stability is and was an illusion, he must have had an inkling why. It is clear from the text what sort of theory of the business cycle was in his head. The main influences were his teachers, Arthur F. Burns (especially *Production Trends in the United States since 1870* [1934]) and John Maurice Clark (especially *Strategic Factors in Business Cycles* [1934]). He had also absorbed Wesley C. Mitchell's *Business Cycles* (1927) and Frederic C. Mills's *Economic Tendencies* (1932), but they seemed to play a somewhat smaller role in his thinking.

There is a faint aroma of Morningside Heights about this collection of influences. I do not know enough to judge whether it reflects a little Columbia University parochialism or merely the absence of any other contemporary guides to the understanding of economic fluctuations. There are a few references to J. M. Keynes's *General Theory of Employment, Interest and Money* (1936) in the second half of the book. But it is not surprising that the Keynesian way of looking at prosperity and depression had not penetrated systematically into Ginzberg's thinking. I know from experience that a freshman taking an elementary course in economics 200 miles north of Manhattan in 1940-41 would have been entirely innocent of any notion about aggregate demand.

Instead *Illusion* emphasizes the idea that any major goods-producing industry in a national economy will trace out a lifecycle beginning with accelerating growth and ending in retardation, saturation, and sometimes even decline. In the case of The New Era in the United States, the principal actors in this drama were the automobile and construction industries, with smaller roles played by electric utilities and the producers of household durables. The main initiating factor was the S-shaped industrial life cycle learned from Burns; and the main transmission mechanism was the acceleration principle learned from Clark. These forces, Ginzberg suggests, were far too strong to be countered by the froth that made up the talk of a New Era.

From this view, the prosperity of the 1920s was carried mainly by the diffusion of the automobile and its accessories, the building of a street and highway network, and the consumption expenditures of the enlarged travelling public as well as the investment expenditures of the businesses that catered to the needs of the travelling public. The consequent shrinking of distance, combined with the growth of the population (natural increase plus immigration), in turn encouraged a boom in both public and private construction, along with a complementary demand for the articles that furnish a house, a store, an office or a factory.

Any such boom will eventually run up against the limits of space, of need, of a lack of new buyers. There is no reason why autos and construction should be replaced by some other industries at just the right time. As soon as the leading industries start to slow down, however, the industries that provide them with plants and equipment will experience absolute declines, because the demand for investment goods is proportioned to the increase in the output of the leading industries. An industry whose production grows *more slowly* needs *less* new capacity. And so the downturn comes.

This kind of account would not carry so much analytical conviction today. It might do as an after-the-fact description once a downturn has occurred. Not all industries will turn down together; those that do will slow before they contract; and the acceleration principle will magnify the effect on the capital-goods sectors. But the analogy to inevitable, almost biological, senescence is not so convincing. We are now more likely to think that income and expenditure can expand together, while the built in, though irregular force of innovation leads to new industries and therefore new objects of expenditure. The dynamics of this process can be very complicated. The business cycle seems less like a determinate sequence, and even less so when it is amplified or damped by the credit mechanism (as the young Ginzberg knew perfectly well).

To take the obvious contemporary analogy: what looks (in March 2001) like the end of the New-Economy boom in the U.S. will very likely take the form of a retardation and then a contraction in the production of computers and peripherals. At least it is the bad news in the sales and profits of Compaq, Dell and IBM, as well as the glamorous software producers that captures the headlines. But a modern macroeconomist would not be content with an explanation that rested on a simple "sooner or later it was bound to happen" argument. Some sort of complete, self-contained model would be required, equilibrium-style or disequilibrium-style. The modern fashion in macroeconomics would not take the aging of a basic industry as an exogenous event requiring no further explanation.

It is worth noting that Eli Ginzberg could not be expected to think in those terms in 1939; the intellectual infrastructure was just in the wings. It is also worth noting that a good causal account of the depression of the 1930s is still a matter of professional controversy, model or no model. What Ginzberg found worse than implausible was the addled belief that it could never happen.

Addled beliefs we have always with us, and they may even have a family resemblance over a time span as long as that between the

1920s and the 1990s. That similarity might be explained by a common source in wishful thinking. Deeper analogies between The New Era and The New Economy are rather less convincing. On the evidence of his book, the young Ginzberg was not given to facile historical parallels.

The very high rate of business investment in the 1990s reflected large purchases of information processing equipment and software, even more so if some communications equipment is added. That category accounted for less than a quarter of non-residential fixed investment in 1991, but just about half in the last quarter of 2000. Headlines suggest that the computer and software industries are major carriers of the assured slowdown and potential downturn of early 2001. The prominently displayed bad news comes from IBM and Dell and Compaq, and Cisco and Yahoo, not to mention the easy-come-easy-go dot.coms.

Is the computer-software complex the source of the economic softness, or does it just reflect sharp deceleration elsewhere? It will take a longer run of data before any careful analysis can be done, but that is not the point I want to make here. It seems very unlikely that medium-to-long-run saturation can be the core of the story of the end of the 1990s, as Ginzberg thought it was at the end of the 1920s. The uses of computers and software seem to be much more open-ended than the uses of automobiles and construction. The analogy to a population of fruit flies expanding into a limited space seems much less appropriate now than it may have been then. On the other hand, the acceleration principle still rings true. It is hardly cause for surprise if the slowdown of consumer spending—which was being actively sought by the Federal Reserve and wished for by others— should be reflected in an absolute decline in the most popular form of investment.

Ginzberg was careful not to dwell on the stock market, and I shall follow his sound example: too volatile, too psychological, too tenuously connected to fundamentals, in the short run at least. It is probably safe to say, however, that the "real" economy and the level of the stock market are not independent of one another. The connection—between the cost of capital and investment, and between personal wealth and consumption—may be somewhat closer today than it was in The New Era, mainly because nowadays a vastly larger fraction of all families owns some equities, directly or through pension funds. If a volatile stock market has an influence on aggregate spending, that is one more reason why the illusion of (automatic) economic stability has much the same status today as it did when Eli Ginzberg wrote. It would be a mistake collectively to forget what we had learned in the meanwhile about the need to work at macroeconomic stabilization.

3

Eli Ginzberg: A Man of Many Parts

Victor R. Fuchs

"One man in his time plays many parts." So wrote William Shakespeare in *As You Like It*, describing the changes in appearance, responsibilities, and capabilities that occur over the lifecycle. Eli Ginzberg has played many parts, but has managed the extraordinary feat of playing them *contemporaneously* for well over half a century. He has been a teacher, researcher, adviser to presidents, mentor to young scholars, prolific author, dynamic public speaker, and wise counselor to scores of friends, colleagues, and heads of non-profit institutions. Moreover, Ginzberg's vigor, enthusiasm, and mental acuity continue unabated as he enters his tenth decade.

To assess Ginzberg's contributions in his many roles (and in many fields) is an impossible task. I shall limit my attention to his work in health, and focus on his special mission as teacher, preacher, and adviser to physicians through his contributions to the *New England Journal of Medicine* (NEJM) and the *Journal of the American Medical Association* (JAMA), two prestigious journals that have published many of Ginzberg's most important attempts to inform and influence health policy discussions. I note in passing that he has also contributed to a wide variety of other health journals, such as *Academic Medicine, American Pharmacy, Arizona Medicine, Health Affairs, Hospital and Community Psychiatry, Israel Journal of Medical Sciences, Journal of Health Care for the Poor and Under-served, Journal of Neurosurgery,* and *Nursing Outlook.*Even limiting my review to the NEJM and JAMA presents a major challenge. Ginzberg

Victor R. Fuchs is Henry J. Kaiser Jr. Professor Emeritus at Stanford University and a research associate at the National Bureau of Economic Research, Inc.

began contributing articles, editorials, and commentaries to these journals more than forty years ago, and has kept up a steady pace of one or two pieces per year until the present. I shall try to sketch a brief picture of the man and his thought that emerges from these contributions, and then review in more detail his discussions of physician supply, competition, and managed care.

The Man and His Thought

Skepticism, realism, and empathy are three central features of Ginzberg's personality and mindset that are evident in the writings I have reviewed. Ginzberg is skeptical that government can effectively manage health care, skeptical that competition will solve the problems of medicine, and especially skeptical of the desirability of managed care (at least as he defines it). While conceding that managed care helped control the growth of health expenditures in the 1990s, primarily by squeezing providers and limiting access to specialists and hospitals, he has no confidence in managed care over the long run.

His skepticism arises in part from a theme that echoes and re-echoes throughout these pages: "The future is uncertain." Thus, he is particularly wary of proposals that rely upon firm predictions about future economic, political, social, and technological developments. Despite his skepticism, however, he thinks it is possible to learn something from the past. He believes that experienced investigators and observers have an obligation to share their *judgments* with those who must make decisions in the face of uncertainty; he is not satisfied with simply calling for "more research." He states his opinions clearly, and he tells the reader the basis for those opinions.Ginzberg's realism shines through in his discussion of public policy and the political process. In discussing the failure of the Clinton attempts to achieve universal coverage, he dismisses most of the conventional explanations that emphasize the role of special interests or poor presentation: Ginzberg attributes the failure to the fact that the public has conspicuously displayed a lack of interest in supporting universal coverage ("Reform in Early 21st Century," p. 2, *JAMA*, 1998). Unlike many other commentators, he understands the difference between the reassuring answers the public gives pollsters and its willingness to accept radical restructuring of the health care system.

I vividly remember a small conference of leading health policy experts that Ginzberg chaired at Cornell University Medical School in February 1992. At the beginning of the conference Ginzberg invited each participant to say a few words about the current policy scene and about the possibility of significant progress during the next few years. Almost without exception, each expert declared that the public was ready for the major policy changes that he or she had been advocating for decades—usually some form of national health insurance. Ginzberg looked at me and rolled his eyes as if to say, "What have they been smoking?" While never wavering in his own belief that the U.S. *should* have universal coverage, he never deluded himself or others that Americans were ready to support the changes necessary to achieve that goal.

In a biting critique of a National Academy of Sciences report on VA health care in 1978, Ginzberg set out his view of the proper way to give policy advice. He wrote, "Sensible policy advice in a democracy requires a carefully reasoned defense of a new goal—the more so if the costs of achieving it involve the elimination of a functioning institution. It behooves the proponents to consider the process of obtaining the necessary political consensus to venture such an attempt...and the staging of the reform must be rooted in reality, not expectations." The NAS committee's recommendation to abolish VA health care was based, in part, on its view that passage of national health insurance was imminent (this was in 1978!). When he read that, Ginzberg's eyebrows must have shot upwards toward the sky. He noted that national health insurance, "has been on and off the nation's agenda since 1912, and it is difficult to identify the political consensus required to turn it from plan into reality" (p. 625, "The National Academy of Sciences Report on the VA: How Not To Offer Congress Advice on Health Policy," *New England Journal of Medicine*, 298(11):623-5, 1978, March 16).

Though a skeptic and a realist, Ginzberg has never lost his empathy for the poor, for the chronically ill, and for the health problems of minorities—especially Blacks and Hispanics. (See, for example, "Medical Care for the Poor: No Magic Bullets," *JAMA*, 259(22):3309-11, June 10, 1988, and "Access to Health Care for Hispanics," *JAMA*, 265(2):238-41, Jan. 9, 1991). He has also written sensitively about the position of female physicians, nurses, and other women in the health field. Many of his contributions address concerns in these areas, but always with a hard-headed view, not seeking villains or imagining that there are easy solutions to difficult problems. In my judgement, Ginzberg maintains a fine balance between optimism and pessimism. A cynic observed that an optimist thinks that this is the best of all possible worlds; a pessimist is sure that it is. Ginzberg does *not* think this is the best of all possible worlds; he believes that a combination of clear thinking and compassion could bring us closer to such a world—but he is not sure that it will.

Physician Supply

Ginzberg has never hesitated to challenge conventional wisdom. Nowhere is this more apparent than in his continued critique of studies and projections that urged a huge increase in the number of American physicians. More than forty years ago in a letter to the *New England Journal of Medicine* (Correspondence, "Cautionary View of Medical Care," *NEJM* 262:367, 1960), Ginzberg expressed great skepticism of the view that "the impending shortage of physicians threatened to undermine the strong American system of medical services." He followed this with a short contribution to the *New England Journal of Medicine* six years later critiquing a series of reports and conferences all recommending substantial growth in medical school enrollments. His reasons show his deep understanding of health economics and the workings of the health care system. To enumerate them is to provide a lesson for all who would venture into this perilous area.

Ginzberg first pointed out that the projections assumed a rate of population increase of 2 percent per annum, even though the rate at that time was only 1.3 percent. (Subsequent growth was even slower.) Second, he questioned whether rising real per capita income would necessarily translate into an increased demand for physicians' services, suggesting that its greatest impact was likely to be on the demand for additional nursing services. He then took up the question of "slack" in the utilization of physicians' time. With respect to surgeons, Ginzberg was right on the mark, as my colleagues and I reported in our study of surgical workloads. We found that the average surgeon was performing the equivalent of four herniorraphies per week (about four hours in the OR), even though most said that ten would be a satisfactory workload, and the busiest one averaged thirteen per week. (Hughes, Fuchs, Jacoby, and Lewit, "Surgical Work

Loads in a Community Practice," *Surgery* 71(3):315-27, March 1972).Ginzberg's fourth point concerned possible gains in physician productivity through more extensive use of physician assistants, nurse practitioners, and other physician "extenders." He thought that pediatric care offered particularly promising opportunity for such gains. One of the arguments advanced by advocates of a huge increase in the number of physicians was the need for the United States to help raise the health standards of developing nations. Here Ginzberg wisely pointed out that "Asia and Africa need sanitarians, veterinarians, and public health nurses" more than they needed physicians (Eli Ginzberg, "Physician Shortage Reconsidered," p. 86). In a similar vein, Ginzberg questioned the argument that a substantial increase in the number of American physicians would do much to alter the imbalance between physician population ratios in wealthy urban centers and poor rural areas.

Next, Ginzberg took on the controversial issue of "over-doctoring." He referred to the suspicion that a great deal of unnecessary surgery was being performed, partly because so many surgeons were underemployed. He also questioned whether there was great virtue in conventional annual physical examinations.

Ginzberg then turned his attention to the question of the relationship between increases in the number of physicians and the health of the population. He pointed out that "It was generally recognized that the control of cigarette smoking, of diet, of sexual promiscuity, and of reckless driving offers potentially large gains in the public health; no connection was made [by those advocating an expansion of physician supply] between this fact and the limited role of physicians in achieving these objectives"(p. 86). Ginzberg's closing arguments were of great importance to all health policy analysts, and particularly to health economists. He stated "Physicians are in a position to create their own demand. They often have wide margins of discretion whether to ask a patient to return to the office for one or more follow-up visits" (p. 87). He noted the rapid rate of increase in health care expenditures and stated "One sure way to accelerate this rise is to increase the number of physicians... The effective use of physician manpower depends in the first instance on a taut supply of physicians" (p. 87). He had special scorn for those economists who naively believed that a big increase in the number of physicians would, through price competition, reduce their average earnings and therefore be socially beneficial. He predicted, "Only a vast oversupply would bring average earnings down, and then only at the individual and social cost of over-doctoring. Given the alternatives of high average earnings for a taut supply of physicians and a loose supply, lower earnings and over-doctoring, I opt unequivocally for the first" (p. 87).

This review of a two-and-a-half page commentary written by Ginzberg more than a third of a century ago illustrates the breadth and depth of his thinking, his ability to focus on central issues, and his skill in anticipating questions that would continue to plague health policy for the rest of the twentieth century.

In a 1983 JAMA commentary (Ginzberg, "A New Physician Supply Policy Is Needed," *JAMA* 250(19):2621-2, Nov. 18, 1983), Ginzberg returned to the physician supply issue with a succinct review of the many factors that must be considered in formulating a rational policy for physician supply. He noted that an increase in the physician/population ratio of 50 percent over the preceding decades had done little to change the "so-called specialty and geographic maldistribution" (p. 2621). He urged the AMA and "its allies" to recommend "at least modest cutbacks in future admissions to U.S. medical schools" (p. 2622), and again criticized those economists who were fixated on driving down physicians' earnings through increased supply.More recently Ginzberg discussed physician supply policies with special attention to the critical role played by physicians with regard to most of the issues of health care reform ("Physicians' Supply Policies and Health Reform," *JAMA* 268(21):3115-8, Dec. 2, 1992). For instance, Ginzberg wrote, "No serious analyst can afford to address the problem of cost-containment without focusing on the training of physicians and how physicians practice medicine" (p. 3115).

In this piece he continues a theme raised in earlier commentaries regarding the improper use of medical care: "There is a growing body of empirical evidence that a large number of questionable, if not detrimental, diagnostic and therapeutic procedures are sought by patients and performed by physicians based on a mistaken confidence in their efficacy… Clearly, quality improvements in health care must start with the physicians" (p. 3116).

While skeptical of, if not downright hostile to, managed care in many other pieces, Ginzberg, in this context, took a more positive tone, writing "Managed care can be defined as an environment in which groups of physicians working collaboratively have the opportunity to practice quality medicine in a way that discourages unnecessary and wasteful procedures" (p. 3116). His role as a skeptic continues, however, when he adds "Whether managed care develops into a major modality of health care provision or sputters along as a promise unfulfilled will depend ultimately on whether physicians find it a satisfactory, in fact a preferred, way to practice" (p. 3116).Ginzberg concludes the piece with three recommendations concerning physician supply policies. First, he would increase funding for the National Health Service Corps with scholarship support conditional on a commitment to future service in an under-served area. He recommends that this service be closely integrated into mainstream medicine by assigning young physicians as staff members to a community health center or clinic with the support of allied health workers and that it be associated with a hospital network. Second, with respect to graduate medical education, he recommends that Medicare "use its power of the purse to try to redress the imbalance between the number of medical school graduates training in the subspecialties and those training in primary care by restricting or limiting its funding for graduate medical education to the period required for initial board certification in a primary care specialty, general surgery, or specialty in short supply such as geriatrics." He would not supply funding for the further training of most specialists and subspecialists. His third recommendation concerns the shortening of the total period required for the training of a physician. He would have medical schools consider admitting college students upon completion of their junior year of college with the award of a baccalaureate degree at the end of their first year of medical school. Along the same lines he recommends that the clinical training sequence integrate the two years of undergraduate clerkship and the first three years of residency training into a unified four-year program. If these recommendations were followed, there is a potential reduction of two years in the normal eleven-year period from entrance to college to initial certification.

In summary, Ginzberg sees the issue of physician supply as much broader and deeper than simply a question of the physician/population ratio. Equally, if not more important, are questions concerning the length of the training period, the kind of training received, the financing of undergraduate and graduate medical education, and the deployment of physicians in medical practice. In all this he hopes to enlist the support of the medical profession itself. As he says, "Without active physician participation nothing will change, surely not for the better" (p. 3116).

Competition and Managed Care

My respect for Ginzberg is so great that I feel he would not want me to ignore areas where we have modest disagreement, most notably in his commentaries concerning competition and managed care. In general, he has been skeptical that competition can play a useful role in health care, but that skepticism must be reconciled with his appreciation that incentives do matter, that government regulation has its defects, and that it is no longer feasible or desirable to return to a guild-like system of complete control by the medical profession. This would seem to leave a significant (albeit not dominant) role for competition. His hostility to managed care seems to be directed mostly toward a particular variant—namely the large for-profit corporations he thinks make unreasonably big profits. He doesn't seem comfortable with the idea that managed care can take many different forms, some of which Ginzberg actually approves, as evident in his own writing.

In an early (1980) commentary on competition, Ginzberg offered a temperate critique of Alain Enthoven's Consumer Choice Health Plan (CCHP). This plan was developed by Enthoven at the request of Joseph Califano, Secretary of Health, Education and Welfare in the Carter Administration, but was ignored by Califano and Carter. Ginzberg approved, in principle, of several of the most important recommendations in the plan: 1) A ceiling on nontaxable employment-based health care benefits; 2) a requirement that employers offer a choice of at least three plans which met minimum standards—employees would bear the extra cost or benefit from the saving depending on which plan they chose; 3) plans should include deductibles or co-payments.Ginzberg's reservations concerned the political feasibility of these proposals as well as a belief that neither the supply nor the demand side of the market would respond quickly to the new incentives. He noted that consumers had repeatedly demonstrated a preference for first dollar coverage; he worried about the effects of competition on teaching hospitals, and he was sure that consumer choice would do little or nothing about the problem of the uninsured. Ginzberg wrote, "Tax revision, consumer incentives to choose among competing plans, and coinsurance all have something in their favor as ways of increasing competition in health care delivery and of slowing the rise in health care costs" (p. 1114). But he added, "I believe that the CCHP vastly overestimates the potential effectiveness of these remedies and vastly underestimates other factors influencing the steady rise in costs" (p. 1114). Although on balance he was not persuaded by Enthoven's CCHP, Ginzberg concluded his commentary by saying, "We are still in his debt for forcing us to think more deeply and more critically about the shortcomings of the existing system" (p. 1115) ("Competition and Cost Containment," Sounding Board piece, *New England Journal of Medicine* 303(19):1112-5).By 1983, Ginzberg's attack on anything suggesting a role for competition in health care had become more fierce, as evident by the title of a JAMA Commentary, "The Grand Illusion of Competition in Health Care." The increase in ire appears to have been provoked by the Economic Report of the President in 1982 which offered a rather simplistic view of how easy it would be to introduce competition into the medical marketplace and how great would be the benefits flowing from such introduction. Much of Ginzberg's piece consisted of a lucid exposition of all the reasons why medical markets differ substantially from markets where competition works well. These reasons are familiar to most health economists and many, if not most, would agree with Ginzberg regarding them. One of Ginzberg's shrewdest observations concerns the fact that even "some of the pro-competitive group recognize that the fair competition that they seek among health delivery systems requires the government to set the rules about such critical matters as benefits, premiums, enrollment periods, subsidy levels, rebates and regional cost differentials." Ginzberg concludes his attack on "radical reform...centered on price rather than quality" by arguing that this is not necessary, nor desirable, and not even feasible (Commentary, "The Grand Illusion of Competition in Health Care," *The Journal of the American Medical Association* 249(14):1857-9, April 8, 1983).

Support for Ginzberg's reservations about the usefulness of a simple price competition model for medical care can be found in a recent article in *The New York Times* about e-business auctions (Tom Redburn, "How Much Am I Bid For This Imperfect Marketplace,"

The New York Times, December 13, 2000, p. 6). The article describes the difficulties encountered by early attempts to create competitive auctions for business-to-business transactions on the Internet. It quotes Stanford University Economics Professor Paul Milgrom as saying, "Price isn't everything...in fact it's rarely the most important thing." The article goes on to state, "Most business deals involve differentiated goods and services turning on factors like quality, convenience, and reliability, as well as price." To all of this Ginzberg would say, "Amen." If this is true of transactions between business firms, how much more true is it of multi-dimensional medical services involving transactions between a professional provider and a relatively uninformed and emotionally involved consumer?The point is well illustrated by the story of the surgeon who was famous for his skill in performing a particular operation and also notorious for his high fees. He was visited by a businessman who was an especially hard bargainer. After the examination, the surgeon confirmed that the businessman did indeed need this operation. The businessman, ever wary, said, "How much will it cost?" The surgeon replied "$25,000." "My," said the businessman, "That's an awful lot of money. Can't you do it for less?" "Certainly," said the surgeon, "I can do it for $15,000." Then the businessman became even more wary. He said, "I don't understand. How is it possible for you to do it for $25,000 and then say you can do it for $15,000?" "Very simple," said the surgeon, "For $25,000 I use my new instruments and my old assistants. For $15,000 I use my old instruments and my new assistants."

In 1995 Ginzberg adopted a more ambivalent tone to express his reservations about competition and managed care (Commentary, "A Cautionary Note on Market reforms in Health Care," *JAMA* 274(22/29):1633-5, Nov. 1995). He wrote "Conceivably, expanded reliance on the market may prove no more efficacious than expanded reliance on the federal government to correct the prevailing ills of our current health care system" (p. 1633).

He conceded that price competition may moderate increases in private health insurance premiums, slow advances in the cost of prescription and over-the-counter drugs, and contribute to slowing the rate of health expenditure increases on other fronts (p. 1635). But he noted that the competitive market cannot provide coverage for the uninsured or speed the adoption of health-preserving behaviors. His final word was one of caution rather than attack: "Without denying that managed care may be able to contribute to the solution, the public should be warned against undue expectations" (p. 1635).Two years later, Ginzberg (with co-author Miriam Ostow) was again a harsh critic of managed care ("Managed Care—A Look Back and a Look Ahead," Sounding Board, *NEJM* 336(14):1018-20, April 3, 1997). This piece, however, far from emphasizing the large profits earned by managed care organizations, predicted that these profits would probably disappear. With regard to future enrollments in managed care, the authors wrote of "the high probability of continuing increases in enrollment" (p. 1019). On the following page, though, they said "Still other signs on the horizon challenge the prospect of uninterrupted growth in enrollment in managed care" (p. 1020). The authors wrote approvingly of efforts of large physician groups or integrated hospital-physician plans to "compete" with managed care plans. Many health policy specialists include such groupings under the concept of managed care.Ginzberg's most recent piece on managed care (as of December 2000) is a celebration of the criticisms encountered by managed care ("The Uncertain Future of Managed Care," Sounding Board, *NEJM* 340(2):144-6, 14 Jan. 1999). Strangely enough, the very first paragraph notes (with apparent satisfaction) the fact that Kaiser Permanente posted a loss of about $270 million in 1997. The not-for-profit Kaiser organization was not one of the Wall Street-driven for-profit corporations that attracted so much of Ginzberg's criticism in earlier writings. Ginzberg carefully recounts all the difficulties encountered by managed care organizations in the second half of the 1990s and notes the complaints and dissatisfaction of patients and physicians in managed care plans. No doubt some managed care organizations have behaved badly, but Ginzberg knows as well as anyone that long before managed care some physicians also behaved badly. No doubt some patients experienced bad outcomes under managed care while others were disadvantaged or inconvenienced. But again, Ginzberg knows that before managed care, some patients had bad outcomes while others were disadvantaged and inconvenienced. For all the buzz about the evils of managed care, there has not been any systematic evidence showing an adverse effect on the health of the U.S. population during the 1990s.

As an explanation of current dissatisfaction with managed care, Ginzberg's critique suffers from failing to analyze the divergent trends in health care expenditures and the growth of GDP per capita in the

1990s. As the nation entered the decade, health care expenditures (deflated per capita) were climbing at over 6 percent per annum; at the same time GDP growth was slowing to less than 2 percent per annum. Both private and public payers demanded restraint of health care expenditures, and managed care did answer that call. The rate of growth of health care expenditures fell sharply, reaching about 2 percent per annum by the middle of the decade. At the same time, the economy was booming. By the mid-1990s health care expenditures were growing less rapidly than GDP, a situation unprecedented in living memory. With profits, wages, and incomes all soaring, it is hardly surprising that the public became unhappy with a health care system whose prime objective was to hold down expenditures. Attention to these divergent trends would add perspective to Ginzberg's critique.I have tried to understand Ginzberg's hostility to managed care, and tentatively offer a "geo-semantic" explanation. The geo portion refers to the fact that Ginzberg is, and has always been, a New Yorker. And more than a New Yorker: a Manhattanite. He knows the great teaching hospitals of Manhattan, where the affluent, the well insured, and the well connected could expect the finest care available. He also knows that these hospitals have a tradition of providing similar care to the very poor who were fortunate enough to be their patients. But what of the working class families in the outlying boroughs or the less affluent suburbs of New York who might be receiving care ranging from very good to very bad? If Ginzberg had been living on the West Coast for the past half century, he would have observed Kaiser Permanente, the Group Health Cooperative of Puget Sound, and other managed care organizations delivering comprehensive, good quality care to millions of working and middle class families at lower cost than traditional providers. He would have seen Kaiser's pioneering efforts to develop a more rational approach to hospitalization, and would have seen them focus on the elimination of care of "dubious value." And he would no doubt have approved of such efforts. Thus, one's view of "managed care" is partly a semantic issue.

Concluding Comments

Eli Ginzberg has been an extraordinary unique force in discussions of health policy for over four decades. He has used his experience, wisdom, and formidable expository skills to provide physicians with superb "continuing education" through his contributions to the NEJM and JAMA. It is to the credit of the editors of these journals that they readily made space available to him, even when he was critical of medicine's conventional wisdom.

Personally, I have benefited enormously from Ginzberg's insights and advice and from his encouragement of my own forays into health economics. A letter from him saying that I seemed to be on the right track or that my research was useful meant more to me than acceptance of an article by a journal. Although most of this essay is written in the past tense, it is with great joy that I note that Ginzberg is writing, teaching, lecturing, and advising at an astonishing pace. Long may he continue! As the rabbis said, "His work was before him; his reward was with him."

4

Thinking about Health Care in the United States and Great Britain: A Half-Century Perspective

Rosemary A. Stevens

It would be nice to say that if Eli Ginzberg did not exist, he would have to be invented. Alas, no one could. He is unique: towering figure in health policy analysis, slayer of the sacred cows of mainstream thinking (his own words), sounder of the alarm, voice of reason. "Our society has a high level of tolerance for arrangements that work," he once remarked, "even if there is little logic to commend them." He says such things with fire and vests them with the force of truth, never bored with educating new audiences and adherents. The sheer size and range of his work is staggering. Last summer I noted 150 book titles attributed to Eli Ginzberg in the Stanford University library holdings. One of them, *The House of Adam Smith* (1934), was in the rare books collection. The library did not yet have Eli's latest book, *Teaching Hospitals and the Urban Poor* (2000), which greeted me in the mail when I arrived home in Philadelphia.

As a long-time admirer of Eli Ginzberg's brilliance in defining large themes for a culture led by narrower specialists, I want to attempt some comparative thoughts about the history of British and American health care over the past half-century. (For the sake of simplicity, I will concentrate on England.) In the Ginzberg tradition, let me incorporate some personal history into this quest. I come from

Rosemary A. Stevens is a member of the faculty of the College of General Studies at the University of Pennsylvania.

England, worked as an administrator in the National Health Service (NHS) in my twenties (I am now in my sixties), and have written about it on many different occasions, though most of my career in the history of medicine and health policy has been in and about the United States. I was an English schoolgirl when the NHS was implemented in 1948. Like other children, my siblings and I had suffered a raft of infectious diseases, including whooping cough, chickenpox, mumps, and scarlet fever—conditions that have long been eliminated from normal childhood. Like other middle-class children, I had been raised on good nutritional principles, and had consumed the ubiquitous wartime supplements of black-current puree and cod-liver oil. Like others, I had benefited from the new wonder drugs: the sulfa drugs from the late 1930s and penicillin after World War II. Health and medicine were entering a new phase. Infectious diseases were on the wane; chronic conditions increasingly visible. On neither side of the Atlantic were the professional and organizational institutions of health care appropriately designed in 1948 to deal with these new conditions.

The fifty-four years since 1948 have been a testing ground for organizational and economic experimentation in health care on both sides of the Atlantic. For much of this period, though, comparative historical analysis was constrained by Ginzberg's "sacred cow" of ideological and political perceptions. There seemed little to say about health care in Britain that might be useful to Americans, except in its role as part of the British welfare state, with its in-built assumptions of universal access to health services, care provided free at the time of use, top-down budgeting, and government control of health providers. Celebratory comparisons could be couched in the political virtues of capitalism, stressing proud reliance on the private sector for health insurance and health provision in the United States—and often ignoring the fact that this was also a policy strongly buttressed by government through direct subsidy and tax provisions. Before the end of the Cold War and the reconstruction of welfare states in many western countries, including Great Britain, the NHS provided a useful ideological gloss and cautionary tale in debates about health care reform in the United States. The "socialized medicine" that Americans sourly observed in post-war Britain—bastion of the welfare state—seemed to express more general privations associated with socialism: lack of choice, rationing, regimentation, and drabness. In contrast, the American free-enterprise health care system was overtly associated with technology, innovation, and consumer choice—and higher costs and waste seemed a small price to pay for this exuberance.

In 1946, when the NHS Act was passed (it was implemented two years later), the U.S. Congress was in the midst of considering the Wagner-Murray-Dingell proposals for universal health insurance. By 1950, national health coverage was a dead political issue in the United States. Private health insurance became the norm of coverage for working age Americans, supported by tax breaks to employers, and later by Medicare and Medicaid. Also in support, major federal investments have been made in infrastructure over the years, notably in biomedical research (transforming medical schools around a model of medicine as science and encouraging medical specialization); in construction subsidies to community hospitals (confirming the central importance of hospital medicine); and in professional education. Compared with the overt and central role of the government in health in England, with its nationalizing of hospitals and regulation of practices, the role of government in health in the United States was downplayed, decentralized, and covert. Today, tax money accounts for 60 percent of America's health budget (this includes the health insurance paid for government workers), while the funds flow mainly through private insurers, as in many countries, and private vendors largely provide the actual health services.

So distinctive have the political arrangements for health care been in the two countries that it has been easy to assume differences rather than similarities in all aspects of health care. Two basic points deserve more attention than they have been given. First, there *are* common long-term themes. For example, in both countries there has been a blurring of public and private roles, continuing attempts to link primary and specialist services, concerns about chronic conditions and serious deficiencies in long-term care, and more recently about bringing medicine fully into the information age and providing effective consumer information. Second, no one has, or has had, a definitive road map for change. The world of health care has changed rapidly since World War II, and there has been no simple baseline against which success or failure can be measured. As Rudolf Klein has observed, the cognitive framework for thinking about health services has shifted too. It has become common to talk about purchasing and commissioning, providers and performance indicators, clinical guidelines and outcomes assessments—a vocabulary unfamiliar for health care only half a century ago.

A major common theme has been (and still is) how to organize hospital, specialist, and primary care, and their relations to each other. In the first twenty-five years of the NHS (1948-73), the greatest organizational success of health care on both sides of the Atlantic was the development of hospital services; and the greatest failure was the relative neglect of general practice—actually of primary care as a whole. Hospitals became more important centers of medicine in the 1950s and 1960s. Private health insurance took off in the United States after World War II, supported by federal policy, and this spectacular growth of insurance coverage fueled the expansion of hospitals and specialists. Concurrently, England set up hospital regions under the NHS, and though it controlled the number of specialist positions and their distribution by specialty and by area, here too specialization became a major theme over the next decades, together with supporting hospital resources. NHS attempts to rationalize hospital and specialist services in its first twenty-five years may be judged a qualified success. Meanwhile, the U.S. was learning that expansion through subsidizing institutions was relatively easy, while rationalizing (or rationing) health services was only effective where it was linked to major money streams. And the money streams were largely in the private sector.

Actually, the American goal for hospitals in the 1940s and 1950s, like that of the NHS, was rational hospital planning, under the Hill-Burton legislation of 1946. However, the states (which were supposed to carry this out) had too little economic or political leverage over jostling interests and little incentive to plan effectively. Hospitals, like other health services in the U.S., continued to develop piecemeal, place by place, eventually becoming ripe for takeover and mergers. Systemic coordination of hospitals, nursing homes, community and other services at the local level was proposed in U.S. legislation in 1966, which provided incentives to set up comprehensive health planning agencies at the local level. There were at least 150 such local planning agencies in 1974. That same year the NHS was reorganized for a similar purpose: to provide a more unified and integrated health service at the local level by coordinating hospitals, community services and family practice. Government-sponsored planning efforts were to founder in the United States and quietly disappear. In England, the effort was abandoned in favor of the idea of more powerful managers, and later by efforts to redesign the health service on more competitive principles through creating a so-called "internal market" of providers and purchasers. In both countries, by the 1990s, there was much greater belief in the efficiency or magic of market mechanisms than in previous decades. Internal markets failed as a political stratagem in the NHS, leading it to upheaval once again, while managed care is still with us in the U.S., though discredited in many ways and ripe for greater regulation.

Parallel problems existed in medical practice over the decades. General practice, with or without part-time specialist work, was the dominant form of medical practice in both countries in the late 1940s (about 75 percent of British doctors and 60-65 percent of American practitioners). In Great Britain, the NHS sustained the GP's function in primary care, but isolated primary from specialist care. In the United States there was a free-for-all competition for patients among generalists and specialists in private practice, tipped toward specialization by the availability of insurance for specialist services and strong public belief in experts. By the 1970s, virtually all American doctors were specialists, though many of these were doing at least some primary care.

In England, the initial top-down organization of the NHS into separate hospital/specialist and primary care services made it difficult to coordinate GP and hospital services effectively. In the United States, an obvious organizational solution to growing medical specialization was to link GPs and specialists together into multi-specialty groups. However, Congress had rejected national health insurance proposals (which might have effected this) in the 1940s, and group practice was officially opposed by organized medicine. There were no major economic or organizational levers for such change until the potential of managed care in the 1990s, and this proved illusory too. Current patterns are of predominantly small-scale medical practices and groups comprised of single specialties. Looking back, it seems odd that in both countries the potential scientific roles of primary care were subordinated for so long to the more visible accomplishments of hospital practice, for the role and potential efficacy of the generalist was changing, demonstrated by an armory of new medications and the expanding usefulness of diagnostic tests. In the

U.S. in the late 1950s, an estimated 40 percent of the drugs then being prescribed had not been available five years before. Today the costs of prescription drugs are rising more rapidly than any other item of health expenditures.

In England there has been the organizational anomaly that the GP was able to prescribe powerful drugs but not, on the same day as this, to order an x-ray, have it read, and be able to give the results to the patient. The anomaly in the U.S. was fragmentation by specialty. Middle-class parents, for example, take their children to the pediatrician, and themselves to specialists in internal medicine, obstetrics, orthopedics, or any other field, scattering their treatment as well as their family's medical records. How to coordinate services, in the interests both of better patient care and professional satisfaction, and the practical difficulties of achieving coordination, have been powerful common themes of the past half-century. The difficulties range from meeting major capital requirements for start-up costs, to bringing together unwilling, even warring parties (doctors versus doctors and doctors versus hospitals) and expecting them to mesh together smoothly. Recent experience of Physician-Hospital Organizations (PHOs) in the United States shows how difficult this is. It was left to the market in the 1990s to try to reinvent and empower primary care through the etiquette of insurance rules, but a simple "gatekeeper" model (a model not unlike the model in England), with restricted access to specialists, was doomed to failure in the American setting, with managed care the convenient villain.

Why has it been so difficult over the years—in either country—to organize primary care as a branch of high-technology medicine? In-built conservatism—resistance to change by the health professions—may be part of the answer. Lack of financial incentives to change is clearly important (including lack of funds for health centers in the early years of the NHS, and a similar lack of funds for health centers under the American Hill-Burton program). But part of the answer has to be the enduring power of cultural myths in medicine. The archetype of the old-style GP in Great Britain—counselor, confidant and friend—a myth valued by both GPs and patients, presumed a role for primary care that was antithetical to the specialist culture, as well as to the organizational constraints imposed on other parts of the health care system. Even now, the shift to large-scale organization of primary care practices, a computer on every desk, standard clinical protocols, and clinical information networks, are sources of concern to doctors who should stand to gain from the information revolution. The United States has had its own myths. Primary care has long been regarded as "unscientific," despite the fact that the formal specialty of family medicine was ratified by a specialty certifying board over thirty years ago. "Research," as valued by the culture of the medical school and reinforced by funds flowing from the National Institutes of Health, tends to mean research based in the laboratory and on highly specific clinical research, rather than broader outcomes research with a sociological or population focus. On both sides of the Atlantic, the last fifty years have demonstrated a need for primary practitioners who are sophisticated scientists and who can work in systems or networks, but have offered few guidelines as to how to get there. The current NHS experiment of creating and empowering primary care groups as the central organizing mechanism for medical care looks promising, at least for that medical culture where primary doctors and specialists remain distinct species. In the U.S., multi-specialist practice is a more logical development, but not one that can be foreseen at present.

Comparisons of health care (or other subsections of the economy) between countries may, of course, tell us much more about the culture of each country than about the subject under investigation. Is it because of, or despite, the NHS that public opinion polls in Britain compare health services with the police and schools? Is it because of the belief that we have a private health care system that Americans are more inclined to compare health services with airlines or banks? Historically, the social goals of health care in the two countries have been different. A primary U.S. goal has been to spread medical technology across a vast nation, on the analogy of democratizing access to electricity, TVs, or (now) computers, while the English have seen health care more as a social service. However, today neither rationalization really works. Technology is expensive, and social services are out of the mainstream. It would be easier to compare the two countries if one could evaluate more clearly what each has achieved in relation to the broader economy. The U.S. commits twice as much of its GDP to health care as Britain and tolerates the existence of a large uninsured population, but supports a high level of care for those within the system and thriving pharmaceutical and biotechnology industries, and there is little overt rationing of technology. What would happen in each country if their relative health expenditures were equivalent? We do not know. At the risk of oversimplification, the last half-century of the NHS can be described as a constant search for rational organization of primary and population care without antagonizing the medical profession or spending too much tax money—and the U.S. system has a similarly constant search for a way to cover the entire population without limiting high-technology medical services, or their growth in a high-tech economy.

From the British perspective, the U.S. system has had the advantage of being able to change direction without blaming government. A basic pragmatism enables Americans to use government programs *or* the market as situations change. The existence of the NHS has ritualized change as government fiat, and led to constant upheavals in the organization of the NHS. The market-oriented managed care movement of the last decade in the U.S. followed the failure of public efforts to integrate services and provide them more efficiently. Now the insurance companies, not government, are shouldering the blame for rising costs, demoralized professionals, and disappointed consumers. Meanwhile, NHS leaders have been struggling as how to best achieve a structural balance between the perceived advantages of decentralized competition (with potential variations in organizational style and efficiency) and government guarantees of comprehensive, universal service. A new vocabulary has marked these various changes: consensus management, general managers, internal markets, and clinical governance. Historian Charles Webster has called the last decades of the NHS a period of continuous revolution: a phrase that carries undertones of exhaustion, frustration and yearning—either for the apparently more settled past or a new status quo in the future. But one might also use this catchy phrase here too. In the United States, changes in the organization of health care have been more or less continuous since the 1980s. They include the rise of for-profit and not-for-profit hospital systems, corporate organization (and disorganization) of physicians, and the destabilization of the academic medical center. The NHS has been distinguished by continuous turmoil but discontinuous policy shifts, making specific changes more visible. From an American perspective, Britons get overly anxious about change. In England, nevertheless, the organization of health services stands fully exposed to public criticism, while the United States has the advantage of a more diverse, even amorphous set of villains. What the U.S. system will look like five years from now is not clear, but the same could be said about services in England.

Has the NHS been a success or failure? And what about the lavish, inequitable, problematic system in the U.S.? The answer in both places: "It depends." Each country has provided a caricature of itself in its health care system, and neither is happy with the result. The sense of failure in Britain is not fully explained by actual events—and this is probably true here as well. It has been too easy to blame rampant managerialism and the apparent "Americanization" of the NHS for more fundamental pressures: changes in medical science and practice; changing demography, disease and disability; changing consumer expectations; the potential of new technology and pharmaceuticals to improve life and health; the importance for health and disease factors outside the traditional health system, including basic education and income; the role (and limitations) of computer-based information as a vehicle for seeking new knowledge and encouraging clinical effectiveness; and the sheer costs of trying to do everything. Similar pressures are being felt in all nations, rich and poor. In the United States, managed care is a proxy for frustration. Yet at the same time there are often overblown claims of success. The NHS still tends to get described in Great Britain as a "jewel in the crown," the U.S. system as the "finest in the world."

How do any of us define what a health service *is* today? How important are health services, and in what/whose terms? And how much are we willing to pay through taxation or insurance? Britons may claim they are nearer to consensus about health care, but that may be damning with faint praise. The evolving British pattern focuses on performance, the health of populations, and primary care groups. The evolving U.S. pattern is of private health insurance under potentially strict national and state regulation, with contracting for services from networks of providers that compete with each other in local markets. Large-scale organization and standards are the sine qua non of any modern system of health care, and health services are increasingly definable as information services, with health systems as information systems. So far, neither the NHS nor the U.S. system has achieved full success as part of the information revolution. In the NHS, standard information systems are in theory easier to achieve than in the U.S., where health services crisscross in overlapping networks, and where both public and private programs are phenomenally complicated. The U.S. has the advantage of being able to encourage more local variation and to shift directions rapidly; but its current high costs and an environment of cost constriction may give little leeway to do new things. Too heavy a dependence on traditional mind-sets may lead the English to concentrate too narrowly on equality of services; the Americans on the rationing of technology; and members of both cultures on apparent threats to the medical profession and its freedom to act on behalf of the patient.

What, then, can we conclude? That health care is an ongoing, messy experiment whose goals will continue to be contested and whose form may never be resolved. And that comparative organizational and social history of health care may be useful. Let's hope, at the very least, that the more we know of health care in other countries, the more we can learn about our own "tolerance for arrangements that work, even if there is little logic to commend them."

5

In Honor of Eli Ginzberg on His 90th Birthday

Eli N. Evans

I first met Eli Ginzberg in 1978, a year after I became the first president of the Charles H. Revson Foundation.

Our foundation, which had on its agenda the long-range future of the City of New York, had been thinking about a fresh idea that evolved into a program eventually called "The Charles H. Revson Fellowships for the Future of the City of New York." Modeled loosely on the Nieman Fellows in journalism at Harvard, the program was designed to give future leaders in the city an opportunity to deepen their knowledge, gain new skills, be exposed to different viewpoints and experiences, and to step back and reflect, learn and grow. The fellowships were designed to make it possible that "in midlife people can take chances, move in other directions, make choices to do other than what seems set out for them to do."Each year the program selects ten outstanding women and men in mid-career, from all walks of life, who have shown the potential for creating positive change in the city and invites them to come to Columbia University for an "active sabbatical" year in a program of their own design. Fellows choose courses from the full range of the university's offerings and attend weekly seminars where they meet with key leaders in such varied fields as government and finance, the arts and social services. Especially for those never before in the midst of a great university, this is an unparalleled opportunity and a profound personal challenge.

Eli has headed the program since its inception, becoming a spirited advocate for its innovative approach, lending his enthusiasm, vision, and wisdom, and making it matter. Each year he has inter-

Eli N. Evans is president of the Charles H. Revson Foundation in New York City.

acted with a widely diverse a group of people—perhaps as diverse as any he had ever previously known, even given his uncommon range of experience. The program's 220 fellows, about evenly divided between men and women, have been black, white, Asian, and Latino, and—to reflect the growing diversity of New York City's future—include individuals born in Chile, Cuba, the former Czech Republic, the Dominican Republic, Germany, Haiti, Honduras, Hong Kong, India, Iran, Italy, Jamaica, Korea, Puerto Rico, and Russia. They have included public officials, union organizers, educators, clergy, arts administrators, journalists from both mainstream and alternative media, and activists involved in all aspects of the economic, social, and political life of the city, such as the first female New York firefighter, the founder of a neighborhood credit union, and the director of the first AIDS advocacy group. Some have been vocal advocates with street smarts and an attitude toward racial discrimination and social justice hardened by years of working in the trenches with community groups.They were a generation that knew not Eli. Many cared little that he was the author of more than 100 books, a man who has known and served nine presidents, a world-renowned expert on labor policy and manpower, an economist who has journeyed as an advisor to governments all over the world. He would have to prove his empathy every year, and not just for one evening or one lecture, but day in and day out in his interactions as advisor on their careers and shepherd of their intellectual growth. Those who might have thought that no one his age understood their anger or had fought for equal justice as hard as they had learned that he had been deeply involved in the efforts to integrate the armed services, and brought the memory of this battle to the table. Eli was the wise and experienced counselor on controversial issues, with nuanced views of discrimination and justice deepened by years of involvement in labor and education policy in the city and the nation. The impact of such perspectives on participants in the program was summed up by one fellow who stated, "I learned to question my gut instincts and to see an issue with new complexity."

Fellows might have been surprised by the range of Eli's contacts and the esteem in which he was held in various sectors in the City of New York. He threw himself into arranging the guests for the weekly evening seminars, bringing to the program such luminaries as former mayors John Lindsay and Robert Wagner, Congressman Charles

Rangel, Ford Foundation president Frank Thomas, and leading lawyers and bankers, feminists and civil rights leaders, real estate ty-
coons and state legislators, and university presidents and planning
commissioners. Each dinner began with Eli's introduction of the guest
and ended with his final, five-minute summing up, which was always a tour de force of wisdom, insight, statistics, anecdotes, and
parables. On display was a storytelling master teacher who, with
pure Ginzbergian dazzle, could take fellows on a soaring journey of
history, economics, and memory. Even in an era of despair and cyni-
cism during the 1980s, Eli gave fellows hope based on an abiding
faith in America and on the perspective of his astonishingly long,
wide, and deep experience.

Eli always participated in the applicant interviews and assessments
of the program that preceded our periodic renewal of grant support.
As the program's reputation spread and the number of applicants
rose, Eli invited former fellows to participate on the final interviewing team. "Eli was the one who was always pushing us to pick new
kinds of people," said one of the participants. "And he had a real eye
for talent and potential...unclouded by politics or ideology." In both
the selection process and the program's activities, as one fellow commented, Eli was "far and away the most careful listener I have ever
come across (especially impressive since he is no slouch as a talker!)."

Thanks at least in part to the program and to Eli's capacity to
identify and inspire future leaders, former fellows have been making a difference in every area of the city. Among them are the deputy
borough president of Manhattan; the chair of the New York City
Planning Commission; writers for the *Daily News* and *Newsday*; the
executive director of the Asian American Legal Defense Fund; a
justice of the New York State Supreme Court; several members of
the state legislature and of the New York City Council; senior officials at the Ford Foundation, Carnegie Corporation, Soros Institute,
and several other foundations; and heads of neighborhood housing
and other local organizations. The Revson fellowship, former fellows tell us, credentials them for higher levels of public leadership.

Eli took command of the Revson program after his retirement
from Columbia University, and we at the Foundation have considered ourselves blessed with his decision to lead it over the last two
decades. So too, have been the more than 200 fellows who have
come to know and love him. In the late 1930s, the first head of the

Neiman Fellowship at Harvard was the poet Archibald MacLeish, whose creativity gave the program its wings. In Eli Ginzberg, the Charles H. Revson Fellows Program for the Future of the City of New York has had, in the words of the fellows, its own "public intellectual...a bona-fide living history textbook...a Rooseveltian elder who is a beacon of light through this raging American storm." One of them spoke for all in saying: "Thank you, maestro."

6

Eli Ginzberg: A Scholar of Uncommonly Common-Sense

Ivar Berg

Modern social scientists are the heirs of the Enlightenment legacies most readily identified by the late Alvin Gouldner with the academic disputes between St. Simon, the "last of the gentlemen and the first of the Socialists," and his student, August Comte. In his lectures at the Sorbonne, St. Simon applied the Enlightenment's very basic rationalist critique of tradition, superstition, and the aristocratic systems these traditions informed—the governments, the church, universities, armies, and organizations otherwise—in *l'ancien regime*. Comte, meanwhile, countered with a defense of tradition out of his concerns about the challenges of change to social stability, and the stability of spontaneous and emerging structures. Comte thus built an intellectual edifice that Gouldner called "naturalistic" in contrast with St. Simon's "rationalistic" system.

In modern times the two sides have been represented well in internecine contests between behaviorist and managerialists on one side, and marginalist (price) theorists—and economists generally—on the other. Fritz Machlup, a marginalist in this event, reviewed "the Second Battle of Princeton" in his presidential address to the American Economics Association (1957), declaring a victory for the marginalists over the behaviorists using the test of Occam's razor. Elton Mayo, an industrial hygienist, urged that, in their analyses based entirely on the actions of individuals, economists favored a damnable "rabble hypothesis," i.e. a perspective that denied all the truly

Ivar Berg is a member of the faculty of the Department of Sociology at the University of Pennsylvania.

social dimensions of human existence. Economists thus effectively applied Occam's razor to cut themselves off from the entirely evident fact that "man does not live," as Paul Samuelson has written, "by GNP alone." Workers, Mayo argued, from the classic studies at Western Electric's Hawthorne works, would sacrifice significant portions of their income prospects in return for the "psychic returns" earned from the fellowship and from their "belongingness" in social structures—unions among them—that could mitigate managers' unilaterally absolute authority. Loyalties to their coworkers, Mayo continued, should be targeted by social science professionals, counselors especially, with the aim of converting workers from their putatively needless and entirely gratuitously hostile "sentiments" toward, first, owners, and later, their managers. Max Weber's discussion of the different logic of "charismatic" and "rational-legal" bureaucratic systems of authority (just before Mayo's human relations movement began) almost offered a synthesis of naturalist and rationalist systems. As it turns out, most of us lean dispositively toward one or the other system of thought with some backing and filling in much of our thinking about organizations and about other practical economic questions.

Eli Ginzberg, in the meantime, has managed, in his typically undogmatic and practical fashion, to represent an implicit balance of these perspectives such that his student and reader audiences get better purchases on workaday problems by drawing, very substantially, from both the rationalists' and naturalists' perspectives, without troubling themselves with overly subtle, overly nuanced distinctions. Such distinctions distract attention from productive diagnoses and practical solutions by their preoccupations with unproductive and distracting splitting of hairs, and from preoccupations with scholastic theoretical issues. Ginzberg's formulations, in contrast, have taken the form of cautious exceptions to mainline economists' helpful but oversimplified reductions of socioeconomic phenomena to those contemplated in price theory, reductions that leave economists free to plead innocence about capacities to resolve problems of "distributive justice," in favor of total attention to "allocative efficiency." Ginzberg has frequently, and wryly, noted that this innocence fades when economists, in policy posts with client firms or in government, offer their advice. Professor Gary Becker has summarized economists' proud and hard-boiled credo well in his definition of the "market paradigm:" "the combined assumptions," he tells us "of maximizing behavior, market equilibrium, and stable preferences, used relentlessly and unflinchingly form the heart of the economic approach." The "heart," in this event, is economics discipline's core as Becker's formulation clearly eschews the "sentiments" of workers emphasized by naturalists after the Hawthorne Studies. As Sir Edwin Chadwick famously put it, "when the sentimentalist and the moralist fails, he will have as a last resource to call in the aid of the economist."

Eli Ginzberg's career-long rejection of such absolutist rationalism as the exclusive arrow in a social scientists quiver has been attractive to American presidents and their top staffs, to whom Ginzberg, from 1938–1979, offered cogent though entirely implicit syntheses of rationalism and naturalism that were politically less abrasive than the harsh—indeed forbidding—structures of the straight economist. Most of Americas' politicians have learned far better, meanwhile, than most employers, that the practice of management, like politics, is the art of the possible. For Ginzberg, the effective manager does not (or ought not) live by the credo whimsically imputed to economists by friendly critics: "a thing worth doing at all is a thing worth doing until marginal cost exceeds marginal revenue." Though many will resent it, significant numbers of managers are obliged to reign in their impatience, for example, with reluctant subordinates. Ginzberg was as gently impatient with wrongheaded managers as they were quick to anger and to strike out at subordinates.

Consider that Ginzberg and his immediate colleagues have produced library shelves full of studies in which straight economic formulations have been productively broadened, thereby offering counsel to audiences that goes beyond the advice that comes from the very narrowly constrained formulations endorsed, as above, by the Beckers and the Chadwicks. The difference between dogmatic "rationalists" and equally unbending "naturalists" inheres first in the different weights the two traditions accord to explanatory as contrasted with exploratory investigations, and second in the preference for the paradigms in the natural sciences (complete with conceptions of "equilibria," from Newtonian mechanics) as contrasted with a search for behavior patterns, value, systems, norms, and non-economic structures that operate in critical ways as sanctions and inducements.

Thus Ginzberg offered cautious encouragement, regarding his own staff's work on "human capital theory" for example, in the late 1960s, that public policy regarding education ought not be driven by an interesting but risky emphasis on education—especially higher education—*as an instrument of production* with only a vaguely obligatory acknowledgment, of sorts, that education serves other, *"non-economic"* values. Thus Becker, attentive to his commitment to 'relentlessness' (and admittedly using only circumstantial evidence), offered us a dispositive reading on a key issue in 1964: better-educated Americans earn more than their less educated peers because they are more productive, and we know they are more productive because they earn more. Major premise: markets are heavily price competitive; minor premise: employers are 'relentless' maximizers.

The problem, as Ginzberg regularly reminded us in the late 1950s to the mid 1970s, at the core of our economy—from the "labor market perspective" of which Ginzberg was a major architect—was the influential and heavily oligopolized manufacturing sector. One is starting down a slippery slope, Ginzberg urged, when one simply postulates highly robust levels of price competition. In periods during which competition, in a managerial sense, is real but is managed in ways that reduce pressures on employers to be maximally efficient in their uses of human and other resources, managers will exploit such 'easement.' Non-price competition, in short, and as Joseph Schumpeter famously urged, involves substitutes for prices, including the prestige values of exclusive labels, for example, or the banking of inventory for customers so that a labor strike will not impair delivery of customers' needs. These types of competition, *in institutional terms,* offer tradeoffs: higher profits clearly made labor agreements more generous and flexible, and thus afforded employers larger margins for reinvestment, for R and D, for advertising efforts extolling the ('priceless') charms of a given widget, and for the purchase of more education than necessary for production purposes.

This is not to say that Ginzberg believed that non-price competition involved neither private nor social costs. Ginzberg, a lifetime non-car owner, frequently noted that, even under administered prices, car manufacturers cut costs in fashions that gave us fifteen years of massive auto recalls that helped make growing auto markets among Americans for the Germans and the Japanese, starting in the early 1970s. A thoughtful student of families and family consumption patterns long before the sudden current awarding of Nobel medals to new age "behaviorists," Ginzberg reckoned in 1973 (!) that imported cars sold increasingly well, even with import tariffs added to their sticker prices, because they would be cheaper for the family when growing numbers of two family earners would begin to worry about the tax on car repairs, i.e. the forgone earnings of the lowest earning spouse in getting ill-constructed automobiles into usable (and safe!) condition. When Ginzberg talked about these things in the early 1970s, Volkswagen already had 10 percent of the American market and their (and the Japanese') shares were growing apace. The correlation of the growth of auto imports with the growth in the labor force participation rates of mothers was as close to perfect as any social statistic we have ever recorded. Other economists in this period focused instead on the United Auto Workers, the United Steel Workers, and the United Rubber Workers' efforts to inflate the Big Three automakers' own "non-competitive" wage bills in their agonized analyses of car imports.

In both of these instances—education and consumption— Ginzberg's concerns about the character of competition in our economy, as a senior citizen, was informed by his readings, many years earlier, of TNEC hearings in Congressionally sponsored studies (1940s), studies of The Structure of the American Economy, led by Mordecai Ezekial (late 1930s), and also studies by Joseph Schumpeter. Schumpeter had, already in 1942 (a tad more than a decade after Ginzberg's own critique of Adam Smith's admirers— most of whom had either not read or did not understand what they admired), argued that oligopolists—the few who dominated steel, auto, glass, aluminum, and appliance markets—were loath to praise price competition. Compared with the many pros of oligopolistic competition were the risks to entrepreneurship in huge corporate structures, however, and Schumpeter recognized the risk that Americans would someday compare rule-by-unelected corporate managers with rule-by-government agents under socialism, and find the former to be too powerful. Schumpeter was thus concerned about the downside of oligopolies, but he quite reasonably credited administered pricing with being the soon-to-be generator of a much-expanded American middle class—as indeed it was even by the late 1950s! On this point, Ginzberg readily noted in the 1960s that the continuing, almost explosive, expansions in the ranks of the middle class, and the hosts of middle class concerns, was really only in its first phase in the 1920s: the later burst, in the late forties to the mid sixties, was a by-product of the expansion not of assembly line workers, but of the *services component of manufactures' own labor forces*—product stylists, lawyers, marketers, warranty processors, personnel officers, engineers, corporate income tax processors, consumer credit bureaus, and pension funds (GE's single biggest profit center, by 1999-2000, was from the returns on the investments in its employees' pension fund).

The third phase of service workers involved the expansion—entirely outside of the manufacturing sector—of a full-blown service-sector-unto-itself that added significantly to this white collar group's expanding economic role. Once again, Ginzberg saw likely benefits to Americans of more public servants who were operating governmental activities serving the armed forces, veterans, retirees, and science agencies serving needed "R and D," pharmacological research, medical treatments (in NIMH, for example), and more. All this followed upon the development of public bureaucracies as 'back-up' to the uniformed forces during World War II.

During a long period (1950-1980s), most economists worried about productivity and inflation. Indeed, it took economists only a short time *after we could actually 'count and sort' the members of the American work force* (1940!) to worry about the problematical productivity of civil servants; public competition with private producers for credit; the public displacement of profit-making service deliverers; and, finally, mounting inflation rates associated with oligopolistic, i.e. non price, competition. We must remind ourselves that inflation is measured by the dollar value of goods shipped, divided by the hours of (non-top managers, subcontractors, etc.) payroll labor efforts.

Victor Fuchs, among other inventive economists, studied carefully this problem of achieving anti-inflationary productivity increases among service workers and was not optimistic. Ginzberg objected strenuously to all this, to the hand wringing and—to him—the gratuitous assumption that service work simply does not lend itself to manipulation, i.e. to effective management, in the interests of efficiency. Indeed, it was one of the shared sentiments among Ginzberg's staff members that we often found ourselves as impressed by the professional talents of public as by those of private sector managers.

In a well-received address in a prestigious lecture series at Vanderbilt University in 1984, Ginsberg pointed out that the distinctions between physical and non-physical output are without merit. To count the manufacturer of a piano as productive and a concert by Vladimir Horowitz as non-productive is ridiculous, he urged. He went on to offer suggestions for assessing public agencies' prospects for the effective delivery of information, welfare services, research (especially at the National Institutes of Health), and other services. In the process—an interesting one—Ginzberg added rich ideas to a topic he has treated with originality and not a little courage. In 1960, for example, he produced a three volume follow-up study of pros and cons of the management of America's military human resources, 1939-1946, in which he offered another kitbag full of intriguing observations about American government as a rational employer. One nugget: American civilian bureaucrats, in league with their uniformed medical officers, applied substantially more humane standards in diagnosing and managing military personnel with psychiatric-type disorders than did civilian managers of American workers. This is a notable finding from an observer of human resource management at DuPont, General Electric, IBM, and AT&T, among other Fortune 500s. The conservation of the human resources movement's birth-date, and thus the birth-date for the idea of compassion-by-government, was set by government itself, with considerable encouragement from Ginzberg, in the first half of the 1940s—not by conservative presidential aspirants with private sector management backgrounds in 2000! It was Ginzberg's argument that welfare-type policies were by no means exclusively condescending acts by bleeding heart liberals but, rather, sound investments in people—Adam Smith's real "wealth of nations."

In addition, Ginzberg confidently, and ultimately correctly, predicted in 1967 that Lyndon Johnson's "war against poverty" would add millions of minorities to the federal payroll and, *more importantly*, to *middle America's ranks*, and that this development would go unheralded as critics pointed to this war's failure to end poverty. In fact, Johnson's two-front war—in Vietnam and at home—led to the emergence of a new growing middle class that, by the 1990s, encompassed half of the African American population.

Eli Ginzberg's evenhanded treatment of the problem of Americans' public sector inspired him and his research group to make systematic comparisons of the utilization (and underutilization) of the educational achievements of the workforces in the federal civil service with the uses of education in private employment in studies—alluded to earlier—of education and jobs. It was not terribly surprising that Uncle Sam, with mostly indirect competition in labor markets from the private sector, was a wiser and more judicious manager than were profit sector employers in hosts of highly reputable civilian employment settings, across all economic sectors. Analyses of the careers of a large (five percent) sample of the entire population of America's federal civil servants revealed that Uncle Sam had a far, far lower percentage of underutilized educational achievements than those in private employment settings.

And, contrary to the legions of critics of federal regulations with their sometimes admittedly problematic dimensions, the federal government can in fact often 'get it quite right:' when Richard Nixon's Deputy Attorney General for Civil Rights, Stanley Pottinger, temporarily debarred Columbia University's federal contracts and grants (both applications and the renewals) in February 1971 (for a failed Affirmative Action plan), the conservation staff discovered that the only records for assessing the workforce members' employment history began and ended with their original employment form; nothing had ever been added during employees' subsequent careers—many of them many decades long. Several of us from Ginzberg's Human Resources Project were off to the ramparts to right the university's wrongs. Following Ginzberg's many staff meetings, we immediately rediscovered a problem very early in Affirmative Action's history: that very few employers *anywhere* had any running accounts of their employees careers. But "the times they were achangin," as Bob Dylan sang: on discovering long-neglected information about their employees' achievements, employers adjusted many employees' organizational circumstances in accord with the new rules of equity but, more interestingly, with common sense recognition that they were not fully exploiting their employees' talents. By the time it was all over (by 1980), however, the "equality effects" died, as enforcement (i. e. monitoring funds) waned under Reagan, and real human resources conservation efforts through the full application of Affirmative Action obligations terminated. Even under increasing price-competitive pressures in the 1970s and 1980s, employers simply did not count expensive college recruits' (i.e. inflationary) human resources costs as a consequential issue in a growing economy in which low-cost imports offset higher American earnings. The costs of the latter earnings, meanwhile, could be passed through to consumers with trade-offs-in-prices for the goods Americans bought from Mongolia, Indonesia, the Philippines, Malaysia, South Korea and China. In the latter nation the bulk of its "reserve industrial army of labor" was (in ironic contradiction to the strictures in the Marxian rosary), and in large measure still is, actually in the Chinese army!

Space limitations lead me to offer only one more of Eli Ginzberg's misgivings—abiding ones, as the foregoing words suggest—about the limited depth of American managers' real interests in human capital formation, training, maintenance, and performance. If Ginzberg managed to move ahead by drawing upon both the rationalist and naturalist traditions, their companion, actually an enthymeme, has been that we can legitimately ask, "If so many American employers are so rich, why aren't they smart?"

Consider that in the very early 1960s the Conservation Project examined the behavior of employers with collective bargaining obligations in their management of many workplace issues, including vexed and vexing disciplinary problems. It turned out that employers won 60 percent of grievances over disciplinary treatments that were arbitrated in each of three one-year periods during the 1950s, 1960s, and 1970s. The awards to workers were based on arbitrators' rulings that *though employers were correct in their judgments about workers' misbehavior and even their business-like motives*, the losing managers (quite naturalistically rather than rationally) violated the agreed upon rules and procedures by very impulsively and unreasonably disregarding requirements (regarding warnings, for example) of "due process" in 44 percent of the cases. Ubiquitous management rights clauses are safeguarded in union agreements by rules that protect the parties against violations of "due process"—a very fundamental item in the rationalists' calculus that informed our founding fathers' conceptions of constitutionalism (i.e. a government-of-laws-not-men), especially given the wishes and frustrations of supervisors that could understandably rile a sub-alteren! The fact is that employees' contractions of their "zones of acceptance" of managers' initiatives can be re-expanded by intemperate and cloddish employers: employees know very well that they are the only resource problem, among many, many other problems, facing managers that stand, literally, within striking distance. Workers not uncommonly absorb managers' frustrations about employees as *palpable* fixed costs; other plaguesome actors, suppliers, regulators, competitors, and customers are less proximal and, with that, less vulnerable to managers' wrath.

In balance, Eli Ginzberg has blended the rational and the natural systems' logics left to us by the Enlightenment with great intellectual, social, and economic benefits. In doing so, he has assured that there has been a continuingly thoughtful *institutionalist* voice by a long-surviving and practicing economist in a world in which mainliners would otherwise have collapsed all non-pecuniary values under a compendious "term of art"—the *propensity* (to save, invest, etc.) toward which the residual variance in economists' calculations is simply nudged clear off the table in favor of non-dispositive circumstantial evidence and zealous (and "relentless") applications of flawed premises about the hegemony of "market forces."

Price theory is valuable when price competition is robust, and the calculus of price is applicable only under that essential condition—as it was not in what Becker has called Human Capital's "salad days:" the 1960s-1980s. The human capital paradigm works better in 2001 than it did in 1964: with price competition aplenty now, and supplies of college graduates growing each year, employers are now replacing high school graduates with college graduates—50 percent so by 2005—and these underutilized workers were earning a little less, by 1985, then *half* of the 11 percent return, discounted over a lifetime, that was reported about college graduates' earnings by Professor Becker in 1964. With more price competition now, the human capitalist vessel carries a good deal more water—*32 years* "after the fact." So much for the "long run."

The time stretch in the preceding line reminds me that Ginzberg has often pointed out that "the long run," in which all will be well, is a succession of short runs. That indeed was the real message of the institutionalists, John Commons and others, at the turn of the last century. In any given year, decade, or era, there will be a few or several turning points—wars, shifts in birthrates, supreme court holdings, booms or busts, and so on. The *most* stable arrangements, practices, values and norms are by *no* means entirely, *totally* stable, but they *are* embodied in *institutions* that tend to change more deliberately and to be less readily vulnerable to even major forces: abolitionism (alive among Quakers, was a force only days after the Constitution was ratified) was a movement that needed the better part of a *century* to bring us to a dispositive civil war. None of Americans' most dramatic shifts have truly "occurred" at the tail end of anything like a "run"; arriving at the end of *proximal* events *with* consecutive equal intervals *does* make "a long run." As Eli has put it, "the long run is a succession of short runs."

The trick, in a lifetime of successful assessments, forecasts, discoveries, and evaluations—whether in regard to "the pill" (with its triumph over the consequences of undisciplined passions), draft deferments (during the Korean and Vietnam wars, which deeply offended the writer), "double digit" inflation, or "sex between the Bushes"—is to recognize continuities and discontinuities, and clearly observe and carefully note them. We do not have an apt word for one's talent to juggle ideas, like balls, without dropping some, but we can come close with "intussususception"—"the assimilation of new material and its disposal among preexistent matter." That is Eli's intellectual "M.O."—everything is on the table, is a rich mixture, and is open to discussion; received theory is only a guide to a few initial assessments of most interesting and *socially* significant phenomena. Ginzberg watched patterns without the "cowardly historian's dependence on chronology," i.e. as a quasi-Darwinian intervening variable. Eli Ginzberg should continue on his path to yet another Festschrift in thirty years; he should thus live to 120.

Part II

Eli Ginzberg as Scholar

7

The Economics of Discrimination as Applied to Business Development

Ray Marshall

Eli Ginzberg's work has been a model for those of us concerned about human resource policy analysis. Although it is rooted in economics, Eli has demonstrated the value of historical, quantitative, and theoretical methods as well as drawing upon other social sciences as appropriate. Eli has, in addition, demonstrated the importance of understanding policymaking processes and of making scholarly research accessible to politicians, policymakers, and the general public. He taught us that strategies are important if the analyst wants to influence political and policy processes.

My generation of human resource analysts and practitioners benefited greatly from Eli's pioneering work in this field. In addition, he helped us with his insightful personal advice. I first met Eli in the mid-1950s when he presented a paper on black employment at the annual meetings of the Southern Economic Association in Atlanta. Eli had done important work on the economics of discrimination long before most economists discovered the subject.

In subsequent years Eli encouraged work that I was doing on that subject, especially in studies of ways to overcome the exclusion of minorities from apprenticeship programs in the skilled trades during the 1960s and 70s. As chair of the National Manpower Advisory

Ray Marshall holds the Audre and Bernard Rapoport Centennial Chair in Economics and Public Affairs at the University of Texas-Austin, and served as U.S. Secretary of Labor under Jimmy Carter. He is the founder of the Center for the Study of Human Resources at the Lyndon B. Johnson School of Public Affairs at the University of Texas-Austin.

Committee, Eli supported and helped shape the development of the apprenticeship outreach program which grew out of that research. His influence with policymakers helped gain support for those programs, which, together with legal challenges to the apprenticeship system, did much to overcome the institutionalized exclusion of minorities from the skilled trades.

More recently, Eli helped me with a book that I am writing on teachers' unions and school reform. Not only did he encourage me to undertake this project, but provided valuable advice about how to pursue it. I was skeptical, for example, about including New York City in a comparative analysis of cities. It seemed to me that the New York school system was too big and bureaucratic to permit the kind of study I had in mind. Reminding me of my Navy experience, Eli pointed out that innovation often was more likely in a big bureaucratic system than in a small one, that there were in fact many innovations in the New York public school system, and that that city provided valuable lessons about how to negotiate changes that were not likely to be achieved by other means. Needless to say, he was right, and my study benefited greatly from including New York City and from Eli's advice about sources and how to influence education policy processes.

This chapter will explore the subject of my earliest association with Eli—anti-discrimination policy, particularly policies to overcome discrimination against minorities and women in the formation and development of businesses. Two important facts about this subject are: a) minorities are more disadvantaged in business than in any other aspect of economic life and b) there are no federal laws against discrimination in this sector. Instead of anti-discrimination laws, governments at every level have used their contracting powers to combat this form of discrimination. However, these programs are very controversial, leading to extensive litigation. This is therefore an example of how policy analysis can be used to support change through legal processes.

I have focused considerable attention on this question since 1989, when Mayor Andrew Young asked Andrew Brimmer and me to do a study of discrimination against minorities and women in Atlanta businesses. A study was needed because the Georgia Supreme Court, following the U.S. Supreme Court's *Croson* decision that year, had declared the Atlanta Minority and Female Business program (MFB) to be unconstitutional because it gave preference to women and minorities on city contracts. The *Croson* decision subjected race-conscious programs to strict scrutiny, meaning that any such program had to show that there was a compelling governmental interest in adopting race-conscious remedies and that those remedies had to be narrowly tailored to address the specific discrimination that was identified. Andy Brimmer and I assembled a research team to undertake the Brimmer-Marshall study, which formed the basis for a reconstituted MFB program in Atlanta during the 1990s. The Atlanta program was not challenged until 2000, when it was transformed into a different program, the Equal Business Opportunity program (EBO 2000), which I hope will be more effective and less vulnerable to legal challenge. I was a consultant to Atlanta on the development of EBO 2000 as well as to the Clinton Administration's affirmative action review and to the Justice Department in its defense of the federal Disadvantaged Business Enterprise (DBE) program, which originated during the Carter Administration in 1978. In the 1995 *Adarand* decision the Supreme Court extended the strict scrutiny requirement to the federal program.

The 1989 *Croson* decision led to a cottage industry of so-called disparity studies by state and local jurisdictions in an effort to meet the strict scrutiny test. Experts also emerged to challenge the MFB programs and the studies upon which they were based. *Croson* ruled that a disparity between the number of minority business enterprises and the amount of business they get was *prima facie* evidence of discrimination. The Court also made it clear that rigid racial quotas were unconstitutional and that general population statistics could not be used to set racial goals or to identify discrimination to justify race-conscious remedies. There is, however, considerable disagreement among the courts about the methodologies governments must use to measure discrimination to establish compelling interest and narrowly tailor these programs to meet the strict scrutiny test. The U.S. Supreme Court has accepted a review of the *Adarand* case and may resolve some of these questions in its next term. This chapter presents my views about how the Supreme Court should resolve these questions. My views are contrary to those advanced by most federal district courts, but are compatible with the decision of the Tenth Circuit in the *Adarand* case that has been appealed to the Supreme Court. I also outline an alternative approach to the ordinary

MFB program that might withstand constitutional challenge whether or not the Supreme Court agrees with the Tenth Circuit in *Adarand*. This alternative approach has been adopted in Atlanta, so a legal challenge could be forthcoming. The Supreme Court's major problem is not only disagreement over the desirability of race-conscious remedies, but a lack of clarity and specificity about the nature of discrimination and how it is measured, as well as how and why it originates and gets changed.

Defining Discrimination

Courts, scholars, and journalists use various terms to describe discrimination, though they almost never define the term.[1] Discrimination is best defined as taking action against people because of some characteristic unrelated to ability or performance. "Bias" or "prejudice" is often confused with discrimination. Discrimination, however, is an *action* while bias is an *attitude*. Discrimination might result from bias, but not necessarily. And in economic affairs, attitudes are more likely to result from behavior than behavior is from attitudes. That is why public policy should seek to change behavior, not just attitudes. Perhaps we cannot legislate morality, but we can legislate behavior.

One of the most significant requirements for understanding discrimination is to explain why it occurs. There is very strong empirical and logical evidence that discrimination is based on a combination of status and economic motives. Discriminators seek to prevent people who are considered to be "inferior" from working in their occupations or industries on an equal or superior basis. Women and minorities historically have been considered by white males to be inferior, and therefore have been permitted to work with white males mainly in lower-status jobs or industry segments. It was acceptable for blacks to do the same work, or even to train young white males, as long as they did so in clearly subordinate positions and were denied the higher status jobs.[2] In Atlanta, for example, until the 1970s black contractors, vendors, and professionals could primarily serve only blacks or work in relatively small businesses and low-status jobs. A report by the Economic Research Service (ERS 2000) shows these patterns to have continued in the 1990s and into 2000, even though there have been some improvements in business opportunities for minorities and females since the 1980s.[3]

The second major factor involved in discrimination is the short-run economic advantage white male workers and businesses derive from limiting competition from blacks or women for jobs and other economic opportunities or limiting business relations to traditional networks. This factor also explains the existence of the oft mentioned "ol' boy" network that restricts business opportunities for women and minorities, who usually have been excluded from those networks.[4] Exclusion from this network was one of the most commonly cited discriminatory actions we learned of in the Brimmer-Marshall study.

Before we can either detect its presence or fashion narrowly tailored remedies to combat it, we must specify further what is meant by discrimination. For policy analysis I have found it useful to define discrimination as either overt (i.e., based on conscious decisions to discriminate) or "institutional," meaning that formerly overt forms of discrimination have become so entrenched and pervasive that no discriminator needs to make a conscious decision to perpetuate it. This is a different concept from "societal discrimination"—which apparently means discrimination by external organizations like schools, business clubs, and other organizations, though the latter could be a consequence of institutionalized patterns of discrimination. In Atlanta and other places, for example, specific overt decisions were made to restrict blacks to certain geographic neighborhoods, occupations, and types of business. The slave tradition was to prohibit blacks from learning. After emancipation, there were at first no public schools for blacks, and when "Negro" schools were established, they were unequal in every way—length of school year, teachers' salaries, facilities, and autonomy.[5] These patterns constrained the kinds of occupations and businesses blacks could realistically aspire to. Consequently, blacks adjusted to the opportunities available to them.[6] Before the City of Atlanta, the Rapid Transit Authority, and the County opened up their contracting processes to MFBs in the 1970s, local officials never thought of including blacks or women in their contracting activities because, as one such official interviewed for our project put it, "that's just the way things were."[7] It is clear to me that these institutionalized forms of discrimination therefore became systemic and were not likely to be changed without concerted action by black communities and conscious interventions by governments.

Discrimination inhibits businesses from contracting with other firms on the basis of merit, so reducing discrimination contributes to greater efficiency.[8] It could very well be that white male business owners lose some short-run economic benefits they would have received from the monopoly power they derived from discrimination, but in the long run these benefits were detrimental because they deprived everyone of the economic efficiencies and opportunities available in a more competitive business environment. And the system limited incentives for blacks to improve their conditions because discrimination prevented them from benefiting fully from developing their entrepreneurial skills, knowledge, and assets.

Clearly, discrimination is not the only factor affecting labor market and entrepreneurial opportunity, but it is a very important factor. There is no question that race has historically determined where people live, their personal associates, the kinds of schools they attend, the kinds of jobs they can get, and the lines of business enterprise they can aspire to. There is abundant evidence, moreover, that minorities and women not only have inadequate access to jobs and business opportunities, but to work-based education and training—such as apprenticeships—as well.[9] Experience shows that positive interventions can break these cycles and cause minority children from very disadvantaged backgrounds to excel in school and life.[10] But without these interventions very little is likely to happen. A major challenge for public policy is to institutionalize opportunity instead of discrimination.

A Behavioral Theory of Discrimination

A theory of discrimination is essential both to understand what discrimination is and to develop interventions to change it. The best way to judge any theory is the use to be made of it. The neoclassical theory, for example, is useful for reconciling economic discrimination with wage theory and the neoclassical general equilibrium theory.[11] But I have not found it to be a very useful guide to anti-discrimination policy. Indeed, by assuming that competitive markets will eliminate discrimination, that theory creates a bias against positive interventions to combat discrimination, and tends to minimize the importance of discrimination in today's markets. If, these economists argue, women and minorities have limited opportunities, it is because they are less productive; they assume, in circular fashion, that compensation is the only significant measure of competence and often exaggerate the degree to which markets are competitive. The neoclassical theory also emphasizes individual decision making whereas institutionalized discrimination is a social phenomenon. It is not at all clear that competitive markets alone will erode or counteract deeply entrenched social forces in any acceptable time period. The neoclassical theory also has an unsatisfactory conception of discrimination. Indeed, this is more a theory of wages, with an extra term—a coefficient of discrimination—than it is a theory of discrimination. Discrimination is defined as a "taste" for which a discriminator is willing to sacrifice profits or welfare, but there is no satisfactory explanation of "taste" or why it came about, became institutionalized or can be changed, other than to say it will be eroded by competition. To the degree that this "taste" is for physical association, it clearly is not a very satisfactory explanation for discrimination.

To some degree, of course, the impact of competition on discrimination is true by definition. The key neoclassical assumption is that the actors that are preferred and non-preferred by discriminators are equally productive, so that a discriminator will acquire a competitive disadvantage. Competitive markets will erode discrimination only if markets really are competitive, but competition is not a natural condition. To the degree that institutionalized discrimination disadvantages minorities and women and exclusionary networks give monopoly power to white males, competitive markets are not likely to be created by antitrust policies alone. With respect to business development, neoclassical theory assumes away a very important precondition for competitive markets, i.e., how women and minorities can get started and develop in order to become as productive as established white males.

In reality, the exclusion of minority and female contractors by networks of white male contractors in the presence of a combination of overt and institutional discrimination restricts the learning opportunities of MFBs, making it difficult for them to become competitive or to secure contracts when they do. The neoclassical assumptions are perhaps satisfactory in terms of reconciling this theory of discrimination with neoclassical wage theory, but do not offer a very satisfactory explanation of how discrimination occurs in historical and institutional contexts. The neoclassical model likewise fails to specify why women and minorities are not as productive as white males or detail a dynamic process whereby interventions to overcome discrimination and permit minorities to develop their human and physical capital can, through cognitive dissonance, change attitudes and behavior. If, as I believe, discrimination is partly because of status considerations and partly because of perceived economic advantage, the status motive can be overcome partially by demonstrating that the group perceived to be inherently inferior can in fact perform as well as the group that considers itself to be superior. The monopoly power of discriminators can be overcome much more effectively through direct interventions—like the use of government contracting to allow minorities and women businesses to get started— than indirectly through trying to enforce competitive market conditions through antitrust laws. As the groups discriminated against accumulate enough market power they can continue to erode discriminatory barriers as well as the monopoly power of discriminators. When this happens, the discriminators confront a different reality. Total exclusion from certain market sectors is no longer an option and many of those who were part of the pattern of institutional exclusion start doing business with the excluded groups. As this happens, opportunity will become as institutionalized as discrimination is now. This process can already be observed in sports, entertainment, and apprenticeship training, where the problem has become more of addressing specific overt acts of discrimination than of breaking down institutionalized patterns. The neoclassical model assumes that individual economic motives will erode discrimination, eliminating the need for positive interventions, which, it argues, only distort markets. The behavioral model, by contrast, assumes that economic and social forces interact, so that social forces prevent women and minorities from ever becoming competitive with the discriminators.

MFB critics often argue that competitive bidding on public contracts is sufficient to create competitive conditions, making positive interventions unnecessary. There are several problems with this argument. First, if established contractors discriminate against women and minorities in the private markets, they acquire competitive advantages in submitting bids on public contracts. Second, a complete reliance on competitive bids is rare—other conditions, like "responsive" or "competent," are common and provide room for the perpetuation of discrimination. Third, an exclusive reliance on competitive bidding by subcontractors would deny prime contractors the legitimate reason for networks, namely to select subcontractors they know can do the work. Finally, low bidding alone would deny governments the ability to use their contracting power to combat discrimination in private as well as public markets. Competitive bidding can become a more common reality in public markets once institutionalized inclusion has replaced institutionalized exclusion in public and private markets.

Why Minority Business Development Programs are Needed

Business is a source of considerable economic and political power. To deny minorities and women access to this power on the basis of race or gender denies them full participation in the American system. Put another way, as long as minorities and women are denied access to business opportunities, the distribution of wealth, income, and power will continue to be unfair, and even to polarize, with grave consequences for the economy, polity, and society. It also can be argued that discrimination limits the full development of competitive markets and therefore produces inefficiencies.

The disparities between minorities and whites are much greater in business than they are in other economic activities, even though these other disparities remain considerable. The gap is particularly wide with respect to income and wealth. In 1990, for example, blacks represented roughly 12 percent of the U.S. population, 11 percent of the civilian labor force, and 10 percent of total employment. However, blacks received less than 8 percent of total money income, held under 3 percent of the nation's wealth, owned only 3 percent of the nation's businesses, and made only 1 percent of business sales.[12] The situation for black businesses has actually worsened. According to the 1997 Survey of Minority-Owned Business Enterprises, black-owned firms accounted for 3.95 percent of businesses, but only 0.38 percent of sales.[13]

Another reason minority business development programs are needed is because there are no other effective ways to deal with the deeply entrenched patterns of discrimination in construction and other business sectors. There are a number of reasons for this. First, as noted, it is very difficult to document discrimination in private commercial transactions. Business discrimination has therefore not attracted the same public attention as other areas, and "no federal statute has ever been specifically adopted to bar racial discrimination in private domestic commercial transactions between two business firms."[14] The Constitution protects minority businesses from discrimination by federal, state, and local governments, and special legislation and executive orders bar discrimination in federal financial assistance or by government contractors and vendors, but there are no effective federal laws against discrimination in commercial transactions. Because of the difficulties in applying general anti-discrimination measures to businesses, federal, state, and local governments have used their purchasing power as the most effective way to overcome the effects of, and to prevent, discrimination against minority businesses. During the Carter Administration, the federal government adopted this approach after other so-called "race neutral" approaches had failed to overcome the effects of discrimination in the construction industry.

The law is mainly designed to combat specific overt discrimination that can be proved in court. The problem, of course, is that the most pervasive forms of discrimination are institutional—that is, they are embedded in human institutions that cause behavior by victims as well as those who discriminate to perpetuate the patterns. Much of the debate about affirmative action, for example, is over the issue of how to combat institutional discrimination where there is not necessarily a defendant who committed an overt act of discrimination that could be proved before judges and juries. A legitimate question by white-owned firms is whether or not they have responsibility for institutional discrimination. My view is that private companies that contract with the government have special obligations to practice affirmative action—i.e., to take positive measures to include people who have been excluded for reasons having nothing to do with merit. Moreover, local governmental entities have a constitutional obligation to prevent discrimination by companies in their jurisdictions that contract with local governmental organizations.

There is no doubt that various MFB programs have helped minority businesses. Most minority firms continue to get a large share of their business from public projects or where government requirements and pressures influence private contractors. In Atlanta, our study found that minority firms got, on average, about 93 percent of their revenue from the public sector, while their white competitors got 80 percent of their revenue from more attractive and lucrative private markets.[15] I should note, however, that even with an effective MFB program, which provided a relatively large *number* of contracts for minorities, the median size of minority contracts ($24,000) was much smaller than that going to majority firms ($3,838,000).[16] The median size of minority contracts was therefore a small fraction of that of their white counterparts. ERS 2000 revealed that these patterns continued into 2000.

Some critics argue that affirmative action programs not only are unconstitutional and unnecessary because competitive market forces tend to eliminate discrimination, but also "distort" competitive markets and introduce economic inefficiencies. In this view, there is no coherent justification for market interventions other than enforcing antitrust laws. As noted, however, these conclusions are possible only under very restrictive—and, in my judgment, unrealistic—assumptions.[17] In particular, these theories have no way of predicting how long it will take to achieve economic parity. An exhaustive assessment of affirmative action programs by Holzer and Neumark found continuing discrimination and concluded that the evidence against affirmative action on efficiency grounds is "weak at best" because affirmative action that combats continuing discrimination "generates additional efficiency gains."[18] These analysts argue that

> Affirmative action seems to have major redistributive effects [toward women and minorities] that operate in markets in which discrimination still exists, and it may create some positive externalities; it *might* therefore lead to increased efficiency… Although we can by no means fully quantify these…based on the evidence we think this is more rather than less likely. Thus, we regard the current state of the evidence as most consistent with the view that *affirmative action offers* significant redistribution toward women and minorities with relative small efficiency consequences.[19]

Holzer and Neumark likewise found evidence that EEO reporting alone tends to deter discrimination, which would be another positive for the MFB programs.[20]

Evidence Required to Detect and Measure Discrimination

In order to determine whether positive interventions are required to combat discrimination and to determine when positive interventions are no longer required, we must have rules of evidence that can be applied to particular cases. Since *Croson,* courts have stressed the importance of statistics. Moreover, *Croson* held that in determining the presence and extent of discrimination, defenders of race-conscious interventions had to demonstrate the relationship between the number of minority firms ready, willing and able to be public contractors and the proportion of contract dollars they get. In many federal district courts, this general standard has given opponents of MFB programs an easy evidentiary task: all they have to do is point to inherent defects in data and quantitative analyses to show that MFB programs have not proved that disparities—ordinarily large according to most studies—might be accounted for by some factor other than discrimination. Plaintiffs have been able to argue that the statistics do not show whether minorities are "ready, willing and able" to contract with public entities. Plaintiffs also minimize the importance of historical evidence, which naturally presents serious problems for them. There is general agreement that discrimination has existed in the past, but opponents of MFB programs have no way to show when it ceased to exist. They sometimes infer that it was when anti-discrimination laws were passed, but this doesn't help with general business discrimination, which violates no federal law. Even though some state and local jurisdictions have outlawed business discrimination, it is a misreading of the nature of discrimination to infer that it ceases to exist even when it is made illegal. In my view, statistical analyses constitute the main kinds of evidence needed to prove discrimination, but there must be some reasonable rules about how good statistics must be in terms of currency and specificity. There also must be rules about what precisely must be measured and over what markets, as well as the validity of quantitative techniques to control for other factors.

These are important questions because it is well established that few, if any, issues can be resolved by statistical analysis alone. The statistics frequently conceal as much as they reveal—they are never current or specific enough to provide perfect "proof." Critics of MFB programs imply that *Croson* precludes the use of historical and anecdotal evidence, relying almost exclusively on statistics. This is, however, a misreading of *Croson* and the standards for good evidence. The Supreme Court always has been reluctant to require specific kinds of proof in all cases, reflecting an understanding that "discrimination takes a myriad of ingenious forms."[21]

It is equally well established that quantitative tools rarely are powerful enough to disentangle discrimination from other causes, even in employment, which is much less complex than business discrimination. We should try to hold other things constant while measuring the effects of discrimination, but it is not always clear which variables to hold constant. Moreover, where discrimination has become institutionalized and pervasive, it will influence variables like size, funding, education, and experience of managers, which therefore cannot be assumed to be non-discriminatory factors. As Kenneth Arrow observed, with the passage of anti-discrimination laws, we have less gross evidence of discrimination and have to rely more on indirect inferences.[22] Arrow notes that in the pre-legislation period, we have evidence that blacks were excluded from a significant range of economic opportunities and "very strong evidence that these practices persist in some important measure."[23] However, it is equally clear to Arrow that discrimination cannot be explained by measurable market forces alone.

As will be demonstrated below, when the most appropriate data and quantitative techniques available are used, they usually reveal (a) gross disparities between the number of minority contractors and their utilization in the private sector or than would be predicted by standard statistical techniques, like those used by ERS 2000; (b) an increase in the utilization of minority contractors in the public sector mainly while MFB programs are in effect—they have declined greatly when these programs are struck down; and (c) when quantitative techniques are used to control for other logical factors besides discrimination there usually are large residuals compatible with discrimination, even though there is little doubt that these other factors (e.g., education, experience, access to capital, size) are influenced by institutional and overt discrimination. Even though these disparities understate the degree of discrimination, they usually are large and statistically significant.

Appropriate Scope of the Market to be Examined

Thus, although in my view statistics alone provide an incomplete picture, these quantitative findings are strongly supported by the historical and anecdotal evidence, including ERS 2000, as well as the evidence assembled by the Congress and several administrations, to support the compelling interest part of the strict scrutiny test required by the Supreme Court's 1995 *Adarand III* decision.[24]

With respect to the appropriate scope of the market to be examined, I believe that a metropolitan statistical area is most appropriate for a municipal analysis, partly because more reliable statistics are likely to be available for those areas and partly because a local public entity is likely to contract mainly from those areas, though some markets will be larger in scope. Of course, national or regional statistics and markets may be more appropriate for federal programs.[25]

Some MFB critics argue that lists of bidders on government contracts constitute the most appropriate sources to calculate disparity rates. However, these lists are not very appropriate for determining whether MFB programs are justified. Discrimination (overt and institutional) has clearly influenced the number of bidders, not all of whom are available during particular contracting periods. Moreover, where there are MFB programs, minority and female contractors are likely to be over-represented on bidders' lists because of crowding, i.e., people who are discriminated against tend to "crowd" into those market segments that are open to them. It obviously is not appropriate to use program outcomes to ascertain whether or not the programs are necessary. One of the best indicators of the continuing strength of overt and institutional discrimination is what happens when the programs are eliminated.

Finally, bidders' lists ignore the important relationships between public and private markets, as well as the relationship between private discrimination and public contracting. Through their discrimination in much more important private sectors, non-minority contractors have been able to limit the development of minority contractors and thus make it difficult for them to compete effectively for public contracts.[26] In the absence of public interventions, minority businesses are unlikely to develop outside of the narrow markets to which they traditionally have been restricted. It is for this reason that in *Croson* and other cases the Supreme Court has recognized that governmental entities have a compelling interest to prevent governmental contracting from perpetuating the effects of past discrimination.[27]

Qualified, Willing and Able Minority Contractors

The problem of establishing statistical proof of whether or not minority contractors are "qualified, willing and able" is particularly challenging. *Croson* provides limited guidance on this question, though it seems to imply that specific qualifications are important mainly when "special qualifications" are required as the Tenth Circuit held in *Adarand VII*, discussed below. Moreover, qualifications

and willingness to contract are sufficiently judgmental as to pre-
clude credible statistical proof in the absence of licensing or other
examinations. Unfortunately, this lack of guidance has made it possible for courts and opponents of MFB programs to argue that the
failure to produce perfect statistical evidence—i.e., timely and highly
specific, and methodologies that control for everything except discrimination—invalidates these programs despite the fact that the most
reliable statistics and the most appropriate methodologies confirm
the persistence of discrimination. Our evidence for Atlanta suggests
that even highly qualified black contractors are disadvantaged relative to similarly situated white contractors. And ERS 2000 finds statistically significant gaps between expected and actual revenue when
such capacity measures as industry, age, and size are controlled for.
It also is hard to know how to define the qualifications of businesses
in dynamic markets where expertise can be purchased in the open
market and where "virtual" companies are increasingly common.
Once contractors are able to obtain contracts, they usually are able
to expand their capacity.

In a dynamic business environment, it would be difficult to argue,
as some critics have, that qualifications are determined mainly by
size. Indeed, ERS 2000 found size to be a relatively unimportant
factor in business decisions. Since *Croson* mentions qualified contractors, presumably this means minimum qualifications established
by the contracting authority—not that the successful bidder had to
be the most qualified or even, as some plaintiff's experts argue,
equally qualified, a concept that usually defies precise measurement.
There is, however, no precise way to know how many contractors in
a universe meet those minimum qualifications. Moreover, as the Tenth
Circuit Court of Appeals observed in *Adarand VII*, there is no credible evidence that minority contractors who have been hired under
MFB programs have lacked adequate qualifications.

Nevertheless, analyses of available data for *business owners* that
enable personal characteristics and other factors to be controlled for
leaves a residual compatible with racial exclusion. There therefore
is no credible evidence that the large disparities in the utilization of
minority contractors can be explained by the lack of qualifications
or the unwillingness to contract. Indeed, strong historical, anecdotal,
and survey evidence (reported in ERS 2000, discussed below) demonstrates that minority contractors are more willing than white males

to contract with governmental entities, even though they recognize that public contracting is less desirable than the mainstream private sector, where their opportunities are greatly restricted. The greater participation of minorities and women is compatible with the concept of "crowding," mentioned earlier. This is all the more reason not to use participation in these sectors as a measure of discrimination and why broader market areas are more appropriate.

The Importance of Historical Evidence

Historical evidence is important to help us understand how discrimination originates and is perpetuated and changed. History also is an important analytical tool because it can show patterns of behavior when racial exclusion was more open before some of its forms became illegal and therefore less conspicuous. And as Arrow notes, these patterns change very slowly, even though they become more difficult to detect by direct means once they became unlawful or less acceptable.[28]

The historical record also is important in detecting how overt discrimination becomes institutionalized. The U.S. Supreme Court explained this relationship in *Fullilove v. Klutznick* when it upheld the federal minority set-aside program which sought to remove "barriers to competitiveness which had their roots in racial and ethnic discrimination and which continue today, even *absent any intentional discrimination or unlawful conduct*."[29]

Those who believe that historical evidence is unimportant have the burden of showing that present patterns have changed significantly or are caused by factors other than discrimination. My work confirms Kenneth Arrow's conclusions that these patterns change very slowly.[30] In addition, our evidence shows that opportunities for women and minorities have improved as a consequence of positive legal interventions and MFB programs, but have been reversed when these measures were struck down.

The Importance of Anecdotal Evidence

Because of the limitations of both historical and statistical evidence, the Brimmer-Marshall researchers conducted over sixty-nine in-depth interviews with seventy-six interviewees in the Atlanta MSA. The average interview was between two and three hours and the range was from one to four hours. Interviewees were selected because of their experience with or knowledge of Atlanta and Fulton County business activities, and represented diverse attitudes about MFB programs, including representatives of predominantly white male business associations that opposed these measures. Interviewees each signed statements attesting that "any and all responses made by me during the interview(s) shall be truthful, accurate, and correct to the best of my knowledge, information, and belief." In most cases, interviews were conducted by an experienced team of two members. An effort was made to verify specific information by using multiple sources. The interviews were confidential, but available to the courts in camera.

Historical and Qualitative Evidence in Atlanta

Like other sources of evidence, qualitative findings from interviews have limitations, but they are a very valuable source of information, especially where this evidence is carefully evaluated and used in conjunction with statistical and historical data. As the Ninth Circuit concluded, although anecdotes by themselves cannot prove discrimination, "the combination of convincing anecdotes and statistical evidence is potent."[31] I naturally believe our historical, statistical, and qualitative evidence is very powerful, even though we did not have sufficiently disaggregated data to do the kind of analysis permitted for larger geographical areas or for Atlanta by ERS 2000.

Our historical research shows that before the 1970s, black business development was tightly constrained by limited markets, in terms of both geography and the incomes of their customers. Whites not only had much larger and more lucrative markets, but also were able to penetrate black markets. White doctors and lawyers, for example, could have black as well as white customers, but black doctors and lawyers had almost no white customers. Indeed, because of widespread systemic discrimination, black professionals often had disadvantages in attracting black clients.

The Brimmer-Marshall interviews showed that the impact of this disadvantage continued to limit the development of black professionals in Atlanta and Fulton County into the 1990s. Indeed, judges and other Georgia public officials practiced overt discrimination against black attorneys during the 1970s. Our interviews produced evidence of virtually every identifiable form of business discrimination across a wide range of industries. Specifically, we found evidence of denials of opportunity to bid; discrimination in bonding; exclusion from the "good ol' boy" network in development, general contracting, and subcontracting; severely limited access to private sector markets; denials of invitation to bid or quote; slow payment and non-payment; price discrimination by suppliers; double standards in performance and qualifications; discrimination in financing; bid shopping; bid collusion; discrimination in employment opportunities; discrimination by unions; customer/end-user discrimination; and stereotypical attitudes on the part of customers and professional buyers.

Our historical investigations found discrimination in Atlanta to be largely self-perpetuating once it became institutionalized. Before 1967, for example, black construction contractors in Atlanta were restricted almost entirely to repair work, the trowel trades, and work in the black community.[32]

This pattern of racial discrimination extended to public employment by the City, the County, and other state and local entities. Almost all blacks were in labor and blue-collar categories, while most whites held higher level professional and technical jobs. A study by James Hefner of black employment in Atlanta for my "Negro Employment in the South" project found that there were no blacks in official or managerial positions in Atlanta city government in 1967, and that black city employees were heavily concentrated in laborer jobs (78.4 percent for blacks and 8.3 percent for whites).[33] Only 1 percent of blacks, but 16 percent of whites, were in professional and technical jobs; 50 percent of whites and 14 percent of blacks were in craftsmen and operatives jobs.[34]

There also was evidence that very few minority general contractors were able to become prime contractors on large private jobs. The exceptions were a few large companies whose work was desegregated by the civil rights movement during the 1960s and 1970s, and where the mayor and other city officials exerted constant pressure for these companies to use minority firms.

Statistical Evidence for Atlanta

As Orley Ashenfelter and Ron Oaxaca make very clear, the use of statistics in discrimination cases has arisen precisely because disparate treatment is so difficult to detect.[35] Despite the acknowledged impossibility of perfect proof, critics believe that the burden is on program sponsors not only to establish evidence of disparate impact, but also to establish that those disparities are due to discrimination and not to some other non-discriminatory factors.

My own view is similar to that expressed by the Tenth Circuit in *Adarand VII,* i.e., that once credible evidence of disparate impact is shown, the burden should shift to opponents of these programs, as it does in employment discrimination cases, to then rebut the disparate impact statistics, not merely by listing the inherent defects of statistical, anecdotal or historical analyses, but by showing that these disparities are caused by some other non-discriminatory factors that minorities and women just happen to have less of.

To the extent that plaintiffs in post-*Croson* cases *have* attempted to rebut defendants' evidence of disparate impact, they have argued that businesses owned by minorities or women are simply smaller than those owned by non-minority males. They uniformly fail, however, to explain *why* these size differences exist. The only other theory I am aware of to explain these size and age differences is that differences in "cultural" proclivities cause minorities and women to prefer to run smaller, less profitable businesses than their white male counterparts. Those of us trained to appreciate the tendencies for individuals to act rationally to improve their own economic well being find this argument untenable. Moreover, as ERS 2000 demonstrates, there are statistically significant differences between the revenues earned by female and minority businesses even after size and other factors are held constant.

This is not to argue that minorities or women, except for discrimination, would be represented "in lock-step proportion" to their numbers in the general population—or even in the business population for that matter. However, when the best available data are examined, minorities and women—and blacks in particular and most clearly—tend to be *grossly* underrepresented in virtually *all* industries and *all* geographic regions of the country, even after controlling for other factors. Moreover, the disparate impacts tend to persist even when minorities are similar to non-minorities in relevant human capital and financial factors. Jon Wainwright has demonstrated, for example,

…that the disparities facing…minority entrepreneurs at the national and economy-wide level tend to persist when the data are broken down by geography…or industry…—even when other influential factors such as education and experience are held constant. This is especially true for blacks, where adjusted disparities remain statistically significant and large in almost every case examined… These findings are strongest for blacks and Native Americans, although I document positive levels of discrimination against Hispanics and Asians as well. [36]

Recent Atlanta Evidence

As noted, the Brimmer-Marshall study was done in 1989-90, immediately following the *Croson* decision. We understood, of course, that with time, parts of our analysis would become less relevant and would have to be updated, which the City of Atlanta has continued to do. The most up-to-date evidence for Atlanta is provided by ERS 2000, in connection with Atlanta's EBO 2000.[37] This is a very thorough analysis using the best data available, including a survey of Atlanta-area businesses in the summer of 2000. These data enabled Haworth and Thornton to calculate statistical significance and isolate the importance of race and gender by controlling for other things. ERS 2000 confirmed the continuation of the same basic patterns that we discovered in 1989-90: women and minorities, especially blacks, have statistically significantly less access to private sector business than white males. Moreover, controlling for various capacity measures, minority- and women-owned businesses have significantly less revenue than would be expected in a non-discriminating environment and, compared with white males, minority workers are much less likely to become business owners. And even when they are larger and more experienced, African American businesses are less likely to be used on large projects than those owned by white males. Because of limited private sector opportunities, African American- and women-owned businesses rely much more heavily than white males on work for the City of Atlanta and other governments, even though there are no significant racial or gender differences in the interest in working in the more lucrative private sector. ERS 2000 also found that white males were significantly less likely to do business with minorities and women, and that minorities, women, and governments constituted more important sources of work for African American- and female-owned businesses.

What Happens when MFB Programs are Suspended?

Additional strong evidence of the continuing need for MFB programs is what happens to minority and female contracting when these programs are suspended because of legal challenges. The fact that the MFBs have performed satisfactorily before suspension should negate the argument that these contractors are not "ready, willing and able." And the dramatic decline in their participation in public contracts—and rare use on private contracts in the absence of affirmative action requirements—is evidence that institutionalized inclusion of women and minorities has not yet replaced institutionalized exclusion.

Without affirmative action programs, minority and female firms are not likely to be able to develop. This conclusion was highly influential in Congress' defeat of the McConnell Amendment to eliminate the DOT's DBE program in 1997, and is supported by the quantitative evidence cited above and by numerous examples of what has happened when MFB programs were suspended:

- After the Supreme Court invalidated Richmond's minority business set-aside program, minority participation fell from 30 percent to 4 percent, representing a drop of more than 87 percent.[38]

- In Atlanta, minority participation in city contracts declined from about 35 percent in 1988 to 14 percent in 1989 after the Georgia Supreme Court invalidated the city's MFB program.[39]

- In Fulton County, minorities increased their participation in county procurement business from .004 percent in 1977-79 before the county's MFB program was adopted, but declined from 17 percent to 1.7 percent after that program was temporarily enjoined in 1986.[40]

- In Philadelphia, public works subcontracts awarded to MFBs fell by 97 percent during the first month after the city's program was enjoined in 1990.[41]

- In Hillsborough County, Florida, minority contractor participation fell by 99 percent after their program was struck down.[42]

- In the City of Tampa, black participation in city contracting fell by 99 percent and Hispanic participation fell by 50 percent.[43]

- In San Jose, California, minority participation in the city's prime contracts fell by more than 80 percent in 1989 when their program was originally suspended.[44]

- In the City of Elyria, Ohio (a suburb of Cleveland), MFB participation in public works contracting virtually disappeared after their program was permanently enjoined by the court in 1991. Participation fell from approximately $1 million dollars (25 percent) in 1991 to $26,000

(0.6 percent) in 1992. In 1993, participation fell further to a mere $19,000 (less than one-half of one percent of the total).[45]

- Local officials have also confirmed significant drop-offs in one or more areas of MFB participation in Detroit,[46] Columbus, Ohio[47] and suburban Washington, DC.[48]

- In the wake of Proposition 209, the State of California Department of Transportation halved its state-funds DBE goal from 20 percent to 10 percent. Subsequently, DBE participation fell from 25.8 percent in 1995 to 14.7 percent in 1996 to 12.2 percent in 1997.[49]

- One of the most striking examples is for the State of Michigan, which had its state-funded DBE program struck down by the court at the same time that its federal-funds DBE program was upheld. According to the General Counsel for the U.S. Department of Transportation, speaking before Congress in the fall of 1997:[50]

[W]ithin six months of ending the State DBE program, minority-owned businesses were completely shut out of state highway construction. They received no contracts at all. Participation by women-owned businesses also plummeted, to 1 percent participation within 9 months. By 1996, there was only the slightest rebound. DBE's received only 31 subcontracts worth 1.1% of state contracting dollars. Under the Federal-aid highway DBE program the same DBE's received 554 subcontracts worth 12.7% of the Federal-aid dollars. Qualified DBE's were ready, willing, and able to perform the work, but without the state DBE program, they were denied the fair opportunity to compete for state contracts. Unfortunately, we have similar examples from all over the country.

The other examples to which the DOT General Counsel referred include the following ten states, all of which either no longer have, or never did have, state-funds DBE participation goals alongside their obligatory federal-aid DBE goals (all figures are for fiscal year 1996):[51]

- In Arizona, federal-aid DBE participation was 8.9 percent, but state-funds DBE participation was only 3.8 percent.

- In Arkansas, federal-aid DBE participation was 11.9 percent, but state-funds DBE participation was only 2.9 percent.

- In Connecticut, federal-aid DBE participation was 15.7 percent, but state-funds DBE participation was only 5.2 percent.

- In Delaware, federal-aid DBE participation was 12.7 percent, but state-funds DBE participation was less than 1 percent.

- In Louisiana, federal-aid DBE participation was 12.4 percent, but state-funds DBE participation was only 3.8 percent.

- In Michigan, federal-aid DBE participation was 15.5 percent, but state-funds DBE participation was only 1.4 percent.

- In Missouri, federal-aid DBE participation was 15.1 percent, but state-funds DBE participation was only 1.7 percent.

- In Nebraska, federal-aid DBE participation was 10.5 percent, but state-funds DBE participation was only 3.6 percent.

- In Oregon, federal-aid DBE participation was 16.2 percent, but state-funds DBE participation was only 3.8 percent.

- In Rhode Island, federal-aid DBE participation was 12.1 percent, but state-funds DBE participation was zero.

An MFB program is needed not just to overcome the effects of past discrimination, but to prevent future discrimination as well.[52]

Is Affirmative Action Discrimination in Reverse?

Some critics of MFB programs argue that they constitute "discrimination in reverse." Affirmative action programs, according to these critics, are based on the false assumption that minorities should be represented in all occupations and industries in accordance with their share of the population regardless of their capabilities and desires.[53] Although I am a strong advocate of affirmative action defined as positive measures to include people who have been excluded, I do not think it reasonable to assume that minorities and women would be randomly distributed among occupations and businesses in the absence of such measures. It is, however, unreasonable to assume that discrimination is no longer a major factor impeding minority businesses or that minorities would be as underrepresented as they are in the absence of discrimination. It seems equally clear to me that without positive interventions to overcome the effects of discrimination things are not likely to change very much.[54]

We should note, moreover, that there are vast differences between goals, like those established in the DOT's DBE program and "rigid quotas," though most critics of positive actions to include people who have been excluded refuse to see the distinction. Goals are sensible guides to program performance. Indeed, almost all successful businesses establish goals. Goals do not ignore qualifications or good faith efforts by program participants to achieve goals that they agree to try to meet as a condition of being awarded public contracts. While it cannot be done mechanically or with great precision, goals also are set on the basis of the realities in each market to which they refer.

It is, however, disingenuous for critics to argue that DBE programs "are discrimination in reverse" because whites were not allowed to bid on that part of a government entity's business going to minorities who previously had been barred from almost all government and private business. In other words, whites can bid on all of the private and almost all of the public business while a DBE program merely permits minorities to, for all practical purposes, bid on a part of the public work. As ERS 2000 found, however, bids are rarely used as the sole basis for private decision making, a factor that perpetuates networks that exclude minorities and women. Some critics will argue that everybody should be allowed to bid on all work. I agree, but until that time comes, programs are needed to let minority and female firms at a minimum become established and viable through participation in public sector procurement activities.

But what about the damage that might be done to whites because of programs to overcome and prevent discrimination? This is an important question and deserves the kind of careful attention given it by the courts, which seem to have conditioned their support for affirmative action on the extent to which it deprives whites of preexisting rights.[55] However, the courts have held—I think correctly—that whites might have to sacrifice some *potential* short run gains in order to combat the more egregious forms of discrimination against minorities.[56] However, affirmative action plans are entirely prospective and do not disrupt "the settled and legitimate expectations of innocent parties."[57] It should be noted, in addition, that the federal Transportation Equity Act (TEA-21) and its implementing regulations adopted narrow tailoring measures to minimize the negative impact on white males, who are themselves eligible for the program.

Measures to Improve Minority and Female Business Development

Based on extensive evidence, I believe a strong case can be made for race- or gender-specific programs to combat deeply entrenched discrimination. As noted earlier, the basic rationale for a race-or gender-conscious policy rests on three important propositions: (1) Minority and female businesses continue to suffer from overt, identified discrimination as well as from the impact of institutional discrimination. (2) Governments have compelling moral, social, and economic interests in combating business discrimination against individuals and groups for reasons unrelated to merit and ability. (3) Under present laws, there is no other effective way to remedy this discrimination or to prevent its continuation.[58] The rest of this section enlarges on these points.

The basic rationale for a minority business development program is thus to make it possible for minority firms to do business with public entities. This is necessary to provide some assurance that there will be at least a minimal demand to justify their investments, hard work, and risks in building their enterprises. As noted earlier, because of pervasive discrimination in the private sector, without public demand for their products and services, minority businesses are limited primarily to the relatively small and shrinking markets they traditionally have served.[59] Whites not only are likely to have better access to capital and other resources, but also can achieve economies of scale in the larger and more lucrative private markets from which black businesses are excluded.

A second measure governments might adopt would be to establish *"race neutral"* business development programs. Any program should have a "race neutral" component to help all disadvantaged, underutilized, or small businesses. Such a program could furnish information, remove obstacles to contracting, provide management assistance, help gain better access and prices for supplies, speed up payment schedules on public contracts, and provide financial and bonding assistance.[60] A race neutral program might also develop specific formulas to target residents, small businesses, or others on a non-racial basis, as is done both by TEA-21 and Atlanta's EBO 2000. Race neutral approaches have a number of advantages. They are less objectionable to people who believe public policies should be "color blind." Secondly, most legal measures to combat discrimination work only on the demand side of transactions and do little to ensure that supply-side measures are available to make it possible for the victims of discrimination to take advantage of opportunities when discriminatory barriers are lowered. A comprehensive program combining demand side measures with race neutral approaches is therefore likely to be more effective than either demand or supply side measures working in isolation.

Race neutral measures have some disadvantages, however. For one thing, they are likely to be expensive, making it difficult for local governments with serious budgetary constraints to afford them. Moreover, they are likely to have very low benefit-cost ratios.[61] Indeed, this is why government contracting procedures have commended themselves to policy makers—they can be powerful weapons to achieve public purposes with minimal budget costs.

The most serious objection to these "race neutral" approaches, however, is that, standing alone, they are not likely to be very effective. Demand is a powerful driver of economic activities. If there are strong obstacles to the formation and development by DBEs, it is unreasonable to expect these entrepreneurs to incur the financial risks involved unless there is a better chance they will have a market than would be the case without DBE programs. Governments have, in fact, long performed this "assured demand" function for fledgling white-owned businesses in such industries as airlines, communications, and other new and innovative businesses.

The inadequacies of these race neutral activities prompted the federal government to establish race and gender conscious programs like TEA-21 and its predecessors, which provide for flexible combinations of race conscious and race neutral policies.

Atlanta's new Equal Business Opportunity Ordinance creates an Equal Business Opportunity Program. EBO 2000 is carefully tailored to screen contractors for their racial and gender practices and to give preferences to Atlanta-based companies, not to create racial and gender set-asides or quotas. Although the evidence on race and gender disparities in the Atlanta area clearly supports a race- and gender-conscious program, the plan outlined in EBO 2000 has some significant advantages: it affects the private as well as the public sector and, since it does not favor any racial or gender category and employs race neutral outreach, it should be subjected to a "rational basis" test and not "strict scrutiny."[62] In addition, because the EBO program is based on "equal business opportunity for all persons doing business with the city" and gives preference to Atlanta-based firms, it probably will receive broader public support than a more controversial MFB program.

The Federal Programs

The Legal Requirements

In response to the Supreme Court's 1995 discussion in *Adarand Contractors, Inc. v. Pena* (115 S. Ct. 2097), which extended the strict scrutiny requirement to federal affirmative action programs, the Clinton Administration undertook an extensive review of the evidence establishing a "compelling interest" in creating such programs while simultaneously amending regulations to cause them to be more "narrowly tailored" to the achievement of that interest. "Compelling interest" and "narrow tailoring" are the two prongs of strict scrutiny, the most exacting standard of constitutional review. In *Adarand*, in order to dispel the notion that strict scrutiny is "strict in theory, but fatal in fact," a strong majority of the Court (seven of the nine justices) ruled that even under strict scrutiny, federal affirmative action programs were constitutional.[63] Moreover, according to the Court, the government has a compelling interest in remedying the "...unhappy persistence of both the practice and the lingering effects of racial discrimination against minority groups in this century."[64]

Several legal principles relevant to determining the nature and weight of evidence of discrimination needed by the government to establish compelling interest were not changed by *Adarand*:

1.   The government may take race-conscious remedial action without a formal determination that there has been discrimination against individual members of a minority group or class. The basic test is whether the government has a "strong basis in evidence" that affirmative action is warranted.[65]

2.   The beneficiaries of affirmative action need not be limited to individuals who themselves demonstrate that they have suffered identified discrimination.[66]

3.   The Supreme Court has made it clear that general, historical societal discrimination against minorities alone is not an adequate basis for race-conscious remedial measures. However, the federal government would have a compelling interest in affirmative action in its procurement programs if it could show with some specificity how "the persistence of both the practice and lingering effects of racial discrimination" has reduced the contracting opportunities for minorities.[67]

4.   The Thirteenth and Fourteenth Amendments give Congress the unique and express constitutional authority to legislate to ensure the guarantees of racial equality.[68]

5.   The Constitution also gives Congress the authority to remedy discrimination in the private as well as the public sector. According to the plurality in *Croson*, "It is beyond dispute that any public entity, state or federal, has a compelling interest in assuring that public dollars, drawn from the tax contributions of all citizens, do not serve to finance the evil of private prejudice."[69]

6.   Under constitutional spending and commerce powers, Congress likewise can ensure that discrimination is not perpetuated through procurement practices.[70]

7.   Congress also has the power to seek to eliminate the effects of discrimination that restrict minority opportunities; it is not limited to deliberate, overt, intentional acts of discrimination.[71]

8.   And Congress has the power to develop national remedies for national problems. It is not required to make findings of discrimination with the same degree of specificity required by state and local governments, and it is not required to find discrimination "in every industry or region that may be affected by a remedial measure."[72]

The Evidence

The government's evidence was still being collected in May 1996, when the Department of Justice issued its Notice of Proposed Reforms for Affirmative Action, and its Preliminary Survey of the *Compelling Interest* for Affirmative Action in Federal Procurement.[73] However, this report summarized a vast amount of information to support the government's conclusion "that racially discriminatory barriers hamper the ability of minority-owned businesses to compete with other firms on an equal footing in our nation's contracting markets. In short, there is today a compelling interest to take remedial action in federal procurement."[74]

The compelling interest material is divided into several parts: (1) an overview of the legislative record that supports Congressional affirmative action legislation on procurement—"a record that is entitled to substantial deference from the courts given Congress's express constitutional power to identify and redress, on a nationwide basis, racial discrimination and its effects"[75]; (2) relevant Congressional hearings and reports that are not related to specific affirmative action legislation; (3) recent studies that document the effects of racial discrimination in procurement at the state and local level; and (4) academic work that demonstrates how various forms of discrimination combine to restrict business opportunities for minorities.[76]

The *Compelling Interest* concludes:

> All told, the evidence that the Justice Department has collected is powerful and persuasive. It shows that the discriminatory barriers facing minority-owned businesses are not vague and amorphous manifestations of historical societal discrimination. Rather, they are real and concrete, and reflect ongoing patterns and practices of exclusion, as well as the tangible lingering effects of discriminatory conduct.[77]

TEA-21's new implementing regulations provided several mechanisms designed to meet the narrow tailoring standard, including waivers, requiring recipients to rely on race- and gender-neutral measures to the maximum extent possible; allowing recipients to tie annual goals to local conditions; greater emphasis on contractors' good faith efforts in achieving individual contract goals; greater flexibility for recipients and contractors; authorizing mechanisms to address the problem of excessive concentration of DBEs; net worth restrictions to limit participation to small DBEs; and provisions for anyone to challenge the presumption of social and economic disadvantage for specific individuals.

Concrete Works Decision

In *Adarand VII*, the Tenth Circuit Court of Appeals outlines a position that seems to me to be much more compatible with good social science research techniques than the impossible standards established by such federal district court decisions as *Concrete Works of Colorado v. The City and County of Denver.*[78] Defendants in this case presented the best statistical data and employed the most sophisticated analytical techniques available. Among other things, the Court ruled that Denver's program was unconstitutional because the regression analysis used to analyze census data made "no attempt to control such seemingly important characteristics as marital status, veteran status, availability of other sources of income and hours worked."[79] The Court did not explain why these matters were "seemingly important" or where defendants could obtain data that would permit such controls. Ironically, the Court concluded that "Discriminating behavior because of differences in race, ethnicity and gender cannot be proved by objective evidence," but must depend "upon inferences fairly drawn from circumstantial evidence."[80] Statistical evidence is one type of "circumstantial evidence," which the Supreme Court has permitted in employment cases where the statistical evidence is bolstered by "testimony of specific instances of discrimination." However, there are "inherent limitations in attempting to collect and measure useful information about the construction industry because of the nearly infinite number of variables affecting the fate of firms operating within the special business environments of the many submarkets for products and services collectively called construction."[81] The Court also recognized the "intensely competitive and very risky" nature of the construction industry where business is dynamic and firms "shrink their performance capacity according to the volume of business..." However, the firm's ability to expand depends on its "access to information, its reputation in the community and the skills of its managers." Moreover, the decision to subcontract depends on many subjective factors. Because of these uncertainties, "risk aversion causes contractors to rely on their working knowledge of past performances of other business firms when looking for subcontractors and supplies."

What the Court failed to acknowledge is that these are precisely the factors that give contractors both the motive and the ability to limit competition by such an easily identifiable characteristic as race—which is exactly what this industry has done in the past. And the difficulty of proving discrimination in business in general and construction in particular are the main reasons the federal and other governments have used their contracting powers to combat this kind of discrimination.

Despite the *Concrete Works* Court's conclusion that discrimination cannot be proved by objective evidence, it concluded that only objective evidence could withstand strict scrutiny. The Court noted that "disparity studies may be persuasive as evidence in litigation of this type as acknowledged by Justice O'Connor in *Croson*...,"[82] but unfortunately, went on to demonstrate that it was virtually impossible to conduct a disparity study that could withstand its interpretation of strict scrutiny, because no data existed that could determine whether minority contractors were "qualified" and "willing and able to perform a particular service." This, despite its recognition that the dynamic nature of the industry caused "qualification" to depend heavily on the ability to get contracts.

To compound the problem, the *Concrete Works* Court established several threshold tests for discrimination that are impossible to meet:

> To determine whether apparent racial, ethnic and gender differences in the performance of business firms in the construction industry in the Denver MSA are the result of *intentional* discrimination practiced against them by their competitors…these are the questions that must be answered. (1) Is there pervasive race, ethnic and gender discrimination *throughout all aspects* of the construction and professional design industry in the…Denver MSA? (2) Does such discrimination *equally* affect all of the racial and ethnic groups designated for preference…and all women? (3) Does such discrimination result from policies and practices *intentionally* used by business firms for the purpose of disadvantaging those firms because of race, ethnicity and gender?[83]

The Court concluded that the "Denver [disparity] studies do almost nothing to answer these questions because the consultants designing them made no effort to address them or any equivalents to them."

The Court faults these studies for not attempting to account for "cultural factors that may affect the desire or willingness to own a business and there were no controls for access to capital or personal wealth." The studies did "attempt to control for education and amount of work experience without, however, considering the relevance of particular educational credentials to construction work and without regard for the particular type of experience." With regard to the sophisticated research methodology used in Denver's studies, the Court noted that "That might be consistent with scientific methodology but it does not square with applicable law."[84]

The *Concrete Works* decision demonstrates considerable confusion about discrimination and the nature of the evidence required to prove it. The Court made heroic assumptions about racial differences in business decision making. There is, for example, an implication that "cultural" factors probably have affected "the desire or willingness to own a business" and that size, access to capital, and personal wealth have nothing to do with discrimination, but in a comment that can only be described as based on complete ignorance of the economics of discrimination, the Court asks: "Is it fair to assume that male Caucasian contractors will only do business with other male Caucasians even where this is contrary to their economic interests?" The judge seems not to understand that racial discrimination is a group or social phenomenon—not merely individual. As noted earlier, social forces often counteract individual rational decision making. Moreover, by limiting competition to a preferred group of associates, as the judge acknowledges that they do, white contractors are able to restrict competition, reduce risk and enhance their profits. Moreover, the *Concrete Works* Court argued that the best scientific analysis of this problem is irrelevant. This and other post-*Croson* decisions take no note of institutionalized patterns of discrimination that cannot be addressed on a case-by-case basis because it is not possible to identify "who is responsible for such discrimination." Institutionalized discrimination is never discussed—though *Concrete Works*, following *Croson*, speaks of "societal discrimination," which is not the same thing.

Adarand VII

The Tenth Circuit Court of Appeals decision in *Adarand VII*, which was accepted for review by the U.S. Supreme Court in 2001, disagreed strongly with the position taken by *Concrete Works*. In this case, the Tenth Circuit reversed the lower court ruling that the DOT's DBE program was not narrowly tailored and therefore unconstitutional. Actually, the district court decision was on an earlier version of the DOT's DBE program, the Subcontract Compensation Clause (SCC), before the revised rules were issued February 2, 1999.[85] The SCC program employed race-conscious presumptions designed to favor minority and other disadvantaged business enterprises. The district court held that SCC met the compelling interest test, but found it "difficult to envisage a race-based classification that would ever be narrowly tailored."[86] Although *Adarand VII* agreed with the district court that the SCC had not been narrowly tailored, it held that the new DBE program passed constitutional muster. Both courts agreed that DBE and SCC met the compelling interest test.

In *Adarand VII*, the Tenth Circuit noted that the Supreme Court in *Adarand III* decided that there could be a compelling interest for race-conscious programs and interpreted *Croson* to mean that

> The Fourteenth Amendment permits race-conscious programs that seek both to eradicate discrimination by the government entity itself and to prevent the government entity from acting as a "passive participant" in a system of racial exclusion practiced by elements of the local construction industry by allowing tax dollars "to finance the evil of private prejudice."[87]

Adarand, in its brief, sought to use *Croson*'s limitations on state and local governments "in an attempt to limit the permissible scope of Congress's power to redress the effects of racial discrimination, ignoring the substantial differences between the scope of the problems addressed by Congress and those to be addressed by a city council..." Congress's power is not "as geographically limited as that of a local government... The geographic scope of Congress's reach...is 'society wide' and therefore nationwide."[88] *Adarand* and its amici argued "for the necessity of findings regarding both discrimination and the availability of qualified DBEs in a particular local market as a necessary prerequisite to any government action. We disagree, concluding that the absence of such findings is more properly addressed in this case under the rubric of narrow tailoring."[89]

The Tenth Circuit's "benchmark for judging the adequacy of the government's factual predicate for affirmative action legislation [i]s whether there exists a *'strong basis in evidence'* for the [government's] conclusion that remedial action was necessary."[90] Both statistical and anecdotal evidence are appropriate in the strict scrutiny calculus, "although anecdotal evidence by itself is not."[91] Furthermore:

> Although *Croson* places the burden of production on the [government] to demonstrate a strong basis in evidence that its race- and gender-conscious contract program aims to remedy specifically identified past or present discrimination, the Fourteenth Amendment does not require a court to make an ultimate judicial finding before [the government] may take affirmative steps to eradicate discrimination.[92]

The Tenth Circuit concluded:

> After the government's initial showing, the burden shifts to [plaintiffs] to rebut that showing: 'Notwithstanding the burden of initial production that rests' with the government, '[t]he ultimate burden [of proof] remains with [the challenging party] to demonstrate the unconstitutionality of an affirmative action program.'[93]

In evaluating the evidence of discrimination to support a compelling interest, the Tenth Circuit considered "both direct and circumstantial evidence, including post-enactment evidence introduced by the defendants as well as the evidence in the legislative history itself."[94] In addition, "we may consider public and private discrimination not only in the area of government procurement contracts but also in the construction industry generally; thus, any findings Congress has made as to the entire construction industry are relevant."[95]

The Tenth Circuit noted that Congress repeatedly had found that "racial discrimination and its continuing effects have distorted the market for public contracts—especially construction contracts—necessitating a race-conscious remedy."[96] However, the question was "not merely whether the government has considered evidence, but rather the *nature and extent* of the evidence it considered."[97] In this regard, the Court agreed that reports and general statements by members of Congress were not sufficient, but

[c]ontrary to *Adarand*'s contentions…the government's evidence as to the kinds of obstacles minority subcontracting businesses face constitutes a strong basis for the conclusion that those obstacles are not 'the same problems faced by any new business, regardless of the race of owners.'[98]

The Tenth Circuit concluded with an analysis of the numerous state and local disparity studies undertaken in response to *Croson*. The Court was

certainly mindful that 'where special qualifications are necessary, the relevant pool for purposes of demonstrating discriminatory exclusion must be the number of minorities qualified to undertake the particular task.'[99]

But here, we are unaware of such 'special qualifications,' aside from the general qualifications necessary to operate a construction subcontracting business. At a minimum, the disparity indicates that there has been underutilization of minority subcontractors; and there is no evidence either in the record on appeal or in the legislative history before us that those minority contractors who *have* been utilized have performed inadequately or otherwise demonstrated a lack of qualifications.[100]

The Tenth Circuit specifically rejected

The decidedly vague urgings of *Adarand*'s amici curiae to reject disparity studies generally as biased and/or insufficiently reliable. Certainly the conclusions of virtually all social scientific studies may be cast into question by their choice of assumptions and methodologies. The very need to make assumptions and to select data sets and relevant variables precludes perfection in empirical social sciences. However, general criticism of disparity studies…is of little persuasive value…nor does it create 'a legitimate factual dispute about the accuracy of [the government's] data.'

Critics have minimized the evidence that disparity ratios would be larger "but for discrimination." However, the Tenth Circuit concluded that the

…existence of evidence indicating that the number of minority DBEs would be significantly (but unquantifiably) higher but for such [discriminatory barriers that discourage the formation and utilization of minority businesses] is nevertheless relevant to the assessment of whether a disparity is sufficiently significant to give rise to an inference of discriminatory exclusion.[101]

Finally, the Tenth Circuit concluded that the sharp drops or elimination of minority contracting when DBE programs are discontinued, while standing alone is not dispositive, strongly supports the government's claim that there are significant barriers to minority competition in the public subcontracting market, raising the specter of racial discrimination.

In sum, on the basis of the foregoing body of evidence, we conclude that the government has met its initial burden of presenting a 'strong basis in evidence' sufficient to support its articulated, constitutionally valid, compelling interest.[102]

Adarand VII likewise rejected

Adarand's contention that Congress must make specific fact findings against every single sub-category of individuals within the broad racial and ethnic categories designated by statute and addressed by the relevant legislative findings. If Congress has valid evidence, for example, that Asian-American individuals are subject to discrimination…it makes no sense to require sub-findings that subcategories of that class experience particuliarized discrimination because of their status as, for example, Americans from Bhutan.[103]

The Tenth Circuit therefore concluded that the evidence cited by the government, "particularly that…in *The Compelling Interest*…more than satisfies the government's burden of production regarding the compelling interest for a race conscious remedy."[104]

Conclusions

Affirmative action programs are needed to overcome the institutionalized patterns of racial and gender exclusion that have characterized American business. Opponents must assume either that discrimination no longer exists or that there are more effective ways to address it. The evidence suggests to me that discrimination in business continues to be an important barrier to the opportunities of minorities, especially blacks and women. It is, moreover, important for the courts to afford governments opportunities to demonstrate the persistence of discrimination through the use of standard research techniques. Opponents should not be able to defeat these programs by pointing out the inherent problems with this research, as has been done by several lower courts. They should be required to present credible research findings to show that disparities can be explained by factors other than discrimination. I therefore believe that good research procedures and the national interest would be advanced if the U.S. Supreme Court sustained the Tenth Circuit in *Adarand VII*. However, if that does not happen, program sponsors should examine Atlanta's EBO 2000 as an example of a program that might not only be more effective in that it combats private as well as public discrimination, but also would not have to meet an impossible strict scrutiny test. A Supreme Court decision sustaining *Concrete Works* would be "strict in theory but fatal in fact."

Notes

1. See e.g. *Croson*, 488 US 469, 507-10 (using such terms as "identified," "societal," and "historical").
2. See Marshall, Ray, "The Economics of Racial Discrimination," *Journal of Economic Literature* 12, no. 3 (1974): 849-71.
3. Haworth, Joan and Thornton, Janet, *Minority and Female Owned Business Opportunity in Atlanta*, Tallahassee, Fla.: Economic Research Service, Provisional Draft, October 2000, hereinafter referred to as ERS 2000.
4. See Arrow, Kenneth J., "What Has Economics to Say About Discrimination?" *Journal of Economic Perspectives* 12, no. 2 (1998): 91–100. Arrow, a Nobel laureate in economics, explains how these networks prevent market forces from eliminating discrimination.
5. See e.g., Boston, Thomas D., "Unequal Access: Minority Contracting and Procurement with the Atlanta Board of Education," report submitted to the Atlanta Public School System (1991), 102–11; Sjoquist, David L., ed., *The Atlanta Paradox*, New York: Russell Sage Foundation, 2000.
6. See e.g., Boston, Thomas D., "A Post-Disparity Study Review: The Fulton County MBE/FBE Program, 1990–1993," report submitted to the Fulton County Board of Commissioners (1994), 10. As Professor Boston notes: "It is not unreasonable to assume that during the nineteenth century and until the 1960's, prospective black businessmen were rather reluctant to start a business beyond the 'mom and pop' variety. For indeed, any large scale enterprise would have been in all probability dependent in some way upon white suppliers and/or white consumers either or both of which would have probably proved hostile. Furthermore, black entrepreneurs faced the very real possibilities of receiving either physical harm or destruction of their property by antagonistic white competitors or bigots."
7. Brimmer and Marshall Economic Consultants, "Public Policy and Promotion of Minority Economic Development," report prepared for City of Atlanta (1990), Parts I, 2 (hereinafter referred to as the "Brimmer-Marshall Report"). The statistical evidence bears this statement out. In both the City of Atlanta and Fulton County, minority and female participation in contracting and procurement activity was virtually nil prior to the advent of the MFB program.
8. See Holzer, Harry and Neumark, David, "Assessing Affirmative Action," *Journal of Economic Literature* 38, no. 3 (2000): 483-569.
9. Lillard, Lee A. and Ton, Hong W., *Private Sector Training: Who Gets it and What are its Effects?* Santa Monica, Cal.: Rand, 1986; Marshall, Ray and Briggs, Jr., Vernon M., *The Negro and Apprenticeship*, Baltimore: Johns Hopkins University, 1967; Marshall, Ray, *The Negro and Organized Labor*, New York: John Wiley, 1965; Sjoquist, *The Atlanta Paradox*.
10. See Comer, James P., "Educating Poor Minority Children," *Scientific American* 259, no. 9 (1988): 42-48; Action Council on Minority Education, *Education That Works*, Washington, D.C.: QEM Project and MIT, 1990; Marshall, Ray and Tucker, Marc, *Thinking for a Living*, New York: Basic Books, 1990.
11. Becker, Gary, *The Economics of Discrimination,* Chicago: University of Chicago Press, 1971.

12. Bureau of the Census, *Statistical Abstract of the United States: 1992*, various tables. A similar pattern is evident for Hispanics, as well as for other racial or ethnic minorities, with the exception of certain Asian ethnic groups. Hispanics in 1990, for example, were 9 percent of the population, but less than 8 percent of the civilian labor force and total employment. They received only about 5 percent of total money income, held less than 2 percent of the nation's wealth, owned only about 3 percent of U.S. businesses, and accounted for only slightly more than one percent of all business sales.

13. US Census Bureau, "1997 Economic Census: Survey of Minority-Owned Business Enterprises: Black (EC97CS-3), Washington, DC: US Government Printing Office, 2001, 17, 80.

14. Suggs, Robert E., "Rethinking Minority Business Development Strategies," *Harvard Civil Rights-Civil Liberties Law Review* 25, no. 1 (1990): 101.

15. "Brimmer-Marshall Report," Part I, 9–10.

16. Ibid., 99.

17. See Becker, *Economics of Discrimination*.

18. Holzer and Neumark, "Assessing Affirmative Action."

19. Ibid., 569.

20. Ibid., 487, citing Farrell Black, *Antidiscrimination Law and Minority Employment*, Chicago: University of Chicago Press, 1984.

21. *University of California Regents v. Bakke*, 438 US 265 at 307 (1978).

22. Arrow, "What Has Economics to Say," 92.

23. Ibid., 93.

24. *Adarand Contractors, Inc. v. Pena* 515 US 200.

25. *See Adarand III supra* and *Adarand Contractors, Inc. v. Slater* 228 F.3rd 1147, 1155 (10th Cir. Sept. 25, 2000), Petition for Cert. Filed, 69 US L.W. 3346 (US Nov. 7, 2000, No. 00-73).

26. The private sector of the economy is far larger than the public sector. In the construction industry, for example, about 85 percent of all construction work put in place is privately owned. According to the 1987 Census of Construction Industries, the total value of construction put in place in the Atlanta MSA was about $14.4 billion. Of this, only $2.3 billion (16 percent) was publicly owned. A similar ratio was observed in 1992. The Atlanta MSA had construction put in place that year valued at $13.8 billion. Of this, only $3.1 billion (22.5 percent) was publicly owned. See US Census Bureau, *1992 Census of Construction Industries: Geographic Series: South Atlantic States* (CC92-A-5) (1995), GA-8.

27. *Shelly v. Kraemer* 334 US 1 (1948); *Norwood v. Harrison* 413 US 455 (1973); *Fullilove v. Klutznick* 448 US 478 (1980); *City of Richmond v. Croson* 448 US 469 (1989). See also Ayres, Ian and Vars, Frederick E., "When Does Private Discrimination Justify Public Affirmative Action?" *Columbia Law Review* 98, no. 7 (1998): 1578.

28. Arrow, "What Has Economics to Say," 92.

29. 448 US 478 (1980), emphasis added.

30. See Marshall, Ray and Christian, Virgil, *Black Employment in the South*, Austin, Tex.: University of Texas Press, 1976.

31. *Coral Construction v. King Co.* 941 F. 2d 910 (9th Cir. 1989) at 919.

32. Marshall, Ray, *Labor in the South*, Cambridge: Harvard University Press, 1967; *The Negro and Organized Labor*, 87-108; and *Black Employment in the South*.

33. Hefner, James, "Black Employment in Atlanta, Negro Employment in the South," Center for the Study of Human Resources, University of Texas at Austin (1973), 41. See also Hefner, James, *Black Employment in a Southern 'Progressive City': The Atlanta Experience*, Ph.D. diss., University of Colorado, 1971.

34.   Hefner, "Black Employment in Atlanta."
35.   Ashenfelter, Orley and Oaxaca, Ronald, "The Economics of Discrimination: Econo-mists Enter the Courtroom," *American Economic Review* 77, no. 2 (1987): 321–25.
36.   Wainwright, Jon S., *Racial Discrimination and Minority Business Enterprise: Evi-dence from the 1990 Census*, Ph.D. diss., University of Texas at Austin, 1997, 149–150.
37.   Haworth and Thornton, "ERS 2000."
38.   "Brimmer-Marshall Report," Part I, 10.
39.   Ibid.
40.   Ibid., 10, 11.
41.   United States Commission on Minority Business Development, *Final Report*, US G.P.O., 1992, 99.
42.   Ibid.
43.   Ibid..
44.   Ibid.
45.   Telephone interview with L. Johnson, City of Elyria Office of Contract Compliance, Feb. 27, 1998.
46.   Telephone interviews with K. Dones-Carter and D. Teeter, City Council Research Department, City of Detroit Feb. 27, 1998.
47.   Telephone interview with M. Carter, City of Columbus Equal Business Opportu-nity Commission, Feb. 27, 1998.
48.   Telephone interview with B. Kim, Staff Attorney, Maryland Department of Trans-portation, concerning the Washington Suburban Sanitary Commission, Feb. 27, 1998.
49.   Telephone interview with D. Goldberg, Staff Attorney, Office of General Counsel, U.S. Department of Transportation, Feb. 28, 1998.
50.   Statement of Nancy E. McFadden, General Counsel, U.S. Department of Transpor-tation, before the Subcommittee on Constitution, Federalism, and Property Rights of the U.S. Senate Committee on the Judiciary, Sept. 30, 1997, 2.
51.   Telephone interview with Attorney D. Goldberg, Office of General Counsel, U.S. Department of Transportation, February 28, 1998.
52.   In *Adarand VII*, the Tenth Circuit Court of Appeals noted that "There is ample evidence that when race-conscious public contracting programs are struck down or discontinued, minority business participation in the relevant market drops sharply or even disappears... Although that evidence standing alone is not dispositive, it strongly supports the government's claim that there are significant barriers to minor-ity competition in the public subcontracting market, raising the specter of racial discrimination." (48-49)
53.   See, for example, Sowell, Thomas, "Affirmative Action: From Bad to Worse," *Wall Street Journal*, March 6, 1990, A20. Sowell argues that "...affirmative action policies...rest on the assumption that different racial and ethnic groups would be evenly or randomly represented in institutions and occupations, in the absence of discrimination."
54.   Critics of affirmative action also argue that these measures disproportionately favor those minority group members who are already more fortunate (see Sowell, Tho-mas, *Preferential Policies*, New York: William Morrow & Co., 1990, 15). How-ever, this argument misses two realities. First, any self-help policy will naturally help those who are most able to help themselves. As noted, anti-discrimination measures are necessary but not sufficient to help the "truly disadvantaged." Second, as noted, minority businesses are rarely affluent, and certainly are not as well off as similarly situated whites.

55. Haworth and Thornton, "ERS 2000."
56. *Fullilove v. Klutznick*, 448 US 448, at 484.
57. *Wygant v. Jackson Board of Education*, 476 US 267, at 283 (1986). *See also Steelworkers v. Weber*, 443 US 193 (1979).
58. *City of Richmond v. J.A. Croson Co.*, 488 US 469, 550 (Marshall, J., dissenting) (noting that while race neutral measures are "theoretically appealing, [they] have been discredited as ineffectual in eradicating the effects of discrimination" in the construction industry.
59. Historical material and interviews, "Brimmer-Marshall Report."
60. It is not clear whether the *Croson* decision required race neutral remedies—the Court merely criticized the City of Richmond for not having "considered" alternatives. See *City of Richmond* v. *J.A. Croson Co.*, 488 US 469, 507 (1989). Presumably, a jurisdiction must consider alternatives and have a demonstrable basis for showing that those alternatives could not promote that jurisdiction's "substantial interest" as well as race conscious approaches.
61. Holzer and Neumark, "Assessing Affirmative Action," 560.
62. See *Associated Pennsylvania Contractors*, Civil No. 89-0427, 738 F. Supp. 891; 1990 US Dist. LEXIS 7288.
63. *Adarand Contractors, Inc. v. Slater* 228 F.3rd 1147 10th Cir (2000) at 2117.
64. Ibid.
65. *City of Richmond v. J.A. Croson* 488 US 500 (1989).
66. *See Local Sheet Metal Workers International Assn. V. EEOC* 478 US 421, 482 (1986); *Wygant* v. *Jackson Bd. of Educ.* 476 US 267 277-78, 287 (1986).
67. *Adarand* 115 S. Ct., 2117.
68. *Croson* 488 US 488; *Adarand* 115 S. Ct. 2114; *Seminole Tribe of Fla. v. Fla.* 116 S. Ct. 1114, 1125 (1996).
69. *Croson* 488 US 492.
70. Ibid., 490.
71. *Adarand* 115 S. Ct. 2117.
72. *Compelling Interest* 26051 citing *Croson* 488 US 490, 504; *Fullilove* 448 US 502-03 (Powell, J. concurring).
73. *Federal Register* 61, no. 101, May 23, 1996, 26056-26063.
74. Ibid., 26050.
75. Ibid.
76. This kind of evidence is justified because "It is well established that the factual predicate for a particular affirmative action measure is not confined to the four corners of the legislative record of the measure." See, *e.g. Concrete Works v. City and County of Denver* 36 F.3d. 1513, 1520-22 (10th Cir., 1994), cert. Denied 115 S.Ct. 1315 (1995); *Contractors Ass'n. v. City of Philadelphia* F.3d 990, 1004 (3rd Cir. 1993); *Coral Construction Co. v. King County* 941 F.2d 910, 920 (9th Cir. 1991), cert. Denied 502 US 1033 (1992).
77. *Compelling Interest*, 26051.
78. 2000 US Dist. LEXIS 2885, Civil Action 92-M-21, March 7, 2000.
79. Ibid., 46.
80. Ibid., 67.
81. Ibid., 71.
82. Ibid.
83. Ibid., 76, emphasis added.
84. Ibid., 88.
85. 49 CFR Parts 23 and 26.
86. *Adarand Contractors, Inc. v. Pena* 965 F.Supp. 1580, (D.Colo., 1977).

87. *Concrete Works* 36 F.3d. 1513, 1519 (10th Cir. 1994) quoting *Croson* 488 US 492.
88. Ibid., 27.
89. Ibid., 27, footnote 10.
90. Ibid., 28, citing *Concrete Works* 36 F.3d. 1521, quoting *Croson* 488 US500, quoting *Wygant* 476 US 277.
91. Ibid., citing *Concrete Works* 36 F.3d., 1520-21.
92. Ibid., 29, citing *Concrete Works*, 1522, citing *Wygant* 476 US 292 (O'Connor, J. concurring).
93. Ibid., 29, citing *Concrete Works*, 1522, quoting *Wygant* 476 US 277-78.
94. Ibid., 29.
95. Ibid.
96. Ibid.
97. Ibid.
98. *Adarand*, 515 US 237, at 43, quoting Appellee's Brief at 28.
99. Ibid., quoting *Croson* 501-2.
100. Ibid., 45, citing *Concrete Works* 36 F.3d 1528.
101. Ibid., 47-8.
102. Ibid., 49, citing *Croson* 488 US 500, quoting *Wygant* 476 US 277.
103. Ibid., 52, footnote 18.
104. Ibid., 54.

8

Money and Medicine: What Should Physicians Earn/Be Paid?

David J. Rothman

"Underinvestment in assessing the past is likely to lead to faulty estimates and erroneous prescriptions for future action."—*Eli Ginzberg, 1997* ("Managed Care—A Look Back and a Look Ahead," *New England Journal of Medicine,* 333, 1018-20)

No one has traced the relationship between money and medicine more adeptly or convincingly than Eli Ginzberg. In persuasive fashion, he has made certain that no one forgets that health care is (now) a trillion dollar industry, and that any plans to reform medical practice or enhance access to medical care must reckon with this simple, albeit astonishing, fact. Whether the concern is medical education, physician supply, managed care, hospital capacity, or national health insurance, Eli Ginzberg forges the links to economic principles, analyzing within this broader framework what has happened and what is likely to happen. All the while, he fully recognizes that medicine is ultimately about more than money, that however powerful market forces are, health is more than a commodity. The market may well limit choice, he has taught us, but it should not be allowed to dictate choice.

This essay pursues the theme of money and medicine, and in the spirit that marks Eli Ginzberg's interdisciplinary efforts, joins medicine with social history. Specifically, it addresses the money aspect in medicine not in classic impersonal terms, with money as the ultimate in a purely constructed instrument, but rather in sociological terms. It situates money in particular contexts, demonstrating how its meaning in medicine often differs from its meaning in other parts

---

David J. Rothman is professor of history at Columbia University.

of the economy and at different times and places. The sociologist Georg Simmel was among those who most thoroughly explicated the rational quality of money. His 1900 book, *The Philosophy of Money*, defined money as "colorless," coming only in an "evenly flat and grey tone," and serving as the neutral intermediary of a rational, impersonal market.[1] But Simmel's approach fails to acknowledge the many social aspects of money, and ignoring this consideration makes it almost impossible to interpret the complex history of money and medicine.

A contemporary sociologist-historian who has explicated the social meanings of money in particularly skillful ways is Princeton's Viviana Zelizer. As her books *Pricing the Priceless Child*[2] and *The Social Meaning of Money*[3] demonstrate, people think about income and shape commercial transactions in very personal ways. They earmark money by categories that baffle economists (setting money aside in pin money, allowances, burial money, and Christmas clubs), and incorporate money into friendships in odd fashions (using crisp bills for weddings and bar mitzvahs or giving gift money in multiples of the lucky number 18). In this same spirit, they will evaluate the adequacy of personal income not merely in absolute but in comparative terms. Thus, in one, probably apocryphal, account, an economist was asked how much he wanted to earn and replied: "$10,000 more than my brother-in-law."

As this essay will argue, people also conceptualize money differently according to the special character and identity of the recipient. This proposition is particularly relevant to analyzing money and medicine, or more specifically, the issue of how much physicians were supposed to earn (under a fee-for-service arrangement) or are to be paid (since so many physicians are now employees). Only by reckoning with the social character of money can one begin to explain the extraordinary ambivalence that surrounds this question, both in terms of physicians' expectations and public expectations. Indeed, the very fact that this has been and continues to be a vigorously discussed and debated subject distinguishes medicine from other enterprises. Not many people engage on how much money a CEO or a banker should be earning, or how they should be paid. But that is not true for medicine. Physician income and appropriate mode of payment captures a degree of attention that is remarkably different.

These preliminary observations help to establish a fundamental point about money and medicine: a profound social tension has existed and continues to exist between the two. A deep ambivalence has marked the relationship between practicing medicine and making money. The origins of this ambivalence, how it has been manifested in the past, and its implications for the future are the core concerns of this essay.

* * *

The normative principles around money and medicine as explicated in traditional medical ethics—the treatises written and read by physicians—reveal deep inconsistencies. The literature simultaneously places the practitioner above mere money, and at the same time establishes rules of behavior to help physicians make money. The contradictions should not surprise students of professionalism, for they mirror the two conflicting characteristics of professionalism itself: the establishment of high-minded duties on the one hand, and the maintenance of a marketplace monopoly on the other.

Much of the medical literature on professional etiquette and ethics emphasizes the sacred character of medicine, treating money as profane and even contaminating. When in 1808 Benjamin Rush, a noted American physician and signer of the Declaration of Independence, set forth the vices and virtues of the physician, the first on the roster of vices was avarice. It was manifested primarily in a physician's "denial of service to the poor." The greatest virtue was charity, exemplified by physicians who not only refused to take payment from the poor patients but gave them assistance. "Humanity in physicians," concluded Rush, "manifests itself in gratuitous services to the poor."[4]

These attitudes were part of an overarching theme in traditional medical ethics—that ethical practices in medicine were defined as the decisions made by a virtuous physician. Tautologies notwithstanding, it was not a specific action that was or was not ethical; rather, it was the physician himself who was or was not ethical. In effect, a virtuous physician could do no wrong. And what did it mean to be virtuous? To follow a way of life that was free of vice, forswearing wine, women, theater, and gambling—and cultivated virtue, including the practice of religion, honesty, and charity. The virtuous physician earned sufficient income to provide his family with all necessities but certainly did not devote himself to becoming wealthy.

These self-denying precepts, however, are not the entirety of the story. Even normative statements in medical ethics point to a second truth about money and medicine. The classic statement of medical ethics, the Hippocratic Oath, which was so protective of patient well-being and confidentiality, also contains two provisions about money. First, that physicians were obliged to impart the secrets of the art of medicine to the sons of their own teachers "without fee." Second, physicians were not to encroach on the territory of fellow physicians: "I will not use the knife, not even on sufferers from stone, but will withdraw in favor of such men who are engaged in the work." In effect, the Hippocratic Oath established professional courtesy, still followed today, with money not to change hands among doctors; and it also set forth the principle of doctors protecting each other's livelihood. In this same spirit, the first major code of medical ethics in the United States, the AMA code of 1847, insisted that a physician asked to see a patient to give a second opinion should never take that patient for his own.[5] Thus, the guiding declarations of professional principles in medicine were themselves ambivalent about money, at once urging doctors to be selfless and self-interested.

* * *

What about actual practices? Norms notwithstanding, what constitutes the history of money in medical practice, taking the twentieth century American experience as the case in point? From the 1920s until well after World War II, money was not typically the subject of discussion or even interaction between doctors and their middle class patients. The physician's receptionist typically took the patient's payment of a bill, or a rapid and awkward exchange of cash occurred between doctor and patient, evocative of the unease with which a groom slips a clergyman money for performing a marriage or a family pays the officiant for delivering a eulogy. (As one very prominent Johns Hopkins internist, Lewellys Barker, noted in his 1942 memoir, he decided what his charges would be and then "turned the matter of fees entirely to my bookkeepers...who carried all the responsibility for collections."[6]) With the advent of third party reimbursements for medical care, whether by Blue Shield, a corporate plan, or Medicare, money receded even further from the direct doctor-patient relationship. The insured patient might not even know what the physician's charges were, or even care, since someone else was responsible for the payment.

The relative silence around money certainly did not mean that income was irrelevant to practitioners. But the critical fact around income, until very recently, was that medicine was not an especially well-paying profession. It afforded practitioners a middle-class, comfortable income, but through the 1950s, lawyers on average earned more, and so did engineers. Whatever else, medicine was not a paved route to prosperity.

The truth of this statement was well recognized. For example, immediately after the first World War, the office of the Surgeon-General issued a series of pamphlets "for disabled soldiers, sailors, and marines to aid them in choosing a vocation," and devoted one of them to "The Practice of Medicine as a Vocation." After a general description of the duties and obligations of a doctor ("the work of the physician is difficult. There is great mental strain...[and] great physical strain."), it reviewed "the income that can reasonably be expected:"

> The practice of medicine does not hold out the hope of any great financial reward. There are some medical practitioners who have made small fortunes in their practice, but such cases are few. The ordinary practitioner can not count on much more than a comfortable living... Not only is the physician's salary generally small, but it is uncertain as well.

The proof presented was the incomes of Harvard medical school graduates. After ten years of practice, they were making $4000 to $5000 a year, a respectable sum to be sure, about twice that of skilled labor, but not a fortune. To be sure, an occasional surgeon earned more, even much more. But medicine was not the road to wealth.[7]

The financial situation of doctors did not change substantially over time. Addressing his colleagues in the Denver Medical Society in 1927, the outgoing president wanted to warn new physicians that "the same amount of energy, mental and physical, expended in any other field will bring far greater returns."[8] Indeed, as late as 1966, the average physician income after expenses was $28,000.

Moreover, until very recently, the physician was a sole proprietor, an independent shopkeeper who received a fee in return for a service. The fees themselves varied from patient to patient. Physicians typically set their charges according to the patient's income, charging the well-to-do more and the poor, less.[9] (No one who was charged less seems to have protested, but one physician described an angry encounter with a wealthy patient who demanded to know why he should be paying more for medical services but not for bread simply because he was wealthy.[10]) The tactic was not unlike that developed by hospitals after 1945: billing insurance companies at higher rates to compensate for charity work. But in this first iteration, fees were left completely to the discretion of the doctor. Indeed, when the AMA attempted to defeat the passage of Medicare in the 1960s, it argued, not without some justification, that government intervention on behalf of the needy was unnecessary because physicians assumed the burden and set their fees accordingly. Since charity was no match for an ideology of rights, AMA opposition was, finally, overcome, but in terms of daily practice the organization did have a point.

There were rougher edges as well to making money in medicine. Over the first half of the twentieth century, kickbacks were commonplace around referrals for surgery. Surgeons were eager to reward colleagues who referred them patients—how else might they insure a steady supply?—and fee-splitting was prevalent. The AMA and the American College of Surgeons criticized the practice: fee-splitting worked against the best interest of the patient "by introducing a financial consideration into the [general practitioner's] choice of a surgeon, rather than professional competence." Nevertheless, it persisted, and surgeons devised inventive methods to circumvent prohibitions. Rather than pay a general practitioner directly for a referral, surgeons would ask him to "scrub in" for the surgery and, under the pretense that he was a valuable member of the surgical team, pay him a fee for professional services. It required state legislation, federal legislation, and an Internal Revenue Service decision to not accept these fees as deductible items against income to reduce the practice, but probably not eliminate it.[11]

The physician's search for income took other directions as well. It was not unusual in the 1920s and '30s for physicians to own their own small hospitals and send their patients to them. So too, many physicians sold their patients drugs or eye glasses, and in this way, used their position to increase their incomes. Conflict of interest is neither new as a concept nor as a practice. No one should think of pre-World War II medicine as some kind of golden age that should be recaptured.

***

The result of this admixture in medicine of principle and practice, of the sacred and the profane, emerges with particular clarity in the personal accounts of the 1920s and '30s that physicians, and in even more revealing fashion, physicians' wives, wrote about the complicated place of money and money-making in their lives.

From the physicians' point of view, they suffered in very tangible ways from the ambiguous place of money in medicine. They perceived a double standard at work. Patients were happy to tap into a tradition that put physicians as professionals above money (delaying payment accordingly), but they also insisted that physicians as consumers accept marketplace rules and play by them. To read the personal accounts of doctors and their wives is to confront incessant complaints about not being paid on time (victims of what they called "slow pay"), or in a fair number of cases, not being paid at all—yet still being held immediately accountable for their own debts. One 1932 article, "A Doctor's Wife Speaks Up" in *Harper's Magazine*, presents the argument very well. As she bitterly complained: "I had to put the grocer off. What I meant but did not say, was that if any of several patients who owed my husband goodsized and overdue bills would only pay him we would pay our own bills with joy." And because the thought was too acerbic to say herself she had her Irish maid, Nora, declare: The grocer had "no business to bother you.... He's in business and he'd ought to know by now that doctors is always slow pay."

The lament was endlessly repeated. Doctors were required to pay the baker, butcher, and candlestick maker immediately, but they, in turn, had to suffer slow pay. Thus, writing in 1928 in the *North American Review*, one physician opened his article on "The Business of Doctoring" with the statement: "The profession of doctoring is a curious business. It *is* a business. We are expected to pay and pay promptly pay our rent, our grocery bills, our gasoline bills.... This money we must collect from our patients. If we insist on being paid adequately and promptly, we are classed at once as commercial, avaricious, unprofessional." Let a frustrated doctor vigorously protest the unfairness inherent in such a situation and he is certain to be "adjudged half robber and half beggar" (741). An occasional medical society, like one in Toledo, Ohio in the 1930s, organized a collection bureau that aimed to collect delinquent fees.[12] But the idea never caught on. Some medical journals counseled doctors to send out collection letters along the lines of: "Dear Mr. Jones: Will you not show me the same consideration you would your grocer or haberdasher?"[13] But responses failing, doctors simply learned to live with non-paying or slow-paying patients.

At the same time, the public expected physicians to make a highly respectable personal presentation. It would be held against them professionally if they dressed poorly, lived poorly, or rode out to their patients in a broken-down automobile. As one daughter of a physician remarked (in a 1927 article entitled "Why I Would *Not* Marry a Physician"): "We looked prosperous because we had to. A doctor has to be presentable, have a good car and make a good impression or he would seldom have a patient."[14] These attitudes bred genuine confusion among physicians as to how far they could make payment for their services into a strictly market place transaction. As one anonymous physician noted in 1932: "It is outrageous that a sick man should be turned away from a hospital simply because he has no money. But...aren't hungry people turned away from restaurants? Aren't ragged people turned away from clothing stores?" Why did doctors have a special obligation that no one else did? Why were they obliged to give services when others were not?

Physician grievances, for the most part, were lost on the public. In fact, to judge by several best-selling books in the 1950s and early 1960s, the public was generally receptive to an attack on physicians for being too money-conscious and striving to maximize their incomes. Richard Carter, a journalist, reflected this orientation in his 1958 book appropriately entitled *The Doctor Business*.[15] Its opening pages told the story of a young boy who had fallen into a well. Volunteers worked unstintingly for twenty-four hours and successfully rescued him; his parents then took him to a local physician who treated him and proceeded to send a bill for $1,500. A public outcry followed that garnered so much publicity that one U.S. Senator spoke of "the outrage in my soul," and even the AMA found it necessary to declare: "Not one doctor in a thousand would have charged a fee."

Criticism of the profession for venality was popular sport. Selig Greenberg's *The Troubled Calling* (1965) emphasized the intensifying "clash between the priestly nature of his vocation and the economic considerations of his career."[16] And Greenberg, joined by

Martin Gross (*The Doctors*, 1966), denounced doctors for following a life style that would be unremarkable in lawyers or businessmen.[17] They faulted physicians because they gave their wives mink coats, drove Cadillacs, took month-long vacations and traveled abroad, played golf on Wednesday afternoon and had accounts with stock brokers. Seemingly, physicians were to take a pledge of poverty, or more precisely, were to remain very much middle-class.

* * *

By odd coincidence, these critiques appeared immediately before the most critical transformation in doctors' income. Beginning in 1966, physician income rose dramatically, for the first time making the profession as a whole—not just an occasional surgeon—wealthy. In 1970, *average* income for physicians was $41,800, by 1975, $56,400, and in 1982, $100,000. The upward trend persisted until 1997, when the figure reached a record $199,600. Variations, of course, were significant. Specialists on the low end of the income curve—in pediatrics, psychiatry, or family medicine—earned $125,000 to $145,000 a year. Obstetricians and gynecologists had incomes of $196,000, general surgeons, $178,000, orthopedic surgeons, $250,000, and for some cardiac surgeons, well over 1 million dollars.[18] Still, as a group, physicians were high income. The causes for the change are readily apparent: the enactment of Medicare; the rise of specialized procedures that separated reimbursement from the clock; and the emergence of major pharmaceutical companies ready to spend freely to win physician favor.

The favorable impact of Medicare on physicians' income reflected the financial benefits of guaranteed payment of fees for services, particularly when the fees were set by a standard of "customary and reasonable" and physicians were being increasingly visited by an aging population. In order to offset the opposition of the AMA to Medicare, President Lyndon Johnson agreed to pay physicians not a flat, government-fixed fee, but what they were accustomed to receiving. It was, of course, a give-away, an open invitation to doctors to bill at the highest possible level (for example, using the best-paid physicians in the community as the standard), but the political calculation was that passing Medicare was worth it. Indeed, the new federal benefit not only paid physicians regularly and well, but provided them with a blank check for reimbursing diagnostic tests and procedures, a particularly lucrative arrangement when the prescribing physician owned the diagnostic technology (such as an EKG machine) or the laboratory.[19]

The second element was the growing reliance upon procedures, mostly surgical, which brought exceptional financial benefits to those who mastered them. The physician billed for the procedure itself, regardless of how much time was required to carry it out. If psychiatrists, pediatricians or internists had to set their fees with an eye to the clock—e.g. so much for fifty minutes—surgeons (or dermatologists or gastro-enterologists) could ignore the clock and bill for the procedure: a transplant (fifty minutes but $15,000) or a wart removal (one minute, $300) or a colonoscopy (ten minutes and $500). Because of procedures, physician income surpassed lawyers' income, for no matter how expensive legal billing time was, there were only twenty-four hours in a day.

The influence of drug companies was not as determinative as these two other considerations, but they did add a tax-free cushion to physicians' income. As they wooed doctors, expensive dinners became more commonplace, as did free travel and vacations. For an elite group, there were also hefty honorariums for lectures. But even an ordinary practitioner could be reimbursed if he allowed drug detail men to review his charts (say, for the use of growth hormone in children) and pass it off as a research grant.

* * *

Ironically, the new financial status that physicians came to enjoy in the 1970s and '80s did not spark much negative public reaction. To be sure, Medicare reimbursements were constrained both by schedules of prospective payments to hospitals according to diagnostic-related groupings and by setting stricter limits on physician reimbursement. Efforts were also made to curtail the obvious conflict of interest that occurred when doctors owned the diagnostic laboratory, or, for that matter, the nursing home to which they sent their patients. And professional medical societies did set forth policies that reduced, although not substantially, the pharmaceutical companies' giveaways. But these measures, important as they were to doctors, failed to capture significant attention among patient/consumer groups or the new breed of bioethicists. They were avidly pursuing very different issues: if a patient was comatose, should the physician be allowed to keep her tethered to a machine? If a woman was to undergo a biopsy for breast cancer, would the physician await her informed choice before undertaking a radical mastectomy? If a subject joined a research protocol, would he be told that he was in an experiment and what its risks and benefits were? Informed consent and patient rights—these were at the core of concern, not how much physicians were making or how they were making it. In effect, physicians became wealthy at just the moment when attention went elsewhere. Or more precisely put, when the focus was on maximizing patient autonomy against physician benevolence, no one cared about doctors' bank accounts.

* * *

Beginning in the late 1980s and persisting through the 1990s, money in medicine again took center stage, with physician complaints matched by patient hostility, all accompanied by widespread ambivalence. The agent of change was the most maligned innovation in the history of American medicine: managed care through health maintenance organizations (HMOs). The intensity of the invective is well recognized and need not be documented here. What does warrant explication is the relevance of this new framework for physicians' way of making a living, and the public's responses to it.

The new system of managed care had a direct and revolutionary impact on how physicians earned their living. First, it curtailed the entrepreneurial, fee-for-service, self-employed character of physicians—by 2000, 40 percent of doctors had become employees of an organization, a larger percentage than ever before. (Because of this transformation, the question central to this essay has to be rephrased from the historical 'what should doctors earn,' to the contemporary 'what should they be paid.') Second, HMOs superintended medical decision-making and tied physicians' income to their provision of services: the Medicare formula had rewarded them for doing more— the HMO formula rewarded them for doing less. Third, HMOs brought marketplace strategies into medicine, for example, demanding discounts from hospitals and providers for volume business, particularly for expensive procedures. The net effects of all these changes was to reduce physician income slightly, and reduce their discretionary, decision making authority, more considerably. The average income for U.S. physicians was $194,400 in 1998, down from $199,600 in 1997.[20] Although a $5,200 decline in so high a bracket may not seem much of a cause for concern, particularly to people not making six-figure incomes, physicians have reacted intensely. There is the symbolic aspect: why should you be paying us less when for-profit HMOs are paying their CEOs extravagant salaries (the comparative point referred to earlier). Salaries are also viewed as a surrogate marker of public respect, which may be declining as well. And there is also a reality aspect: even a small drop in salary can be painful to the extent that the practitioner anticipated an increase in earnings over time, and may have mortgaged, margined, and borrowed accordingly.

And the HMOs did something else: they subverted the trust between doctor and patient. Consumers, alert to all these changes and understanding the general rules of the managed care game—if not knowing the exact details of the contract with the physician sitting across from him—worried, appropriately, whether the physician was withholding treatment or a referral because his concern with own income was trumping his concern for his patient's welfare. The suspicion that doctors would now do less because of money sparked a hostility that the prospect of a physician doing more for money (under fee-for-service) never had.

The response of the physicians, individually or through their professional societies, has been bitter in terms of invective and ineffective in terms of policy. Although they have tried to mask their complaints about income in terms of their reduced ability to treat their patients, no one has been fooled. When the AMA, for example, issued an anti-managed care document entitled "Putting Patient Interests First," all who read it understand that the organization was really attempting to put physician income first.[21] Moreover, the efforts of the professional societies to teach their members how best to game the system have not yielded significant results. Finally, and most important, neither individually nor collectively have physicians reduced the control wielded by HMOs. It was state legislatures, not professional societies, that compelled HMOs to give new mothers a second night in the hospital, or women undergoing mastectomy one night in the hospital.

The response of patients has been no less bitter, but oftentimes more successful. On an individual level, the patient in need of experimental therapy or determined to continue to use her (out of network) provider can often create enough fuss or negative publicity to gain her goal. Consumer-driven efforts to create scorecards for HMOs have also had some positive impact. Indeed, it appears that some restrictive policies of HMOs are being relaxed: some organizations, for example, are allowing referral without review to specialists. Most observers are confident that the system that has been in place for the past fifteen years will not be the system in place fifteen years from now.

* * *

What does all this portend for money and medicine? Looking ahead, it is not unreasonable to expect:

- Continuing ambivalence about the place of money in medicine, and confusion on how to achieve the right mix of the sacred and the profane.

- Attempts to implement new forms of reimbursement that avoid the pitfalls of fee-for-service and managed care methods. There is no magic formula or holy grail, but some system change may be possible.

- A general recognition among younger practitioners and recruits to medicine that this career choice is not best for those determined to earn great amounts of money. It has been suggested that the increased number of women in the ranks of medicine is an indication of this trend; white males are deserting medicine because of limited financial opportunities.

- A possibility that financial and managed care policies will move medicine from a profession to an occupation. The evidence for this proposition is the small but growing enthusiasm for physician unions. Although unions have not deprofessionalized medicine in some European countries with national health insurance systems, their impact in the United States might well be different.

- A shift in the balance of power between patient/consumer and physician, with patients likely to be more suspicious, distrustful, energized (through the Web or through direct-to-consumer pharmaceutical advertisements), and informed (through the same mechanisms). These developments might even lead patients to price-shop among doctors, a practice that would be without precedent in American health care. Some physicians are already complaining that patients unceremoniously drop them as soon as their companies change plans, refusing to pay a full fee when they could pay a $10 co-pay fee. On the other hand, some observers are suggesting that doctors not only start putting lemons in their water coolers but experiment, like the airlines, with frequent flier miles: after ten procedures, you would get one free.[22] Were we to reach that point, we would immediately know that we have entered an entirely new phase in the history of money and medicine.

Notes

1. Simmel, Georg, *The Philosophy of Money*, New York: Routledge, 1990.
2. Zelizer, Viviana A.R., *Pricing the Priceless Child: The Changing Social Value of Children*, Princeton: Princeton University Press, 1994.
3. Zelizer, Viviana A.R., *The Social Meaning of Money*, Princeton: Princeton University Press, 1997.
4. Runes, Dagobert D., Ed., *Selected Writings of Benjamin Rush*, New York: Philosophical Library, 1947.
5. Code of Ethics, American Medical Association. 1847.
6. Barker, L.F., *Time and the Physician: An Autobiography*, New York: Putnam, 1942, 288.
7. Vocational Rehabilitation Series, no. 17, January 1919, Washington, Government Printing Office, 1919. Quotation p. 6.
8. Van Meter, S.D., "The Shortcomings of the Medical Profession," *Colorado Medicine*, February 1927, 47.
9. White, J.A., "System in Fee-Setting," *Medical Economics*, 17, 1940, 39.
10. Pleasants Jr., Henry, *A Doctor in the House*, Philadelphia: Lippincott, 1947, 196.
11. Rodwin, Marc, *Medicine, Money, and Morals*, New York: Oxford Press, 1993, ch. 2. Davis, Loyal, *A Surgeon's Odyssey*, New York: Doubleday, 1973, 100-5, 299-300.
12. Price, J.L., "Salvaging Fees but Keeping Patients," *Medical Economics*, 11, 1934, 34-37.
13. Droke, Maxwell, "The Patient who Ignores your Monthly Statement," *Medical Economics*, 1, 1924, 14.
14. Palmer, Ruth Maxwell, "Why I Would *Not* Marry a Physician," *Hygeia*, 5, 1927, 22.
15. Carter, Richard, *The Doctor Business*, Garden City, NY: Doubleday, 1958.
16. Greenberg, Selig, *The Troubled Calling*, New York: Macmillan, 1965.
17. Gross, Martin, *The Doctors*, New York: Random House, 1966.
18. Medical Group Management Association, *Physician Compensation Survey 2000*, Englewood, CO: MGMA, 2000.
19. Marmor, Theodore K., *The Politics of Medicare*, New York: Aldine Publishing Company, 1973.
20. American Medical Association, *Physician Socioeconomic Statistics*, 2000-2002 Edition. Physicians' median income also dropped to $160,000 in 1998 from $164,000 in 1997.
21. American Medical Association Council on Ethical and Judicial Affairs, *Ethical issues in managed care. JAMA.* 1995; 273:330-335.
22. Steinhauer, Jennifer, "When Doctors Feel Disposable," *New York Times*, July 15, 2001, Business Section, 11.

9

Danse Macabre:
Poverty, Social Status, and Health

Jeremiah A. Barondess, M.D.

Eli Ginzberg has said that as early as 1934, with the completion of his doctoral dissertation, *The House of Adam Smith*, he was convinced that for economics to be meaningful, it had to be assessed in relation to politics, property, power, and people. Few have held as consistently or as productively to an early conviction as Ginzberg has, especially over a career that has thus far spanned some seven decades. In the process of examining myriad issues in human resources, the roles of government, and medicine and health, he has become an extraordinarily productive icon of a special brand of utilitarian economics, one that has in fact helped to define the public intellectual. It is a privilege to share in honoring him in this *festschrift*.

* * *

The tone poem Danse Macabre, *written by Saint-Saëns late in the nineteenth century, evokes medieval imagery of Death anthropomorphized, playing the violin and forcing the dead to dance. In a deeper sense, the image of humanity in the grip of larger, unknown forces raises an alternative image: poverty, social status, and its various determinants and derivatives impacting the human condition and forcing a different kind of dance.*

To the extent that economics is ultimately about human welfare, its descriptors, theories, and interlacings meet in the arenas of health and life expectancy with particular force. As issues in population health develop increasingly powerful connections to public policy,

Jeremiah A. Barondess, M.D. is president of the New York Academy of Medicine.

121

economics has emerged as perhaps the most important link between the two, offering broad opportunities to help in explicating health trends and to inform public responses. In recent years, economists and the health policy community, together with the public sector, have focused especially on the delivery of health care to the disenfranchised, notably the elderly and the poor. In the former instance, this collaboration has been highly effective in easing discrepancies in access to care; in the case of the poor, less so. While clearly such efforts must be extended to include the entire population, affordable access to care will address only incompletely the immense disparities in health and life expectancy that obtain across subsets of the population.

From the west-facing windows of my office I can look across Central Park to Central Park West, where boys who reach the age of fifteen have about an 80 percent probability of living to the age of 65; for their sisters the probability is 87 percent. Through my north-facing windows I can see much of East and Central Harlem, where boys who reach the age of fifteen have about a 37 percent chance of living to the age of sixty-five; the probabilities for their sisters are about 65 percent.[1] Extraordinary differentials in life expectancy such as these have engaged the attention of social scientists and government cadres, the public health enterprise, and the clinical community for years.

Economic status and its partner, social position, have long been understood as underlying forces tightly linked to disease patterns, mortality rates, and life expectancy. This history has been well summarized by Antonovsky.[2] For more than 150 years studies have demonstrated not only that life expectancy is linked to poverty and social station, but that it is linked monotonically in stepwise fashion. Morris[3] cites Gavin's 1839 study of some 1600 deaths in a London suburb, stratified by social class: "Gentlemen, professional men and their families" died on average at age forty-five; "tradesmen and their families" at age twenty-six; and "mechanics, servants, laborers and their families" at age sixteen. These averages are no doubt skewed to the low side by the fact that infant and childhood mortality rates were high, largely due to infectious diseases, but the class distinctions are nevertheless powerful. The class gap seems, in Antonovsky's view, to have emerged somewhere between 1650 and 1850, as the rate of increase in the world population began to rise, starting slowly but gathering momentum with time; during these two centuries the world population doubled for the second time (the first doubling having occupied the first sixteen centuries of the Christian era), with life expectancy among the middle and upper classes increasing rapidly, while the life expectancy of the lowest strata appears to have increased much more slowly, or even declined as an industrial proletariat emerged. As Antonovsky further notes, at some point, probably in the late nineteenth century, these trends reversed, and the class gap began to diminish, "to what may be the smallest differential in history," although "evidence of a linear gradient remains, with a considerable differential, given man's life span."[2] Considerable differentials in the United States and in England and Wales were likewise demonstrated in studies in the early part of the twentieth century, with differences in life expectancy at the extremes of the social scale ranging from about 7.4 years to more than thirteen.[2] Among American wage earners with life insurance studied in 1915-1916, the death rates per 1000 policyholders were: professionals and semi-professionals, 3.3; skilled workmen, 3.7; semi-skilled workmen, 4.5; unskilled workmen, 4.8. Using the rate of the professional class as 100, the ratios of the other three were 112, 136 and 145, respectively.[4] Altenderfer[5] studied the relationship between income and death rates in the ninety-two U.S. cities with populations of 100,000 or more in 1940, and found that the poorest third of the cities had higher death rates. Other studies between World War II and the present have found the same inverse gradient, with female death rates consistently lower than those for males. Yeracaris[6] studied death rates for the city of Buffalo in 1940, with population subsets stratified based on median rentals, as a marker of economic status. With each successively lower step in the rental ladder the differential between groups increased, so that the largest gap appeared between the lowest and next lowest groups, while a relatively small although definable difference appeared between the two top groups. He noted that if the death rate that obtained in the tracts with the highest rentals had prevailed throughout Buffalo, 19.1 percent of the deaths would not have occurred, and if this rate had prevailed in the tracts characterized by the lowest rentals, 38.5 percent of the deaths would not have occurred!

McCord and Freeman in 1990[7] documented remarkably high mortality rates in the inner city, using New York's Harlem as the study site. The Harlem population is heavily black and notably poor. For example, in central Harlem 96 percent of the inhabitants are black and 41 percent live below the federal poverty line. Age-adjusted mortality from all causes was more than double that of U.S. whites and 50 percent higher than that of U.S. blacks, and the excess mortality was concentrated among those less than sixty-five years of age. Standardized age-adjusted mortality ratios for deaths under the age of sixty-five in Harlem were 2.91 for males and 2.70 for females, with the highest ratios obtaining among women twenty-five to thirty-four years of age and men thirty-five to forty-four. The excess mortality was due chiefly to cardiovascular disease, cirrhosis, homicide, and neoplasms. In a famous derivative of the study, the authors commented that "black men in Harlem were less likely to reach the age of sixty-five than men in Bangladesh."

The famous Whitehall Study of mortality,[8] published in 1991, covered more than 17,000 British civil servants over a ten-year period (p.15) with regard to health inequalities. The British civil service stratifies grades of employment, with unskilled workers at the bottom, clerical workers next, then professional and executive levels, up to top administrators. In this study, relative risk of mortality over the ten-year period of observation increased significantly as employment grade decreased. Based on the mortality risk of the top tier, and controlling for age, the relative risk of mortality was 1.6 for the professional/executive grades, 2.2 for the clerical grades, and 2.7 for the lowest grades. These differences in mortality have been considered to be especially striking, since the sample examined was relatively homogeneous, with employment in the civil service and access to nationalized health care shared by all participants.

Relation to Specific Morbidities

A number of studies have examined the relationships of these gradients to specific diseases or categories of disorders. For example, Susser, Watson and Hopper[9] documented a gradient in mortality rates across five levels of occupational status and across a range of diseases, including malignancies, infectious and parasitic diseases, and diseases of the respiratory, digestive, and circulatory systems. Thus, the gradients appeared to be unrelated to specific disease category, i.e. they obtained for each.

Both individual social class and area-based deprivation have been found to be associated with generally less favorable profiles of cardiovascular disease risk factors, except for plasma cholesterol. Smith, Hart and their coworkers[10] have developed a series of indices of social deprivation characterizing areas in which people live, and found that a number of these are related to mortality and exert impacts on cardiovascular risk beyond the characteristics of the individuals who live there. They include, for example, socioeconomic inequality within the domiciliary area, education, welfare services, voting patterns, medical care expenditures, and local crime rates. The study suggested that individually assigned and area-based socioeconomic indicators contribute independently to some health outcomes, in this case cardiovascular risk factors.

In the MRFIT trial,[11] similar associations between economic status and risk across a variety of diseases were noted. Among 300,000 white men screened in the early 1970s and followed over a sixteen-year period during which nearly 32,000 deaths occurred, age-adjusted all-cause mortality was inversely associated with median family income. Although there was considerable heterogeneity in the strength of the relationships, the gradient was observed for cardiovascular disease, including coronary heart disease, stroke, and other cardiovascular diseases, as well as for cancer of the esophagus, stomach, colon, rectum, and lung. Relative risk estimates were shown to demonstrate similar gradients for AIDS, diabetes, chronic obstructive pulmonary disease, pneumonia and influenza, cirrhosis, homicide, accidents, and suicide, although the gradient in the latter instance was somewhat smaller. No association was noted for carcinoma of the prostate or lymphatic tumors. The authors made a summary point of the fact that the degree "to which known risk factors explain socioeconomic differentials in mortality should not be taken as a measure of reduced intrinsic importance of the differentials. The fact that smoking accounts for some of the difference in mortality rates between income groups does not mean that social causes themselves are less important. Smoking—like alcohol use, exercise and diet—does not occur in a social vacuum. ...the determination of socially patterned behaviors should be seen as part of the process generating socioeconomic differentials in health, not as a reason for considering social interventions unnecessary."

Sharp associations between the incidence of AIDS and economic deprivation have been demonstrated at the state level.[12] Most of the AIDS cases in Massachusetts for the years 1988 through 1994 were found to occur in block-groups where at least 10 percent of the population was living below the poverty line, population density exceeded 10,000 people per square mile, and fewer households had incomes of $150,000 or more. There were monotonic patterns of increasing AIDS incidence with decreasing economic resources and increasing population density; the cumulative incidence of AIDS in the total population was nearly seven times higher among individuals in block-groups where 40 percent or more of the population was below the poverty line. It should be noted that gender and race/ethnicity were also found to be important correlates, with the highest rates occurring among non-Hispanic black men in areas with the greatest population density, followed by non-Hispanic black men and Hispanic men living in the most impoverished areas. The lowest rates occurred among white women in the least impoverished areas.

Age

The interaction of age with health and socioeconomic status is not simple or straightforward. Individuals of higher socioeconomic status tend to have the onset of health problems later in life, whereas they are more prevalent in those of lower socioeconomic status by middle age. House, Lepkowski and their coworkers[13] have noted that, overall, health differences related to socioeconomic status are not prominent in early adulthood but increase with age until relatively late in life, when they decrease due to selection or greater equalization of health risks and protections. These authors found that results previously reported for indices of socioeconomic status hold separately for education and income, and that the interaction between age and socioeconomic status, specifically education or income, in predicting health "can be substantially explained by the correlations with greater exposure of people of lower socioeconomic status to a wide range of psychosocial risk factors to health, especially in middle and early old age, and, to a lesser degree, the greater impact of these risk factors on health with age." Thus, health problems potentially susceptible to prevention activities are increasingly concentrated among individuals of lower socioeconomic status in middle age and early old age. The authors note that "higher socioeconomic strata are increasingly approximating the ideal of postponing significant increases in morbidity and functional limitations until relatively late in the life course."

Gender

The interplay of gender, socioeconomic status, race, and area-based pressures has received some attention in the literature. In a study of health inequalities among men and women in welfare states the degree and patterning of such inequalities were studied in Britain, Finland, Norway and Sweden.[14] The posit was that structured social position, including social class, employment status, and material living standards are determinants of the health of men, but additional determinants of women's health include family roles. Contrary to expectations, inequalities in health were more pronounced for both employed men and employed women in the Nordic countries than in Britain. For men in all four countries and for Finnish and Swedish women, age and social class were strongly associated with ill health, though the evidence was less clear for Norwegian women. Among British women, a family role framework complemented the structural one, in that, in addition to age and social class, marital status and parental status were associated with their health: the health of previously married women was poorer than that of single and married women; British women with young children were healthier than childless women, a finding not borne out in the Nordic countries. For reasons as yet unclear, the degree of class differential in illness, both for men and for women, was smaller in Britain than in the Nordic countries, although the latter presumably have more egalitarian welfare models than the former. Other studies[15] of women's health in the United Kingdom found high mortality for women associated with working in manual occupations and living in rented housing with no car in the household (putative measures of economic status). Low mortality was associated with non-manual occupations and living in owner-occupied housing and having a car. With socioeconomic status defined in this manner, the disadvantaged group experienced death rates two and a half times that of the advantaged group.

Women's heart disease mortality has been studied with relation to social context in the neighborhood as well as racial differences. Leclere and coworkers[16] noted that although black women experience rates of heart disease morbidity similar to those of non-black women, they have higher rates of heart disease mortality. These workers found that women who live in communities with high concentrations of female-headed families are more likely to die of heart disease, net of other characteristics. While for younger women this effect appeared to be grounded primarily in poverty, for older women the effect of female headship rates remains after other neighborhood characteristics are accounted for. The study highlights the importance of examining the effect of neighborhoods and their social content on mortality. Jargowsky[17] has noted that a consistent demographic feature of black neighborhoods, especially those characterized by high rates of poverty, is a high rate of female family headship. Thus, in 1990, in metropolitan neighborhoods with over 40 percent of the families in poverty, nearly three-quarters of black families were headed by females. The social networks of black families, especially those that contain single mothers, provide supports of several kinds, but these are frequently inadequate due to the number of situational and economic stresses on such families. As a result, older blacks, particularly women, find themselves facing substantial social support demands with limited resources, making these social networks a series of obligations for middle-aged and older black women which they cannot adequately serve.

Lifestyle

Health behaviors and lifestyle have been increasingly associated with a variety of diseases in recent decades. Lantz and her coworkers[18] examined the degree to which cigarette smoking, habitual alcohol use, sedentary lifestyle, and relative body weight explain the observed association between socioeconomic characteristics and all-cause mortality. The distribution of these four behavioral risk factors varied substantially by educational attainment and annual household income, after adjustment for age. Persons with the least education and the lowest incomes were significantly more likely to be smokers, to be overweight, and to be relatively sedentary. The data suggested a high degree of stability in the health behaviors of individuals over time. Importantly, despite the presence of significant socioeconomic differentials in health behaviors, these accounted for only a modest proportion of social inequalities in overall mortality. Health-related behaviors are likely to reflect a number of psychosocial forces operating on the individual, and in this sense should be viewed as responses to social environments rather than more strictly as individual choices.

Further to the impact of adverse health behaviors, the National Longitudinal Mortality Study,[19] which tracked some 530,000 persons twenty-five years of age or more surveyed between 1979 and 1985, followed this cohort for mortality for the years 1979 through 1989. Higher mortality was found in blacks than in whites less than sixty-five years of age, and in persons not in the labor force, with lower incomes, with less education, in service and other lower level occupations, and in persons not married or living alone. The study concluded that employment status, income, education, occupation, race, and marital status have substantial net associations with mortality, with employment status showing the largest likelihood ratio statistics and the largest relative risks after multivariate adjustment. Income and education were separately related to mortality, with differences in income apparently the more powerful of the two factors. Individuals at the bottom of the education and income distribution were two to three times more likely to die during the ten-year follow-up period than those at the top. The authors concluded that, while the pathways through which income and education affect mortality are complex, they are likely to be linked to purchasing power for health services, healthy habits and behaviors, and the knowledge and empowerment that come with education. There were no major differences between men and women in these relationships. While blacks had higher mortality than whites, the risk attached to each of the various examined factors was evident within each racial group. The relative risk of all the factors considered was considerable, especially in comparison with established risk factors, including cigarette smoking (the relative risk of death for cigarette smokers versus non-smokers was less than 2 percent).

Education

Other studies have found associations between death rates and educational level. Thus, the decline in death rates in the United States between 1960 and 1986 was greater in more, as opposed to less, educated groups, and the resulting health gradient by socioeconomic status was thus steeper in 1986 than it had been in 1960. Pappas and his group[20] have noted that education, along with occupation and income, shape the individual's life course and are enmeshed in critically important domains of life, including the physical environments in which one lives and works, associated exposure to pathogens, carcinogens and other environmental hazards, vulnerability to interpersonal aggression and violence, and socialization and experiences that influence psychological development and ongoing mood, affect and cognition, and, ultimately, health behaviors.

Coping and Stress

There have been few studies of the effect of various efforts to cope with economic and psychosocial stresses as related to health outcomes or to attenuation of the impact of such factors. James and his coworkers[21] have invoked in this connection the folklore related to John Henry, a legendary nineteenth-century railroad laborer whose capacity as a "steel driver," and his famous contest of driving steel spikes as new rail was laid, with a steam-powered machine brought in for the same purpose, has been celebrated in ballad and song. According to the legend, John Henry, using his hammer, was able to drive more steel than the machine, but died in the effort. James has called the effort to cope actively with stresses in the psychosocial environment "John Henryism," and has constructed a John Henryism active coping scale. The John Henryism hypothesis suggests that, in contrast to high socioeconomic status environments, those individuals with low status, with their diminished supply of problem solving resources, exist under imposed conditions generally unfavorable to successful active coping with the stresses under which they live. In light of the known inverse association between socioeconomic status and blood pressure, James and his group investigated the posit that associations between socioeconomic status and blood pressure would be modified in relation to the level of John Henryism in the individual. They found that at low levels of John Henryism, socioeconomic status differences in hypertension prevalence were small (1.6 percent), whereas at high levels of John Henryism, low socioeconomic status blacks were nearly three times as likely to be hypertensive as higher status blacks (31.4 percent versus 11.5 percent). The study hypothesis was not supported among whites. These authors concluded that John Henryism in American blacks has a cultural as well as an economic basis, and amounts to a cultural adaptation, in this case one with adverse health implications.

Stresses of daily life, and those that obtain more chronically, appear to be handled with more difficulty at lower socioeconomic levels, where influence on or control over life events is likely to be more limited. Thus, as Williams has noted,[22] stresses at the lower end of the socioeconomic scale are likely to be absorbed with more difficulty due not only to economic deprivation but to the associated characteristics of the lives led at such levels: social relationships and supports are more easily disrupted, and risky health behaviors more readily adopted, due not only to individual vulnerability, but also to the increased marketing of cigarettes, alcohol, drugs, and less healthful foods in poorer areas. Further, socioeconomic differences in exposure to some risk factors may increase with age as socioeconomic status becomes more fixed and its effects more cumulative. As Williams notes, there may be some attenuation of these differences in later old age because of recent societal investments in the social, economic, and health care status of the older population. It is argued that these changes may attenuate differences in exposure to psychosocial risk factors across socioeconomic levels in the older age groups. He suggests that the very processes by which health changes with age may be importantly stratified by socioeconomic status. The largest health differentials across socioeconomic levels are likely to be seen in middle and early old age, as Williams notes, because these age groups are most likely to be characterized by sizable socioeconomic differentials in exposure to risk factors as well as by substantial impacts of risk factors. He notes that, by contrast, in early adulthood socioeconomic differences in exposure may be sizable, but the health impact in the individual is blunted, while in older age groups socioeconomic differences in exposure diminish although the health impact remains strong. This perspective, examining relations among socioeconomic status, age, and health in terms of changes over the life course, as well as socioeconomic differences in exposure to psychosocial risk factors and in the impact of those factors on health, are important elements in a complex series of interactions.

Race

The impact of socioeconomic status on health is made more complex by its association with race. The median family income of African Americans was 63 percent lower than that of whites, as the 1990 census demonstrated. In addition, American blacks are more than twice as likely to be unemployed, three times as likely to be poor, and twice as likely not to have graduated from college.[23] In addition, racial differences frequently persist even after adjustment for socioeconomic status.[24] Further, measures of socioeconomic status are not equivalent across racial groups. Thus, there are racial differences in income returns for given levels of education as well as in the quality of education, the level of wealth associated with given levels of income, the purchasing power of income, the stability of employment, and the health risks associated with working in particular occupations.[25] Socioeconomic status is not simply a confounder of the relationship between race and health, but part of the causal pathway by which race affects health.[26] This is to say that race is an antecedent and determinant of socioeconomic status and socioeconomic differences between blacks and whites reflect in part the impact of economic discrimination as produced by large scale societal structures.[27] The health-related implications of racial bias and related social stratification are beginning to be investigated. Williams notes the non-random distribution of stress in the American population, and its linkage to social structure.[27] The implication is that the location of blacks in the structure of American society would lead them to have higher levels of stress than whites. While studies in the area of racial discrimination and health are still limited, a few are available. One study has suggested that racial discrimination is associated with higher levels of blood pressure.[28] Williams, Yu, Jackson and Anderson[27] found that discrimination in daily life was positively related to ill health among blacks. Further, in their study, they found that blacks have significantly higher scores than whites with regard to measures of discrimination, financial stress, and stress in life events. As noted above, levels of educational attainment vary by race (blacks are 1.6 times more likely than whites to have completed less than twelve years of education and whites are almost twice as likely as blacks to have graduated from college). The lower average income of blacks provides for households that are on average significantly larger than those of whites. Blacks are more likely than whites to be in the worker category (61 percent vs. 51 percent) and whites are almost twice as likely as blacks to be managers (24 percent vs. 13 percent). Blacks are more likely than whites to report major experiences of discrimination in employment and in contact with the police; they are twice as likely as whites to report two discriminatory experiences, and seven times more likely to report three. Finally, blacks report higher levels of poor health than whites, a finding reduced by almost 25 percent when adjusted for education. The race effect is dramatically reduced when economic status is considered, but remains significant.[27]

Fundamental Social Causes

The association between socioeconomic status and mortality has persisted despite dramatic changes in social and health conditions over the last 150 years, and despite dramatic changes in risk factors and life expectancy, in the disease pattern and in health care systems, as Link and his coworkers have noted.[29] The impact of poverty on health is tightly bound to other expressions of disadvantage which appear to exert their effects both individually and, to varying degrees, in concert. Thus, gender, race, level of educational attainment, personal health-related behaviors, and the social circumstances of individual lives have all been implicated as powerful eroders of health and life expectancy. Link and his coworkers have argued that a set of fundamental social causes underlies these phenomena. The question of whether social conditions operate by exposing people to risk factors which in turn cause disease, or whether social conditions operate through other, or additional, mechanisms has been a focus of considerable interest in recent years. Addressing and ameliorating obvious risk factors, such as poor housing, sanitation, and working conditions have not been associated with blunting of the relation between socioeconomic status and many disease outcomes, even though the dominance of infections in nineteenth- and early twentieth-century mortality statistics has been sharply reduced, and even though access to health care for the poor has been to a degree enhanced. What appears to have happened is that risk factors that formerly obtained and that related primarily to infectious diseases have been replaced by other risk factors, such as smoking, exercise, and diet. As risk factors relating socioeconomic status to some diseases came under control, others have emerged.[30] In Link's view, higher socioeconomic status enhances awareness of and ability to mobilize personal resources and behaviors to avoid risks for diseases and death, and this results in a socioeconomic status gradient related to health-protective factors. Link and Phelan[30] believe that social conditions whose associations with mortality persist in this manner are fundamental social causes of inequalities in health.

To test their theory that the health effects of socioeconomic status are tied to the effective use of resources that bear on health at higher levels on the socioeconomic scale, Link's group examined the differential use of pap smears and mammography, and found, with relation to both education and income, differential use of these technologies, with greater use among those higher on the socioeconomic scale. The effect of education was slightly more powerful than that of income. As Link notes, "The fundamental cause approach predicts that, once discovered, beneficial innovations like these, which require individual agency and access to health resources, will, upon implementation, come to be associated with socioeconomic status and thereby play a role in socioeconomic status gradients in mortality,"[29] and further, "When innovations beneficial to health are developed in our society, their implementation necessarily occurs within the context of inequalities in knowledge, money, power, prestige, and social connections. These inequalities shape the distribution of the health benefit." The authors conclude that individuals benefit from high status not only because it is less stressful to be at the top, but also because being there leads to benefits that translate into better health.

* * *

Most theories addressing interrelations of socioeconomic status and health have focused on individual behaviors, psychosocial stress, and fundamental social causes. Adler and her coworkers[31] have emphasized that, in addition, the relation of socioeconomic status to health is not a threshold phenomenon, but a graded relationship occurring at all levels of social status. While socioeconomic status is a composite measure that includes economic status measured by income, social status measured by education, and work status measured by occupation, Adler believes that these are not fully overlapping variables, and the fact that associations between socioeconomic status and health are found with each of the indicators suggests some broader underlying characteristic or dimension of social stratification as the potent factor. Importantly, she notes that studies that examine the health effects of socioeconomic status by comparing the health of individuals at the bottom of the hierarchy either with those above the poverty level or with those at the top miss the continuum or the gradation that obtains. "Not only do those in poverty have poorer health than those in more favorable circumstances, but those at the highest level enjoy better health than do those just below."[31]

At another level of detail, per capita income appears to be less strongly related to life expectancy than is income distribution. That is, overall, relative status appears to be more important than absolute status. As Wilkinson notes,[32] social hierarchies are nearly universal among human social groups and tend to be stable over time. He suggests that responses to hierarchical position may be encoded into the behavior or repertoire of individuals and may have direct effects on physiological processes which may in turn influence individual biological vulnerability to disease. Further, he suggests that the health effects of dominance status may be largely dependent on characteristics of the larger social context to which position is assigned, particularly stability.

At a fundamental level, the question of how social and economic forces translate into ill health and premature mortality in this graduated manner is the pressing dilemma. Plainly, economic status and social stratum operate through complex networks, at the level of the individual, the family and other social networks, and the community. Susser, Watson and Hopper, in an important observation in 1985,[9] noted that "Societies in part create the disease they experience and, further, they materially shape the ways in which diseases are to be experienced. Cross-cultural studies of disease consistently show that the varieties of human affliction owe as much to the inventiveness of culture as they do to the vagaries of disease. If disease is seen in its full dimensions as a phenomenon besetting persons in communities, its status as a culturally constituted reality becomes apparent." Societies and cultures, in other words, shape to a substantial degree the disease pattern that obtains in the population. Health is a social problem. The economic gradients in our society exaggerate inborn differences that in turn translate into adaptability to environmental and social circumstances which are unevenly distributed with regard to their health implications.

None of this is to say that efforts should not be made to alleviate the striking gradients that obtain in community conditions, for example the effectiveness and frequency of garbage pickups, air and water pollution management, roach and rat infestation control, and so forth. Nor is it to say that efforts should not be made to alleviate the equally striking gradients in access to clinical care, especially high quality clinical care, or that intense programs to alter health-adverse behaviors should not be undertaken. These things clearly must be done, but, equally plainly, attacking the socioeconomic gradients in health will involve far more than the health enterprise. Important issues of national policy are involved. Link and his coworkers[29] have noted that the aura of inevitability attached to social inequalities in health is the case only "if one presumes that social inequalities are immutable." They note further that policy approaches to issues such as the minimum wage, housing for the homeless, parenting leave, Head Start programs, and capital gains taxes bear directly on the extent of inequality in our society and have led them to conclude that levels of social inequality are in fact responsive to policy. McCord and Freeman[7] likewise recommend direct attacks on poverty and inadequate housing, as well as intensive educational campaigns to improve nutrition and reduce the use of alcohol, drugs and tobacco, directed particularly at children and adolescents, and merging of educational efforts directed toward the control of epidemic drug use and associated crime, in combination with coordinated police and public action. They particularly emphasize effective education concerning AIDS and its relation to intravenous drug use.

At the same time, the focus on social systems and social justice, as linked to health improvement, must acknowledge the realities of American politics and the ascendancy of conservatism in recent decades. Efforts to link social progress to health will have to find a way to deal with a tendency to put the onus on the poor and homeless and their unhealthy habits—to, in effect, blame the victim. The likelihood, as Lantz, House and their coworkers[18] note, is that "increasing health promotion and disease prevention efforts among the disadvantaged is not a magic policy bullet for reducing persistent socioeconomic disparities in mortality." Emanuel[33] agrees when he says "health care is unlikely to be the horse to carry social justice measures over the finish line." He notes that health issues in the United States have won broad support in recent years—for example in the budget of the National Institutes of Health, and also in Medicare and other health programs—and views this support as deriving from a view of health care as benefiting the entire society. Health programs are not viewed as special interest programs or as programs for the poor, minorities, or other groups. He thinks that, "it is precisely because health care is viewed as key to equal opportunity without overtly or intentionally redistributing income that it garners such strong public support." Incrementalism, in his view, will have to be the order of the day, as it already is, but our efforts will clearly have to involve health economists and state and federal government in a far more muscular way than has obtained to this point.

The reorientation or, perhaps better, the additional orientation that must obtain more strongly should be less focused on disease and more on erosions of health and life expectancy. The former is an arena that is primarily biological, scientific, and clinical, with important public policy supports; the latter is primarily a public policy issue with supports from the medical and public health side. Orchestrating this realignment is a central task in addressing health in the decades ahead.

Ultimately, the focus at the national level, on biomedical research on the one hand, and financing access to health care on the other, must be joined by policy applications of the trends that have been documented with regard to the impact of socioeconomic status and caste. Funding must be provided for efforts to get to social adversities at a deeper level. These include, very importantly, promoting education as an important substrate for health improvement, strengthening communities through enhanced community services, and providing widespread progressive health education for school children and their families. Racism remains ubiquitous in American society, and should be addressed not only for reasons of social justice, but because of the extraordinary health impacts and other human cost implications. Ultimately, "Solutions to public health problems will require redress of the fundamental causes of economic deprivation and further research regarding the pathways through which these economic conditions are related to disease and death."[19]

All of these are, to substantial degrees, fraught with economic implications. The links among the clinical, public health, and policy communities must include fundamental efforts at disease prevention and health promotion, in which the economics community must be prominently involved. A significant enhancement of a more tightly linked profile for public health, the health-related social sciences, and a broadly conceived health economics is needed. Such a linkage will have to be articulated with national policy to be effective.

Notes

1. Geronimus, A.T., Bound, J., Waidmann, T.A., Hillemeier, M.M., Burns, P.B., "Excess mortality among blacks and whites in the United States," *New Eng J Med.*, 335:1552-1558, 1996.

2. Antonovsky, A., "Social class, life expectancy and overall mortality," *Milbank Memorial Fund Quart.*, 43:31-73, 1967.

3. Morris, J.N., *Uses of Epidemiology*, Second Edition, Edinburg and London, E & S Livingstone, 1964, pp. 161-162.

4. Bruno, F.J., "Illness and dependency," *Miscellaneous Contributions*, 9, The Committee on the Costs of Medical Care, Washington, 1931, cited in Sydenstricker, E., *Health and Environment*, New York, McGraw-Hill Book Co., 1993, p. 94.

5. Altenderfer, M.E., "Relationship between per capita income and mortality in the cities of 100,000 or more population," *Public Health Reports*, 62, 1681-1691, November 1947.

6. Yeracaris, C.A., "Differential mortality, general and cause-specific, in Buffalo, 1939-41," *J. Am Statistical Assn.*, 50:1235-1247, 1955.

7. McCord, C., Freeman, H.P., "Excess mortality in Harlem," *New Eng J Med.*, 322:173-177, 1990.

8. Marmet, M.G., Smith, G.D., Stansfield, S., Patel, C., et al, "Health inequalities among British civil servants. The Whitehall II Study," *Lancet*, 337:1387-1393, 1991.

9. Susser, M., Watson, W., Hopper, K., *Sociology and Medicine*, New York, Oxford University Press, 1985.

10. Smith, G.D., Hart, C., Watt, G., Hole, D., Hawthorne, V., "Individual social class, area-based deprivation, cardiovascular disease risk factors and mortality: The Renfrew and Paisley Study," *J Epidemiol Community Health*, 52:399-405, 1998.

11. Smith, G.D., Neaton, J.D., Wentworth, D., Stamler, R., Stamler, J., "Socioeconomic differentials in mortality risk among men screened for the Multiple Risk Factor Intervention Trial: I. White Men," *Am J Pub Health*, 86:486-496, 1996.

12. Zierler, S., Kreeger, N., Tang, Y., Coady, W., et al, "Economic deprivation and AIDS incidence in Massachusetts," *Am J Pub Health*, 90:1064-1073, 2000.

13. House, J.S., Lepkowski, J.M., Kinney, A.M., Mero, R.P., Kessler, R.C., Herzog, A.R., "The social stratification of aging and health," *J Health & Social Behavior*, 35:213-234, 1994.

14. Lahelma, E., Arber, S., "Health inequalities among men and women in contrasting welfare states," *European J Pub Health*, 4:213-226, 1994.

15. Moser, K.A., Pugh, H.S., Goldblatt, P.O., "Inequalities in women's health: Looking at mortality differentials using an alternative approach," *Brit Med J.*, 296:1221-1224, 1988.

16. Leclere, F.B., Rogers, R.G., Peters, K., "Neighborhood social context and racial differences in women's heart disease mortality," *J Health & Social Behavior*, 39:91-107, 1998.

17. Jargowsky, P.A., *Ghettos, Barrios and the American City*, New York, Russell Sage Foundation, 1997.

18. Lantz, P.M., House, J.S., Lepkowski, J.M., Williams, D.R., Mero, R.P., Chen, J., "Socioeconomic factors, health behaviors and mortality. Results from a nationally representative prospective study of US adults," *JAMA*, 279:1703-1708, 1998.

19. Sorlie, P.D., Backlund, E., Keller, J.B., "US mortality by economic, demographic and social characteristics: The National Longitudinal Mortality Study," *Am J Pub Health*, 85:949-956, 1995.

20.   Pappas, G., Queen, S., Hadden, W., Fisher, G., "The increasing disparity and mortality between socioeconomic groups in the United States, 1960 and 1986," *New Eng J Med.*, 329:103-109, 1993.
21.   James, S.A., Strogatz, D.S., Wing S.B., Ramsey, D.L., "Socioeconomic status, John Henryism and hypertension in blacks and whites," *Am J Epidemiol.*, 126:664-673, 1987.
22.   Williams, D.R., "Socioeconomic differentials in health: A review and redirection," *Social Psychology Quarterly*, 53:81-99, 1990.
23.   *Health, United States, 1992.* National Center for Health Statistics, Washington DC, US Government Printing Office, 1993.
24.   Lillie-Blanton, M., Parsons, P.E., Gayle, H., Dievler, A., "Racial differences in health: Not just black and white, but shades of gray," *Ann Rev Pub Health*, 17:411-448, 1996.
25.   Williams, D.R., Collens, C., "Socioeconomic and racial differences in health," *Ann Rev Sociol.*, 21:349-386, 1995.
26.   Cooper, R.S., David, R., "The biological concept of race and its application to public health and epidemiology," *J Health Politics, Policy & Law*, 11:97-116, 1986.
27.   Williams, D.R., Yu, Y., Jackson, J.S., Anderson, N.B., "Racial differences in physical and mental health," *J Health Psychology*, 2:335-351, 1997.
28.   Kreeger, N., Sydney, S., "Racial discrimination and blood pressure: The CARDIA Study of young black and white women and men," *Am J Pub Health*, 86:1370-1378, 1996.
29.   Link, B.G., Northridge, M.E., Phelan, J.C., Ganz, M.L., "Social epidemiology and the fundamental cause concept: On the structuring of effective cancer screens by socioeconomic status," *Milbank Quarterly*, 76:375-402, 1998.
30.   Link, B.G., Phelan, J.C., "Editorial: Understanding sociodemographic differences in health—the role of fundamental social causes," *Am J Pub Health*, 86:471-473, 1996.
31.   Adler, N.E., Boyce, T., Chesney, M.A., Cohen, S., Folkman, S., Kahn, R.L., Syme, S.L., "Socioeconomic status and health. The challenge of the gradient," *Am Psychologist*, 49:15-24, 1994.
32.   Wilkinson, R.G., "Income distribution and life expectancy," *Brit Med J.*, 304:165-168, 1992.
33.   Emanuel, E., "Political problems. Response to: Daniels N, Kennedy B, Kawachi I: Justice is good for our health," http://bostonreview.mit.edu/BR25.1/emanuel.html.

10

Managed Care and the Prospects of Health Reform

David Mechanic

I first met Eli some thirty years ago; by then he had already written some thirty books. Of these, I was most familiar with his three-volume study of the ineffective soldier (Ginzberg 1959), a resource I depended on when writing my first book on mental health policy (Mechanic 1969). Eli, an expert on manpower, was one of the first to recognize the devastating effects of psychiatric disorder on effective performance and to understand the many failures of selective service screening during World War II. Despite the fact that almost two million men were rejected for service because of alleged psychiatric disorders, such conditions were a major cause of separation from the services. I suspect that Eli's long involvement with, and his understanding of, human resources issues made him particularly sensitive to the importance of chronic disease much earlier than most other social and economic scientists—a theme that has continued to interest him over his career.

It is humbling to realize that Ginzberg's vast output on issues of health and health care that began in the 1940s with studies of nursing and hospital care (Ginzberg 1949), and ranged over almost every important issue in the subsequent decades, has been only one part of his prodigious output. In this essay I focus on health care issues, the only facet of Ginzberg's work on which I am competent to speak.

David Mechanic is director of the Institute for Health, Health Care Policy and Aging Research at Rutgers, the State University of New Jersey.

In his various studies and many books, Eli has always addressed troublesome questions, and the theme of the potential for health reform runs through his writings over the decades. As a young man optimistic about the future and the prospects of change, I approached Eli's analyses, and his views of the limits of health reform, with some impatience. In reviewing his book with Miriam Ostow, *Men, Money, and Medicine* (Ginzberg and Ostow 1969), I wrote:

> Ginzberg and Ostow accept gross inequalities in medical care and different systems of medical care for the rich and the poor as a reasonable and permissible cost of preserving the autonomy of the professional in respect to where and how he practices. Although fully appreciative of the irrationalities and inefficiencies that result, they see little sign of public intolerance toward entrenched professional institutions...with increased inflation in medical care prices and persistent maldistribution of resources, it is not inconceivable that others will support growing protests about the organization and distribution of medical care. As such voices become organized, they will be heard by government, and the third of the medical-care dollar that government provides, if used judiciously, will be no insignificant wedge in the health industry. We are a long way from anything resembling a revolution in medical care, but I, for one, am not betting on the status quo (Mechanic 1970).

Thirty more years of trying to encourage needed changes have taught me that Eli was talking from much experience and acquired wisdom and that he understood better than I the fundamental interests and enormous barriers that held back needed social change.

Eli viewed medicine within the context of a pluralistic and democratic society, and his pessimism about major reform was premised on the notion that as long as entrenched institutions could command the respect and tolerance of the majority of the population, significant change was unlikely (Ginzberg and Ostow 1969; Ginzberg 1977). He believed that until the majority of Americans were dissatisfied with their medical care, things would go on as before despite the issues of concern to experts. Achieving change through the political process has become more complex over the years—especially with growth in the power of television and other mass communications and the influence of big money. Some believe that the Clinton health care plan, though it failed, was our last opportunity for many years to come in achieving comprehensive health reform (Skocpol 1997).

Perhaps, not surprisingly, Ginzberg, writing recently in the *New England Journal of Medicine* (Ginzberg 1999), reports on the growing numbers of uninsured and underinsured, the many problems attributed to managed care, and the possible consequences of a fall in the economy. Following this scenario, he notes that:

Since managed-care plans will not be in a position to constrain rising health care costs in the face of consumers' demands for more choices and reduced interference in the patient-physician relationship, and since future health care costs must be controlled, at least as far as government expenditures are concerned, the best alternative is for government to provide essential coverage to the entire population and then let persons who want more and better care to cover the additional costs out of their own pockets through privately purchased insurance, or through employer benefits (p. 146).

Some may puzzle over why Eli Ginzberg is now contemplating major reform. Apparently, he has come to believe that a growing proportion of voters are losing faith in the private health insurance system and are troubled by developments in managed care. The tolerance and respect that shielded the system from the inroads of reform are being undermined—due to the loss in confidence in it—making it possible to have transformative changes. This essay explores these circumstances and assesses whether our system of care has reached the point of impending implosion. In some ways I change places with my friend in taking the view that, while many significant changes in health care will occur by iteration, we are unlikely to have anything resembling the kind of changes Eli describes in the foreseeable future.

The Growth of Managed Care and the
Problem of the Uninsured

There are many analyses of why the Clinton Health Care Reform failed (Skocpol 1997; Starr 1995; Mechanic 1996; Johnson and Broder 1997). It is ironic that the American public allowed private corporate medicine to do what they would not have allowed government to do—and its intrusions have gone beyond anything government could have contemplated. Business embraced managed care because it promised to reduce growing health care costs and until recently, with much fat in the system, managed care could deliver on that promise. Much of the fat has been eliminated, and the costs of varying managed care plans are now rising. Hospitals and other institutions are complaining bitterly about insufficient reimbursement, and corporate medicine now abandons markets and populations when they appear unprofitable. Some of the biggest and most esteemed HMOs are experiencing large financial losses and there is fear that the competition to contain costs is driving quality down.

Americans are not used to being told that they cannot have what they want in the way of medical care. Rationing, which was always present but is now stricter and more explicit, is bringing the lesson of constraints home. The result is a significant loss of trust in medical institutions and a tremendous backlash (*Journal of Health Politics, Policy and Law* 1999). Politicians know that bashing managed care is immensely popular and has few political risks. There has been much managed care reform activity in the states and on the federal level. Even the President of the United States, many governors, and countless legislators are into micro-management of care affecting delivery services, mastectomy, the use of "gag" rules in contracts, and other matters.

Although representatives of health care plans, and managed health care organizations in particular, initially showed little astuteness in their public relations, they seem to have learned a great deal and have become more proactive in addressing some of the problematic aspects of implementing managed care approaches and strategies. Large health care plans have also demonstrated ingenuity and flexibility in devising new products (Robinson 1999) that respond to public alarm about less choice of physicians, restricted access to specialists, benefit design restrictions, and "experimental therapies." This adaptability has the potential to defuse some of the hostility to managed care, but managed care organizations still face significant challenges in their public relations and increasingly in their relations with physicians.

Managed care includes a wide range of structures, approaches, strategies, and reimbursement arrangements, and patient satisfaction varies a great deal from one to another. However, in public discourse managed care is depicted as a monolithic concept and negative attributions taint the entire industry (Mechanic 1997a). With the centralization of health care and the development of large managed care organizations, there is a persistent tendency in the press, and in the public mind, to generalize misdeeds in particular instances to large national plans or to the industry overall. Thus, care could very well be improving but appears much worse in the public discourse.

Ginzberg, in his various recent writings, makes much of the growing numbers of uninsured and underinsured persons, and he is quite right in focusing on this deficiency of our employment-based health care arrangements. It is perhaps surprising how willing Americans have been to accept the rising ranks of the uninsured although there has been support for federal and state efforts to extend health insurance to children and poor adults. The irony is that the number of uninsured people continues to grow despite these efforts and extraordinary economic growth. The uninsured remain concentrated among low wage employed workers, children, young people, and the near poor. But should the economy turn sharply, this problem may extend deeper into more politically active population groups, and anything might happen. Early momentum for the Clinton reform efforts at the beginning of his administration came from a lagging economy and growing anxiety among middle-class Americans about possible loss of insurance and about "job-lock" due to fears about losing insurance. It is difficult to know how large an uninsured population the electorate will tolerate, and already many of our major medical institutions feel under great pressure in providing indigent care. It is clear, however, that we are nowhere near the threshold for any comprehensive federal intervention.

Managed Care: Rhetoric and Reality

With the large variety of structures, approaches, and strategies included under the managed care rubric, it is difficult to track and monitor it in a valid way. Although some managed care companies share data with researchers, much of relevance is now seen as proprietary products and are not available. Moreover, most of the studies that have been done have been focused on cost and not quality, deal with limited outcomes such as enrollee satisfaction, and have been short-term, rarely allowing sufficient time to observe important changes in outcomes. Recognizing the limits of such studies, one can only fairly conclude that they show no large differences between managed care and non-managed care settings (Miller and Luft 1997, 1994; Reschovsky 1999; Kemper et al. 1999). Although respondents consistently report modestly greater satisfaction in relationships with physicians in non-managed care settings, they prefer the cost advantages and limited paperwork of HMOs. On access, utilization, and quality measures, HMOs sometimes perform better and sometimes worse than comparison groups. In short, the data are a wash. The variations within structures of comparable kinds are much greater than variations among particular types of organizations.

There seems to be one major exception to this general observation of little difference: the arena of serious mental illness (Mechanic 1997b; Mechanic and McAlpine 1999). Managed Behavioral Mental Health Organizations (MBMHOs) have been the single most aggressive component of the managed care industry and appear to have reduced consumer and professional requests for services much more sharply than in medical or surgical areas. There is also evidence from a variety of studies that patients with serious mental illness have had poorer outcomes within managed care than within more traditional relationships. Here, however, the comparisons are commonly with more traditional publicly organized services (Mechanic 1998). More broadly, there is indication that managed mental health care has the effect of "democratizing services" in a way that has deleterious effects on those most in need. The data show less-than-expected differences in services utilization among persons with more and less serious illness within managed care (Mechanic and McAlpine 1999). The reasons for such homogenization remain obscure but they are disturbing nevertheless.

There are indications and fears, as well, that the problems in dealing with serious mental illness extends to other disabled groups, to the elderly, and to persons with chronic disease (Ware et al. 1996). As the argument goes, managed care does well in dealing with the healthy population but less well in dealing with those who are sick. The evidence remains unclear here. Some studies find that persons with chronic disease and the elderly do less well in HMOs but others do not, and the evidence does not support a clear assessment. While there are complaints about HMO care among advocates for disabled children and other special categories of ill individuals, the basis for these problems are complex.

One of the most significant disincentives for quality under managed care in our present health care system is the inadequacy of risk adjustment methodologies. Small proportions of sick patients account for most health care expenditures. A capitated health plan or medical facility that attracts many such patients could find itself in serious financial difficulty. Health providers, thus, have little incentive to seek credit as the best providers of services to very sick people because they fear they will attract too many patients whose costs far exceed the capitations they bring (U.S. General Accounting Office 1996). Persons with disabilities who are part of support groups and client networks commonly share information on the best and most responsive providers. If such perceptions become widely shared, the selective flow to particular provider groups could be highly problematic. Health plans and providers understand—however sympathetic they might be to high risk groups—that they do better for their financial health when they limit enrollment of high risk patients. In current circumstances, plans and providers are rewarded better for competing on risk avoidance than on quality. Some progress is being made on risk adjustment approaches to capitation, but this is an area that still requires considerable developmental effort.

Another reason for the drop in intensity of care for high risk patients in managed care may be the inexperience of many new plans in managing such complex patient groups. For example, many of the managed behavioral health care companies have evolved from private sector work, where they had to deal with relatively few of the most serious and persistently disabled patients. Many of these patients have extremely high rates of service utilization and depend on care from a variety of service sectors. Less experienced clinicians and case managers from the acute care sector may have pushed these seemingly high utilization rates toward the mean, not sufficiently appreciating that many of these patients are fundamentally different from the typical cases they managed from the private insurance sector. Several of the MBHCOs have become very large and have acquired the technical expertise to manage the severe and persistently ill person traditionally found in the public sector. Thus, we might anticipate improved performance with enhanced experience. This obviously will require careful monitoring.

Some Physician Reactions to Managed Care

An important feature of the managed care backlash is the extreme hostility toward managed care by physicians and many other health professionals. With the growth of corporate medicine and managed care, health professionals have significant fear of loss of future income, reduced autonomy, and dependence on outside organizations for their professional livelihoods. Surveys of physicians show increasing reports of loss of freedom on many dimensions of care, including spending sufficient time with patients, hospitalizing patients who they believe require it, ordering tests and procedures whenever they want to, and the like (Burdi and Baker 1999; Hadley et al. 1999). Doctors certainly are experiencing large changes in their conditions of work, and much larger uncertainties than in the past, but it is not clear that their reports accurately reflect changing conditions as compared with their own needs and wants.

Take the issue of common complaints that doctors have too little time for each patient and that the demands of managed care require more productivity and seeing more patients. The complaint is hardly new; such complaints of insufficient time have been evident for decades (Mechanic 1975). But, more important, is that the apparent consensus that the length of doctor-patient encounters have decreased in the era of growing managed care is incorrect. Clinical encounter time actually increased between 1989 and 1997 (Mechanic et al. 2000a). This trend is consistent for both HMO and non-HMO practice and primary and specialty care. Although average encounter time is somewhat shorter in HMOs than in non-HMO practice, it was also shorter prior to the expansion of managed care. HMO encounter time between 1987 and 1997 showed the same pattern of increase as is evidenced in non-HMO practice.

Take another example—the common complaint made by many doctors in surveys that they cannot hospitalize patients who, in their opinions, require it. This is a more difficult claim to assess because it is possible that the fact of managed care strategies themselves serve as a deterrent to questionable decisions and doctors learn the acceptable criteria for hospitalization. However, even surveys of physicians that focus on specific behaviors and experiences, and not general attitudinal reports, find that few hospital admissions are denied and even fewer after appeal (Remler et al. 1997). There is much evidence, of course, that concurrent review of inpatient care has reduced length of stay, but the implication that the gateway to the hospital that the doctor requires is now blocked is exaggerated.

Health care surveys and polls have become commonplace, and the media and various health care interests have come to depend on them, but too often, without sufficient appreciation of their limitations. It is well established that when respondents feel strongly about some issue, they generalize their reaction in responding to other areas in the survey as well. Doctors do not like managed care and they tend to be negative in their attitudinal responses to most items that refer to it. Such "halo" effects can be quite large. Moreover, survey responses can be magnified by the salience of the issues and the social context in which questions are asked, by question wording, by the ordering of questions in the survey, and other aspects of survey format (Sudman and Bradburn 1982; Bradburn and Sudman

1988; Sudman et al. 1996). Surveys, of course, are useful but they have to be understood in their proper context.

The Employer Revolution

No one would have anticipated thirty years ago that the assault on traditional concepts of medical professionalism and on the power of medical authority would come, not from government and not from the growing legitimacy and success of the group and staff model HMO, but rather from the private marketplace and large employers. Weary of ever increasing premiums for medical care insurance for their employees, and distrustful of government, employers were quite willing to encourage a competitive marketplace to bring down costs. It is ironic that large employers, many who initially favored the Clinton reform, so distrusted government that they turned against it despite its potential advantages for them. Employers and the general public sat on the sidelines, and even cheered, while the private sector usurped medical authority and imposed constraints and rules that would have made them apologetic had government been the perpetrator.

Many employers not only decreased their costs by contracting with managed care companies, but they also transferred a greater proportion of the premium to employees and sometimes modified the benefit design as well. Moreover, with changing employment patterns, there were more workers in small firms that did not provide health insurance or excluded coverage of dependents, or made it extremely expensive. Many part-time workers in firms that provided insurance were excluded as well. Efforts to build community coalitions to decrease health care costs and to develop voluntary insurance pools to encourage small firms to provide coverage have proved disappointing (Brown and McLaughlin 1990; McLaughlin and Zellers 1992). In the public sector, changes in welfare programs, and the severance of welfare and Medicaid resulted, perhaps inadvertently, in large numbers of poor children losing their health insurance. If anyone ever believed that employment without government mandates would be the basis for universal health insurance entitlement in the United States, that illusion should be ragged by now.

Emasculated Reform Marches On

It is now a cliche that universal health insurance is part of all developed Western countries save one, our own, unless one wants to also include South Africa. It is a sign of our times that when candidate Bradley advocated a health proposal not very different from the one supported by the father of the Republican candidate when he was President, the Democratic opposition saw it as too much, too soon. In the earlier period, it was too little, too late. It seems like we can no longer have an intelligent political conversation in America about universal health coverage without being seen as outside the ken. While the common view from abroad that the uninsured go without care is exaggerated, many studies show repeatedly that they are significantly under-treated and have worse health outcomes than those with insurance (Weissman and Epstein 1994). The care we provide the uninsured is highly inefficient and wasteful as well and distributes the burden of supporting such care unfairly.

It is difficult to know precisely how much damage the public safety net has sustained, in part because definitions of the safety net vary so greatly from one community context to another (Baxter and Mechanic 1997). Clearly, however, the burden of care for the uninsured and underinsured falls substantially on major university health centers, public hospitals, and a relatively small group of not-for-profit hospitals located in or near poverty areas. For some years indigent care has been subsidized by shifting costs to private insurers and the Medicare program. Increasingly, the growth of managed care and its capacity to drive down hospital reimbursement has made it more difficult to shift these costs. Hospitals depended on Medicare to offset some of the pain induced by managed care, but now Medicare also has become a tougher payer, facing hospitals with their first real financial challenge. Although federal disproportionate share payments and some state programs have helped relieve some of the burdens of uncompensated care, changing conditions make it more difficult to sustain a reasonable safety net for a growing uninsured population.

Whatever the hostility to managed care approaches and strategies, managed care provides a context that would allow, if we had the political will, movement toward universal health coverage. Patients are still resisting the mechanisms that protect against open-ended consumption and probably will continue to do so for some time, but any affordable system in the future will have to live with such constraints. The rich, no doubt, as Eli told us many decades ago, will continue to acquire what they wish and where they wish, but the public challenge is to provide everyone with a decent minimum. Achieving this is not space science and outside our ken. The politics, however, are quite another matter.

There is much emphasis these days in the social science literature on growing inequalities in an era of plenty and the pervasive effects of such inequalities on health outcomes (House and Williams 2000; Mechanic 2000b). Building on the observed gradient in the relationship between socioeconomic status and health, there is an emerging political hypothesis that if the public could understand that the well-being of all of us was tied to reducing income inequalities, we might have more political will to do so. However we might regret income inequality, the evidence that inequality itself, and not income and educational disadvantage, is the cause of poor outcomes is not persuasive. The need remains to focus our efforts on the real deprivations experienced by those of lower SES and those in greatest need of health care, as well as other important services, such as child care, education, housing, and nutrition.

The hypothesis that little is likely to happen until many more of us feel at risk may be true. Perhaps a coalition will emerge when many diverse groups—the uninsured, hospitals, doctors, employers, employees—feel more pain as costs rise again and are subjected to increasingly tough constraints. The interests in America have always benefited economically from major health reform. One significant analysis of the failure of the Clinton reforms argued that it failed because it did not promise the major interests enough (Skocpol 1997). Perhaps when the going gets tough enough health plans and pharmaceutical companies will join doctors, hospitals, and the uninsured in supporting universal coverage. If and when we get it, it won't be on the cheap.

When I first established the Institute for Health, Health Care Policy and Aging Research at Rutgers University in 1985, I selected Eli as our inaugural speaker. In celebration of our tenth anniversary we asked him back again and he generously, on both occasions, gave our students and faculty the wisdom of his long experience in health policy and health affairs more generally. Eli still toils in the vineyards and we look forward to his return on future occasions to continue to inspire us with his knowledge, experience, wisdom, and enthusiasm for our common endeavor. And, not least, Eli, in his person and in his work, represents a model of aging gracefully.

References

Baxter, R.J. and Mechanic, R.E. (1997). "The Status of Local Health Care Safety Nets." *Health Affairs* 16(4):7-23.

Bradburn, N.M. and Sudman, S. (1988). *Polls and Surveys: Understanding What They Tell Us*. San Francisco: Jossey-Bass.

Brown, L.D. and McLaughlin, C.G. (1990). "Constraining Costs at the Community Level." *Health Affairs* 9(4):5-28.

Burdi, M.D. and Baker, L.C. (1999). "Physicians' Perceptions of Autonomy and Satisfaction in California." *Health Affairs* 18(4):134-145.

Ginzberg, E. (1999). "The Uncertain Future of Managed Care." *New England Journal of Medicine* 340(2):144-146.

Ginzberg, E. (1977). *The Limits of Health Reform*. New York: Basic Books.

Ginzberg, E. and Ostow, M. (1969). *Men, Money, and Medicine*. New York: Columbia University Press.

Ginzberg, E., et al. (1959). *The Ineffective Soldier: Lessons for Management and the Nation*. New York: Columbia University Press, Three volumes.

Ginzberg, E. (1949). *A Pattern for Hospital Care*. New York: Columbia University Press.

Hadley, J., Mitchell, J.M., Sulmasy, D.P., et al. (1999). "Perceived Financial Incentives, HMO Market Penetration, and Physicians' Practice Styles and Satisfaction." *Health Services Research* 34, No. 1 (Part II):307-321.

House, J. and Williams, D. (2000). "Understanding and Reducing Socioeconomic and Racial/Ethnic Disparities in Health." Institute of Medicine Conference on Capitalizing on Social Science and Behavioral Research to Improve the Public's Health. Atlanta, GA, February.

Johnson, H. and Broder, D. (1997). *The System: The American Way of Politics at the Breaking oint*. Boston: Little Brown and Company.

Journal of Health Politics, Policy and Law. (1999). Special Issue: The Managed Care Backlash. *Journal of Health Politics, Policy and Law* 24(5).

Kemper, P., Reschovsky, J.D. and Tu, H.T. (1999). "Do HMOs Make a Difference? Summary and Implications." *Inquiry* 36(4):419-425.

McLaughlin, C.G. and Zellers, W.K. (1992). "Shortcomings of Voluntarism in the Small-Group Market." *Health Affairs* 11(2):28-40.

Mechanic, D., McAlpine, D.D. and Rosenthal, M. (2000a). "Are Patient-Physician Visits Getting Shorter? 1989-1997." Under review.

Mechanic, D. (2000b). "Rediscovering the Social Determinants of Health." *Health Affairs*, in press.

Mechanic, D. and McAlpine, D.D. (1999). "Mission Unfulfilled: Potholes on the Road to Mental Health Parity." *Health Affairs* 18(5):7-21.

Mechanic, D. (Ed). (1998). *Managed Behavioral Health Care: Current Realities and Future Potential*. New Directions for Mental Health Services, No. 78. San Francisco: Jossey-Bass.

Mechanic, D. (1997a). "Managed Care as a Target of Distrust." *Journal of the American Medical Association* 277(22):1810-1811.

Mechanic, D. (1997b). "Managed Mental Health Care." *Society* 35(1):44-52.

Mechanic, D. (1996). "Failure of Health Care Reform in the USA." *Journal of Health Services Research & Policy* 1(1):4-9.

Mechanic, D. (1975). "The Organization of Medical Practice and Practice Orientations among Physicians in Prepaid and Nonprepaid Primary Care Settings." *Medical Care* 13(3):189-204.

Mechanic, D. (1970). "Crisis in the Health Field." *Science* 168:1563-1564.

Mechanic, D. (1969). *Mental Health and Social Policy*. Englewood Cliffs, NJ: Prentice Hall.

Miller, R.H. and Luft, H.S. (1997). "Does Managed Care Lead to Better or Worse Quality of Care?" *Health Affairs* 16(5):7-25.

Miller, R.H. and Luft, H.S. (1994). "Managed Care Plan Performance Since 1980: A Literature Analysis." *Journal of the American Medical Association* 271(19):1512-1519.

Remler, D.K., Donelan, K., Blendon, R.J., et al. (1997). "What do Managed Care Plans do to Affect Care? Results from a Survey of Physicians." *Inquiry* 34(3):196-204.

Reschovsky, J.D. (1999). "Do HMOs Make a Difference? Access to Health Care." *Inquiry* 36(4):390-399.

Robinson, J.C. (1999). *The Corporate Practice of Medicine: Competition and Innovation in Health Care*. Berkeley: University of California Press.

Skocpol, T. (1997). *Boomerang: Health Care Reform and the Turn Against Government*. New York: Norton and Company.

Starr, P. (1995). "What Happened to Health Care Reform?" *The American Prospect* 20 (Winter): 20-31.

Sudman, S., Bradburn, N.M. and Schwartz, N. (1996). *Thinking About Answers*. San Francisco: Jossey-Bass.

Sudman, S. and Bradburn, N.M. (1982). *Asking Questions: A Practical Guide to Questionnaire Design*. San Francisco: Jossey-Bass.

U.S. General Accounting Office. (1996). *Medicaid Managed Care: Serving the Disabled Challenges State Programs*. Washington, DC: U.S. Government Printing Office, GAO/HEHS-96-136.

Ware, J.E., Bayliss, M.S., Rogers, W.H., et al. (1996). "Differences in 4-Year Health Outcomes for Elderly and Poor, Chronically Ill Patients Treated in HMO and Fee-for-Service Systems." *Journal of the American Medical Association* 276(13):1039-1047.

Weissman, J.S. and Epstein, A.M. (1994). *Falling Through the Safety Net: Insurance Status and Access to Health Care*. Baltimore: Johns Hopkins University Press.

11

The Imperatives of Training Older Workers:
A Massachusetts Report and Recommendations*

John T. Dunlop

On a state level, the Massachusetts Blue Ribbon Commission Report of April 2000 is reminiscent of reports and recommendations on a national scale of the late 1960s and 1970s that appear to have gone out of fashion. Most notable was the position paper addressed to the new administration taking office in January 1969 by the National Manpower Policy Task Force, which is comprised of eighteen academic experts, including Eli Ginzberg, of course.[1] The annual Manpower Report of the President, prepared by the Labor Department, to which Eli Ginzberg contributed extensively, served as an overall policy forum while it lasted. Occasional chapters in the *Economic Report of the President*,[2] while useful, are not currently adequate to highlight on a continuing basis the national issues confronting public programs and private policies related to the rapidly changing labor force and employment patterns. Moreover, individual states and regions reflect somewhat distinctive patterns, hence a case for presenting the recent Massachusetts report.

The Massachusetts Jobs Council—the governor's advisory board on workforce development—established the Blue Ribbon Commission on Older Workers in 1997 to study the labor market for older workers in the Commonwealth and to recommend policies to improve the economic status of the older labor force.[3]

*I gratefully acknowledge a major role of Professors Peter B. Doeringer of Boston University, Andrew Sum of Northeastern University and David Terkla of the University of Massachusetts, Boston, the Research Staff of the Blue Ribbon Commission, in the preparation of the Commission's reports and in assistance with this chapter.

John T. Dunlop is emeritus professor of economics at Harvard University.

It may be appropriate at the outset to make reference to Eli Ginzberg's substantial writings on the theme of Older Persons.[4] He wisely stated almost fifty years ago that "much that transpires in the lives of older workers can be understood only in terms of developments that occurred earlier. But it is also true that the later years of life are very much influenced by factors embedded in the aging process itself. The adjustments people make in their later years is a result of the interaction of these two factors."[5]

My earlier work emphasized that "older workers tend to confront a major problem, in a sense analogous to continuing inflation. Their educational assets reflect an earlier currency, now often relatively depreciated. This is a continuing problem, and in truth it applies at all educational levels from the laborers to the professional worker. The rate of obsolescence may be as great, or even greater, at high educational levels as with low levels of formal training."[6]

The initial focus of the Massachusetts Commission was to design programs for economically disadvantaged workers over fifty-five—the group singled out for special consideration under the federal government's Job Training Partnership Act. However, it soon became apparent to the Commission that the employment and training issues involving older workers are often rooted in their earlier employment experiences—just as Eli Ginzberg stated—so the Commission amended its usage and analysis of "older worker" to begin at age forty-five.

This chapter is organized into four sections: the first projects the changing characteristics of the Massachusetts population and labor force over the next decade; the second projects the changing demands for employment by private and public employers and the labor force constraints to meet these demands. The third section describes the resulting mismatch between supply and demand over the next decade. The final section summarizes in some detail the recommendations of the Blue Ribbon Commission to redress this mismatch and produce the requisite workforce with the necessary skills and training.

Changing Population and Labor Force

The country is well alerted to the fact that "phenomenal demographic change" will occur as the post World War II baby boom generation enters its fifties.[7] The number of older persons (defined by the Commission as those aged forty-five to sixty-nine) in the

Massachusetts population began to rise in the 1990s as the first wave of the baby boom generation reached its mid-forties. This trend will accelerate over the decade 2000-2010, as shown in Table 1.

Table 1. Number of Massachusetts Residents Age 16-69, and Age 45-69, 1970-2010, in Thousands

Year	Age 16-69	Age 45-69	Age 45-69 as a Percent of Age 16-69
1970	3,559	1,399	39.3
1980	3,953	1,391	35.2
1990	4,229	1,374	32.5
1995	4,164	1,440	34.6
2000	4,233	1,567	37.0
2005	4,390	1,771	40.3
2010	4,551	1,974	43.4

Between 1995 and 2010, the older population in Massachusetts (forty-five to sixty-nine) is projected to rise by 534,000 and its share of the state's working age population (sixteen to sixty-nine) will reach an historical high of 43.4 percent, up from 32.5 percent as recently as in 1990.

Similarly, the fraction of the workforce accounted for by older workers (forty-five to sixty-nine) is projected to grow from 28 percent in 1990 to 39 percent by 2010. Despite the trend towards earlier retirement among male workers, projections prepared for the Commission show that all of the net increase in the labor force to 2006 would come from older workers. The aging of the workforce is particularly severe in Massachusetts among the states.

It took Massachusetts nearly a decade to grow its labor force by 50,000 in a state with a resident labor force of 3.3 million people. "That translates into an anemic 1.5 percent growth from 1990 to 1999, ranking Massachusetts 47th out of all 50 states. Meanwhile, the national labor force growth rate was nearly 11 percent over the same period."[8]

In the period 1990-99 over 140,000 immigrant workers arrived in Massachusetts from abroad. This influx not only allowed the Commonwealth to replace a net loss of 90,000 native-born workers over the period, but it enabled the state to post the net gain of 50,000 workers. Without foreign immigration, the Massachusetts labor force would have declined by 3 percent instead of growing by 1.5 percent in the past decade. These elements of Massachusetts demography enhance the attention to the older workforce.

Economic Growth and the Constraints of Labor Supply

Massachusetts has experienced substantial job growth and declining unemployment in the 1990s. From an unemployment rate of 9.0 percent in 1991, the unemployment rate by 2000 had declined to below 3 percent. Future economic growth is clearly seriously constrained by labor supply.

The Massachusetts Division of Employment and Training projects that the state's economy will grow from an employment level of 3,252,000 total jobs in 1996 to 3,656,000 in 2006, an increase of 400,000 new jobs, or 12.4 percent. An additional 740,000 jobs will need to be filled to replace workers who retire, move up the career ladder, or change careers. In total, more than 1.1 million jobs should result.[9] But the Commission's labor supply projections for the same period show that growth in the workforce would be less than one-half of the requisite amount in the absence of measures to attract, retain, or retrain the labor force.

While the labor force participation rates of older females in Massachusetts have been steadily increasing, those of older men have fallen. Labor force participation rates for older male workers, once the highest in the country, have dropped by almost 11 percentage points since 1970 (Table 2), and Massachusetts now ranks only about twenty-fifth in the nation in terms of the participation rates of older men. This alone represents a loss of about 72,000 older male workers to the Massachusetts economy.

Fortunately in the three-year period 1997-99, with unemployment in Massachusetts in the 3-4 percent range, the civilian labor force participation rates for older workers reversed themselves and showed increases rather than a continuing decline. The participation rate for those forty-five to fifty-four was 83.7 percent in 1996 and increased to 86.4 percent on average in 1998-99; the participation rate for those fifty-five to sixty-four was 59.8 percent in 1996 and increased to 63.8 percent on average in 1998-99; and the participation rate for those sixty-five and over was 11.3 percent in 1996 and increased to 13.0 percent on average in 1998-99.

Table 2. Trends in the Civilian Labor Force Participation Rates of 45-69 Year-Old Men in Massachusetts, 1970 to 1997, By Age Group, Numbers in Percent

Age Group	1970	1996-97	Absolute Change
45-49	94.9	90.9	-4.0
50-54	93.3	87.6	-5.7
55-59	90.0	80.7	-9.3
60-64	71.1	55.8	-15.3
65-69	46.7	28.6	-18.1
45-69 all	84.5	73.6	-10.9

But the longer term declines in labor force participation rates actually understate the shrinkage in labor supply of older workers because they do not reflect the decline in hours worked and the doubling of the fraction of older workers who have been employed in part-time employment since 1970. The extent to which declines in labor supply in Massachusetts represent preferences for more leisure and more flexible hours of work or a response to deteriorating employment opportunities is not easily determined from the data. In any event, the contraction in the labor supply of older men through the mid-1990s contributed to the Commonwealth's current shortages.

If Massachusetts is to achieve its projected and potential economic growth and solve its problems of skill scarcities, it has few alternatives to utilizing its older workforce more effectively. Attracting more younger workers (from graduates of educational institutions from other states or from other countries) will require stronger compensation incentives. Massachusetts already ranks twelfth among the top states in terms of the participation of females in the labor force. More reliance on foreign immigrants is a further alternative to older workers, but Massachusetts is already the fifth highest in the nation among states in the contribution of immigrants to labor force growth, and almost all the net growth in labor supply in the Commonwealth during the last decade has come from outside the country.

The only labor force group of sufficient size to meet the growth needs and aspirations of the Commonwealth is the growing pool of workers forty-five years and over.

Labor Market Mismatches

Older workers have been disproportionately employed in the classic Massachusetts industries of textile, apparel, leather, shoes, etc. The projected sectors of growth include health care, biotechnology, financial services, and computer services. These high-end sectors will continue to utilize a considerable proportion of professional, managerial, and technical employees. While low-end growth industries, such as eating and drinking establishments, personal services, retailing, and home health care, more readily accommodate workers with less education, recent occupational projections suggest that almost half of all new jobs in Massachusetts will require a bachelor's degree or higher.

Today's cohort of older workers ages fifty-five to sixty-four is better educated than its predecessors and will be replaced by an even more educated cohort as today's forty-five to fifty-four year-olds age over the next decade. However, fewer of these older workers are as well educated as the young adults who have been available to growth employers in the 1990s. For example, only 30 percent of workers fifty-five to sixty-five have at least a bachelor's degree—below the 40 percent for workers twenty-five to thirty-four years. Among the underutilized older workers, one quarter of the unemployed and almost one-third of the underemployed lack a high school diploma or its equivalent.

Labor scarcities and skill mismatches of the magnitude projected for Massachusetts will impose major adjustment costs on employers in terms of higher wages needed to recruit workers and additional training expenses. Employers are aware that labor markets have become much tighter in Massachusetts, but few appreciate how much greater these adjustment costs are likely to be in the future.

Because there will not be enough of the relatively well-educated workers in their twenties and thirties that many employers have relied upon for decades to fill entry-level job vacancies, employers will have to learn how to hire and train older workers for entry jobs. This greater reliance on older workers is coming at a time when employers are investing less in older employers compared to those who are younger, and cutbacks are being made in federal training funds for older workers.[10] Moreover, the training shortage is most acute among smaller employers.

Under any scenario that allows the Commonwealth to achieve its growth potential, the majority of employers will have to substitute at least some older workers for the traditional entry workers. Hiring and selection practices will have to be adopted to a workforce that has more experience, but less up-to-date education. Training and promotion practices will need to be attuned in how recent school graduates and experienced workers learn new job skills. Wage and fringe benefit structures will need to accommodate differences in the compensation preferences of younger and older workers, and more flexible working hours will be needed for older workers who have different family or caregiver responsibilities than younger workers. These changes are not likely to be made easily for managers, supervisors, or workers, be they young or older.

"If the economy is to operate at a high level of employment, say in the range of 3 to 4 percent unemployment, then programs for treating shortages have no less an integral role than those oriented toward the unemployed and the disadvantaged. The interrelations between general economic policy and manpower policy cannot be ignored."[11]

Summary of Recommendations of the Massachusetts Blue Ribbon Commission

1. Recommendations on Assessment and Placement

- Use quantifiable criteria, such as whether wages and working conditions meet prevailing labor market standards, how much training is required, and the permanence of employment prospects to determine which jobs should be the targets for training and placement efforts.

- Adopt job development and job placement standards for all publicly-supported occupational education, skill training, on-the-job training programs, and approved training programs for persons receiving extended unemployment benefits based upon the goal that participants be employed in jobs that pay at least 85 percent of their previous earnings, or in which pay is equal to at least 50 percent of the median family income in the Commonwealth, whichever is greater.

- Adopt rigorous standards of accomplishment and competency for pre-vocational programs, such as basic literacy and GED preparation.

- Offer intensive assessment to all Workforce Investment Act participants, unemployment insurance recipients, and other job seekers who are "at risk" because they are unlikely to be able to obtain employment which pays at least 85 percent of the earnings of their previous jobs, or that results in annual full-time income equal to at least 50 percent of the median family income in the Commonwealth, whichever is greater.

- Ensure that all unemployment insurance recipients receive intensive employability assessment and that those who are "at risk" of not being able to earn 85 percent of the wages on their prior jobs or 50 percent of the Massachusetts median income, whichever is higher, are clearly informed of opportunities for extended benefits under the provisions of Sec. 30 of the unemployment insurance system. Sufficient time must be provided to apply for such benefits and assistance must be available for completing the application process.

- Require One-Stop Centers to conduct annual surveys to identify all education, training, and employability support service opportunities in their service areas.

- Require One-Stop Centers to provide information on program size, costs, participant characteristics, and program performance to applicants.

- Use the One-Stop Centers to determine whether older workers have special support service needs, such as community-based work and family counseling, and to identify the availability of such programs in the community.

- Create a technical assistance capacity in One-Stop Centers for identifying "best practice" experience among employment assistance programs for older workers and for disseminating this information to local providers of employment and training services.

- Require that One-Stop Centers establish web sites with comprehensive program data that are updated annually and job openings data that are updated at least weekly.

2. Recommendations on Occupational Education and Training

- Expand the five-year statewide comprehensive strategic planning process under the WIA to include all major occupational education and training programs. The goal should be to create a fully integrated workforce development system to coordinate programs operated under the WIA and the Wagner-Peyser Act, the Workforce Training Fund, adult basic education, occupational education provided by community colleges, training under the Transitional Assistance Program for welfare recipients, and training supported by the Social Security system.

- Develop uniform oversight procedures and incentives to ensure that all organizations receiving federal and state funding for skills training, occupational education, or work experience activities for older workers coordinate these programs with skills training and work experience provided through adult skills training programs under the WIA, the Workforce Training Fund, and other statutorily supported training programs.

- Require that the training and employment services offered by the different providers in this integrated system respond fully to the needs identified by the employability assessment process.

- Ensure that older workers receive the same opportunities for training as younger workers by training staff to facilitate the enrollment of older workers in workforce development programs, by monitoring the levels of service provided to older workers, and by conducting regular "client satisfaction" interviews with older program participants.

- Authorize changes in administrative rules and procedures to encourage persons eligible for extended unemployment to enroll in approved skills training and occupational education programs and require that such programs be approved as allowable training activities even if the overall length of the program exceeds the current 18 months, if such additional training is necessary to secure reemployment at comparable wages.

3. Recommendations for Workplace Training

- Educate employers and unions about the severe labor market mismatches and supply deficits emerging in the Massachusetts economy and encourage them to increase their human resource development efforts, particularly for older workers.

- Provide incentives and technical assistance to expand outreach programs and partnerships between the public workforce development system and employers and unions to better meet the employment and training needs of older workers.

- Target training and technical assistance resources under the state Workforce Training Fund on employers most in need of building their training capacity, such as those with fifty or fewer employees.

- Ensure that low-wage, low skilled workers are recognized as a priority group for service in determining which programs are funded under the state Workforce Training Fund.

- Designate set-aside funding for training initiatives involving employers and/or labor organizations that cut across the JTPA and the WIA regional Service Delivery Areas.

- Request that employers provide an assessment of the training and development needs of their employees, as well as their firms, as part of the application for support under the state Workforce Training Fund.

- Support the enactment of legislation to provide training and technical assistance in state and municipal government workplaces comparable to those available to private sector workers under the state Workforce Training Fund.

4. Recommendations for Supported Work Experience

- Use the work experience slots under the Senior Community Service Employment Program (SCSEP) as an on-the-job training component for workforce development and integrate work experience with other skill training programs.

- Encourage SCSEP work experience programs to provide transitional employment experience by limiting individual participants to fifty-two weeks of subsidized employment experience in any three-year period.

5. Recommendations on Planning, Coordination, and Oversight

- Establish an adequately staffed Workforce Investment Board to plan for, implement, and monitor the Commission's recommendations.

- Require this Board to develop uniform oversight procedures for coordinating and evaluating all publicly funded workforce training programs in the Commonwealth, including adult skills training for older workers, adult basic education, incumbent worker training, supported work experience, training for welfare recipients, and advanced skills training and occupational education provided through community colleges.

- Appoint to this Board one or more members who have an in-depth knowledge of older worker employment issues to identify special service needs of older workers and to identify special barriers to the successful upgrading of older workers.

- Designate a single, high-level executive in state government to be responsible for implementing Workforce Investment Board policies.

- Create a Massachusetts "21st Century Workforce Development Commission" to monitor how technological change, workforce demographics, and other structural changes are affecting the Massachusetts economy and its workforce development system. A standing advisory committee on older worker issues should be established within this Commission.

6. Recommendations for the Coordination and Delivery of Services at the Local Level

- Establish local workforce investment boards that can undertake the same degree of comprehensive planning as recommended for the state-level Workforce Investment Board and provide these local boards with sufficient resources to accomplish this goal.

- Require these local boards to develop uniform planning and oversight procedures for coordinating all publicly funded workforce training programs within their planning areas.

- Appoint one or more members to these local boards who have an in-depth knowledge of older worker employment issues to identify special service needs and barriers to the successful upgrading of older workers.

- Complete the planned network of One-Stop Centers throughout the state and determine whether or not additional centers will be required.

- Use community-based organizations and other placement organizations to supplement the one-stop system until it is fully implemented and its effectiveness has been demonstrated, particularly with respect to serving low income communities.

7. Recommendations for Improving Program Accountability and Performance

- Devise a common management information system incorporating detailed demographic and socioeconomic characteristics of participants for all publicly funded employment and training programs for older workers in Massachusetts.

- Require that all programs document both the types and the intensity of services received by program participants, including weeks and hours of program participation in each component, modeled after the management information system that has been required under JTPA.

- Develop performance indicators that measure success in improving the economic status of participants in terms of wages and earnings as well as employment. Correlate these performance indicators with the characteristics of participants and the intensity of services to estimate the degree of economic improvement relative to the severity of employment barriers.

- Develop counterpart indicators to measure the extent to which programs are addressing labor scarcities and skill mismatches through employer surveys and the analysis of the industrial and occupational characteristics of job placements.

- Adopt performance standards for certifying WIA training programs, for approving training programs for persons receiving extended unemployment insurance benefits, and for evaluating the performance of all other publicly-supported training programs based upon the goal that clients be employed in jobs that pay at least 85 percent of previous earnings, or in which pay is equal to at least 50 percent of the median family income in the Commonwealth, whichever is greater.

- Provide incentives to programs to serve persons with the most serious obstacles to employment and employers with the most serious skill scarcities.

- Establish an independent evaluation program, incorporating federal standards for maintaining confidentiality of information on individuals, to conduct long-term assessments of how well workforce development programs are performing. This evaluation should be based on both the income improvements achieved for older workers and success in meeting critical skill scarcities. Follow-up should rely upon both unemployment insurance wage records and direct surveys of participants and employers. These follow-ups should be conducted at intervals of three months, six months, one year, and two years.

- Conduct regular process evaluations of a representative cross section of programs.

- Provide incentives for building linkages between programs such as public-private partnerships and programs that combine basic education with vocational preparation.

- Create set-aside funding at the state level for research and demonstration programs to address labor market mismatches through the training of older workers.

8. Recommendations on Resources and Priorities

- Provide sufficient supplemental state funding to meet the labor market scarcities and skill mismatches of the Massachusetts economy.

- Provide sufficient supplemental state funding to harmonize eligibility criteria among employment and training programs operated under different legislative authorizations.

- Develop a sliding scale of fees for employment and training services based on ability to pay, with those most in need receiving services without charge.

- Use state-level planning and coordination mechanisms to ensure that older workers receive their proportionate share of training resources.

- Give priority to serving those with the lowest incomes and most serious barriers to employment if resources prove insufficient to close the Commonwealth's employment and training gap.

The preceding eight-part summary of the Recommendations of the Massachusetts Blue Ribbon Commission on Older Workers has been presented here in such detail since few readers of this volume are likely to have encountered the *Report* or its *Key Findings and Recommendations*.

The significant elements of the *Report*, it seems to me, are to address the mismatch in the demography of the Massachusetts workforce with the aspirations for economic growth of the Commonwealth in the next decade. The retraining and use of its older workforce is its only recourse in attaining its growth objectives; this course requires the reversal of programs of early retirement and necessitates a bundle of policies encouraging part-time and flexible work schedules and fringe benefit packages oriented toward older workers, with more conventional programs for younger workers. While larger enterprises have begun to adopt retraining and related programs—internally or through outside arrangements including community colleges—smaller enterprises and public agencies seldom have even thought about these issues.

This view of Massachusetts problems in the next decade places a heavy burden on the Workforce Investment Board and staff to develop a close and influential relation with various segments of the employer and union management communities to monitor the emerging mismatch and to implement policies that retrain older workers and adopt congenial personnel policies. The use of the unemployment insurance system, within permissible limits, to provide training also requires special attention since the employer community generally seeks lower utilization and tax rates.

Notes

1. *The Nation's Manpower Program, A Position Paper by the National Manpower Policy Task Force, January 7, 1969.* John T. Dunlop was chairman of the Task Force. Also, see two publications of Eli Ginzberg: *The Manpower Connection, Education and Work*, Cambridge, MA: Harvard University Press, 1975; *Manpower Agenda for America*, New York: McGraw-Hill Book Company, 1968. The Massachusetts Blue Ribbon Commission Report has no reference to military manpower issues that were a necessary component of studies and statements on a national level in the 1960s and 1970s in the Vietnam era.

2.   See *Economic Report of the President, Transmitted to Congress, February 1999*, Washington, D.C., Chapter 3, "Benefits of a Strong Labor Market," pp. 99-129, and Chapter 4, "Work, Retirement, and the Economic Well-Being of the Elderly," pp. 131-169.

3.   The twelve-member Commission, appointed in 1997 by then-Lieutenant Governor Paul Cellucci was an independent panel drawn from industry, labor, education, and public interest organizations chaired by John T. Dunlop with Warren Pepicelli, vice president of U.N.I.T.E. as co-chair. The able research staff was comprised of Professors Peter Doeringer, Director, and Andrew Sum and David Terkla. See Commonwealth of Massachusetts, Blue Ribbon Commission on Older Workers, *Older Workers: An Essential Resource for Massachusetts*, and a summary report, *Key Findings and Recommendations*, April 2000.

4.   In summarized form see, Ginzberg, Eli, *Understanding Human Resources, Perspectives, People, and Policy*, Lanham, Maryland, Abt Associates, University Press of America, Inc., 1985, chapters 21-25, pp. 275-336; chapters 46-47, pp. 615-54.

5.   Ibid., p. 278.

6.   Dunlop, John T., "Technological Change and Manpower Policy - The Older Workers," in *Technology, Manpower, and Retirement Policy*, Juanita Kreps, Ed., Cleveland and New York, The World Publishing Company, 1966, p. 18.

7.   See Dohm, Arlene, "Gauging the Labor Force Effects of Retiring Baby-boomers," *Monthly Labor Review*, July 2000, pp. 17-25.

8.   Sum, Andrew and Mello, Neil, "Picture of Labor Force Growth Isn't as Rosy as It Seems," *Boston Globe*, August 13, 2000, p. F3.

9.   Massachusetts Division of Employment and Training, *The Massachusetts Job Outlook Through 2006*, Economic Analysis Department, December 1998.

10.   Fragis, H., Gittleman, J., Horrigan, M., and Joyce, M., "Results from the 1995 Survey of Employer-Provided Training," *Monthly Labor Review*, June 1998, pp. 3-13. Also see, Patrick J. Purcell, "Older Workers: Employment and Retirement Trends," *Monthly Labor Review*, October 2000, pp. 19-30.

11.   Dunlop, John T., "An Overall Evaluation and Suggestions for the Future" in Robert Aaron Gordon, ed., *Toward a Manpower Policy*, New York, John Wiley & Sons, Inc., 1967, pp. 355-72, at p. 368. (The volume summarized four annual conferences of the Berkeley Unemployment Project.)

12

Health Services in a Transforming Metropolitan Economy[1]

Thomas M. Stanback, Jr.

At my first staff meeting after joining the Conservation of Human Resources Project at Columbia University in the early sixties, Eli Ginzberg announced that the study of employment and labor markets had thus far seriously neglected the urban dimension and that henceforth in our work there should be a major emphasis on cities. Over the years that followed, Eli was the enthusiastic champion of a number of urban-oriented studies and, often, a contributor.

Two studies, in particular, stand out in my memory. The first was conceived in the early seventies when it seemed that New York was facing bankruptcy and when no word of optimism could be heard over the din of the naysayers. Eli called the staff together and invited us to contribute chapters to a book about New York City. The title, he said, would be *New York is Very Much Alive.* It was a good book, and of course, Eli was right.

The second study was *The Corporate Headquarters Complex in New York City.* The principal investigators were Matthew Drennan and Robert Cohen, but Eli played a key role from beginning to end. To my mind, this little book still stands as the best study of the New York economy of the last forty years.

Eli was the best editor a writer could ever have. He read wonderfully fast but always with keen perception. A manuscript was returned with a shower of comments—always within a day, and often sooner. Working with him was a privilege. He has been a mentor, an

Thomas M. Stanback, Jr. is professor of economics emeritus at New York University.

inspiration, a friend, and always, a source of sound advice and warm support.

* * *

Since World War II the U.S. economy has undergone a dramatic transformation during which manufacturing declined from about a third of non-farm employment in 1950 to around 13 percent today, while services have become ever more important as a generator of both jobs and income. Throughout this period the health services sector has played a critical role. It has experienced major structural change and rapid growth, with its share of GNP rising from 5 percent in 1950 to about 14 percent at the end of the nineties and selectively, as in the case of New York City, to as high as 20 percent.

A conventional view of the organization of health services focuses on the large medical center with little attention given to the arrangement of subordinate levels of health services delivery systems. In this study, however, I analyze employment and other measures at the level of metropolitan areas, making it possible to examine the extent to which health care systems vary in employment size among different metropolitan economies.

Two principal findings emerge. The first is that there is a hierarchical ordering of metropolitan places in terms of the concentration of health care personnel. The second is that the economic contribution of the health care sector to the metropolitan economy is magnified because an important part of the payment for these services is provided by Medicare-Medicaid, an "export-sector" type flow of dollars from outside the area that is not simply the result of a re-spending of resident earnings. Medicare-Medicaid payments (adjusted by level of total earnings) vary widely among metros, providing additional evidence of a hierarchical arrangement of health care delivery systems within the national economy.

The U.S. Economy, 1974-1997

It is the share of job increases that show most clearly the major sources of U.S. employment growth.[2] In 1974 retailing, business/professional services, and non-profit services together accounted for 28 percent of total non-farm employment, respectively, yet during the period 1974 to 1990 they accounted for 63 percent of net job increases. Of the 24 percent contributed by nonprofit services, health services were the major source of new jobs (about 15 percent).

During the nineties, job increases were dominated by business/ professional services (25 percent) and nonprofit services (27 percent), while retailing accounted for a sharply reduced share. Once again, health services were responsible for a major share of job creation—more than 18 percent.

Health Services and the Metropolitan System

In my study of the role of services in the metropolitan system, upon which much of this analysis is based, metropolitan areas (metros) of the continental United States were classified and grouped according to industrial specialization (1990) and these groups were broken down by metro population size.[3]

An initial finding is that health services' shares of employment rose among all type-size metro groups during the years studied. In 1974 shares calculated separately for each group ranged from roughly 3 to 7 percent of employment; in 1997, from 9 to 12 percent.

What is of special interest, however, is that shares of employment accounted for by health services varied quite widely among individual metros. This is readily observed when metros are ranked according to size of health services share of employment and the array of metros is broken into quintiles. The highest and lowest share values (percentages) are shown below for each quintile:[4]

Highest and Lowest Share Size (%) within Quintiles of Metro Rankings of Health Services Employment Shares, 1997

	Highest	Lowest
Quintile I	30.9	11.5
Quintile II	11.5	10.2
Quintile III	10.2	8.8
Quintile IV	8.8	7.7
Quintile V	7.7	4.5

We observe that among the top two-fifths of metros in the system, health services accounted for above 10 percent of all jobs in 1997; among the top one-fifth, from 12 to 31 percent. For the lower ranking metros, shares ranged downward to less than 5 percent—smaller but by no means unimportant shares of total employment.

What these measures indicate is that for a considerable number of metros the health services sector constitutes an important part of the economic base. These metropolitan economies with relatively large concentrations of health services may be regarded as playing a role within the system of places as intermediate level providers of specialized medical services, even though they are not major centers for the training of medical personnel and the delivery of highly specialized services.

Health Services as an Economic Base Activity

To understand why this is so we must recognize that metropolitan areas are very open economies that must provide, through exports, to a much greater extent than national economies, a stream of income to pay for imports of goods and services from the outside world. Moreover, exports drive the local economy (i.e. those activities that provide for the everyday needs of the populace and the businesses and institutions that provide for them). Increases in exports may be expected to result in a multiplied effect on local income and employment.[5]

An important distinction between goods and services is that while goods are usually exported, services, for the most part, are not. Goods, being physical and transportable, are typically produced for a market extending beyond the city or metro borders. Services, on the other hand, are typically performed for customers who must be dealt with directly, viz. the patient with the doctor, the client with the lawyer, the supermarket with the daily or weekly customer. This need for direct dealings between provider and customer means that the bulk of services are delivered locally and that services constitute most of the activities within the local sector.

This does not apply to all services, however. A number of services may be exported. In some cases, the service provider travels to the customer or the customer to the provider. In other cases s/he is able to deal with the customers through modern communications systems or by direct mail (e.g. Internet marketers, direct mail retailers).

Urban economists and economic geographers have long recognized that there is a hierarchical ordering in the delivery of many services. Those services that are routine and in frequent demand, and in which providers are relatively unspecialized (i.e. lower order services), will be found in all urban places and will be exported to only a very limited market, if at all. On the other hand, where the service is less frequently demanded and requires a higher level of specialized personnel and/or specialized equipment or facilities, it cannot operate on an economically efficient basis. Producers of such services will need to be concentrated in a limited number of places, each of which will serve a broader market than if it produced only local services.

What this means, of course, is that urban centers providing "higher order" services will also provide "lower order" services for their own populace so that the total share of employment accounted for by combined higher order and lower order services will be larger than if the range of services were more restricted.

The hierarchical nature of financial and business services is well established. For example, in New York City, the range of financial services extends from routine banking to the city's stock market and investment community. Not surprisingly, the total share of its financial services is quite large—more than three times the national average. Specialized financial services are clearly a major part of its export sector while more routine financial services must be regarded as part of its local sector.

The distinction between routine local sector services and more specialized "exported" services is equally applicable to medical services. Major medical centers offer an array of highly specialized services: training health care professionals, carrying out research, and providing sophisticated treatment to patients. Yet, at the same time, many doctors' offices and other facilities within these same metropolitan areas are providing less specialized services.

The existence of a limited number of major medical centers is, of course, common knowledge. What is less widely recognized is that there is within the American health care system a large number of metros in which the level of concentration of health service employment indicates a significant "exporting" of health services. While some of these are major medical centers, others must be regarded as subordinate, regional or sub-regional centers.

Examples of such places are readily observed among the ten metros ranked highest in terms of shares of employment accounted for by health services (1997):

Rank	Name of Metro	Type of Metro	Health Services Share (%)
1	Rochester, MN	Resort/Retirement	31.0
2	Punta Gorda, FL	Resort/Retirement	18.9
3	Alexandria, LA	Government/Military	18.5
4	Wheeling, WV	Diversified/Service	15.5
5	Iowa City, IA	Government/Service	15.5
6	Sherman-Denison, TX	Manufacturing/Service	15.0
7	Pueblo, CO	Government/Service	14.3
8	Tyler, TX	Diversified/Service	14.2
9	Chico Paradise, CA	Resort/Retirement	13.9
10	Asheville, NC	Manufacturing/Service	13.8

While the top ranked metro is Rochester, MN, home of the world famous Mayo Clinic, and the fifth, Iowa City, IA, is the home of the University of Iowa and of its medical school and medical center, the remaining eight are by no means well known. They are located in various parts of the country and have been classified according to overall industrial structure under several different heads. What they have in common is that for each health service employment is relatively large, indicating delivery of health services on a scale larger than needed for local requirements and thus "exporting" to regions or sub-regional markets, outside of metropolitan boundaries.

Analysis of the entire top quintile shows that these places are found among virtually every type-size group of metros. Of special interest is the finding that included within these high ranking metros are a number of manufacturing/service (thirteen out of forty-three) and government/military (seven out of twenty-one) places. It is metros among these groups that have been hardest hit by loss of manufacturing jobs and military base closings and, accordingly, have been provided the most needed support by relatively high levels of health services employment.[6]

To fully appreciate the role played by health services within the export base of metropolitan economies it is useful to compare them with retailing. Retailing is, for the most part, a local sector activity, except in the case of metros specialized in tourism, retirement, or conventions. A quintile analysis of employment share in retailing for 1997 of the type already discussed for health services bears this out. It was among the resort/retirement groups that the largest percentage of metros was ranked in the top quintile: over 46 percent of the larger population resort/retirement group and over 83 percent of the smaller. This contrasts sharply with the distribution of metros specialized in health services. As noted above, these metros are more broadly dispersed among the various type-size groups of places.

Non-earned Income and Health Services

It was emphasized earlier that metropolitan exports provide a stream of income to pay for imports of goods and services from the outside world. What was not noted was that there were sources of dollar income other than exports of goods and services. For many metropolitan economies non-earned income—defined here as dividends, interest and rent payments (DIR), and transfer payments (TP) (principally Social Security, Medicare, Medicaid, and welfare payments)—also provide major dollar flows that, like export sector earnings, may be spent in the marketplace. These flows have varied somewhat among metros, but have increased in importance everywhere:

	1974		**1997**	
	U.S.	Range*	U.S.	Range*
Earnings	73.6%	65.1%-77.9%	66.4%	54.8%-69.3%
DIR	13.8%	10.8%-14.9%	17.2%	14.8%-26.5%
TP	12.5%	11.1%-14.8%	16.4%	13.2%-22.1%
Personal Income	100.0%		100.0%	

*Range among type-size metro group totals.
Source: Bureau of Economic Analysis

The size of these flows suggests that they have been an important factor in stimulating metropolitan economies generally and in stabilizing some of the weaker metros for whom the loss of manufacturing or military employment has seriously weakened the export base.

DIR. The growth of DIR payments is indirectly related to the growth of health services in a number of places. As individuals' investments have come to provide a greater share of income and thus to permit retirees to move more readily to retirement-type communities, these communities have experienced a greater demand for those goods and services related to the needs of senior citizens, particularly the demand for health services. In addition, these new arrivals bring with them eligibility for Medicare coverage (see below), which largely provides payment for their health services.

Transfer payments. As shown above, transfer payments increased substantially as a share of personal income over the 1974-1997 period. Like DIR, transfer payments varied in importance among metro groups, ranging in 1997 from as high as 22 percent of personal income to as low as 13 percent. The highest levels relative to personal income were in the government/military and resort/retirement groups, where metros were more frequently hosts to retirees.

Medicare-Medicaid payments. These payments, a subcategory of transfer payments, are paid directly to providers of medical services for the elderly, disabled, and poor. Accounting for about 18 percent of total national health expenditures in the early days of these programs (i.e., in the beginning of the 1970s), Medicare-Medicaid payments have grown to account for more than a third of national health expenditures since the mid-1990s.[7]

Accordingly, Medicare-Medicaid payments must be seen as important dollar inflows to metropolitan economies. Levels of these payments vary widely among metros, however, as indicated by the quintile distribution (1997) below. In this distribution the highest and lowest levels of Medicare-Medicaid payments are shown for each quintile of payment. In order to adjust for size of metros, these payments have been expressed as a percentage of comparable metro earnings levels.

Highest and Lowest Medicare-Medicaid Payments, by Quintile Rankings of Metros, 1997 (expressed as % of metro earnings levels)

	Highest	Lowest
Quintile I	27.9	11.6
Quintile II	11.6	9.2
Quintile III	9.2	7.3
Quintile IV	7.3	5.8
Quintile V	5.8	2.6

The difference among metros in levels of Medicare-Medicaid payments is striking, the top fifth receiving payment of magnitudes ranging from 11.6 to as high as 27.9 percent of the level of comparable metro earnings (i.e. wages and salaries), while the bottom fifth received payments ranging downward from 5.8 to 2.6 percent.

Here again there is evidence of variations in the roles played by metros but expressed this time in terms of Medicare and Medicaid payments. While it may be true that some variations are due to differences in demographic structure (with a larger proportion of Medicare patients in some metros than in others), it seems evident that those metros in which medical payment levels are high are providing a wider range of specialized services (in addition to more routine care) to Medicare-Medicaid patients than are other metros and thus are providing services to patients drawn from a wider market area. If such is the case, then those metros that are providing higher levels of medical services to Medicare and Medicaid patients should also be numbered among those previously identified on the basis of employment shares as more specialized in delivering health services.

An analysis was made of the extent to which metros ranked in the top quintile, on the basis of shares of health services employment, were also ranked on the basis of Medicare-Medicaid payments. Taken as a whole, the analysis showed that those metros with relatively large shares of employment in health services also ranked relatively high in terms of level of Medicare-Medicaid payments. Of the sixty-two metros ranked in the top quintile for shares of health service employment, thirty-one (50 percent) ranked in the top quintile for Medicare-Medicaid payments, and another seventeen (27 percent) in the second quintile.

Additional insights are gained by examining the ranking for Medicare-Medicaid payments (adjusted) of the same ten metros shown above as top-ranked for health services share of employment:

Rank and Quintile Based on Health Services Employment	Metro	Rank and Quintile Based on Medicare-Medicaid Payments
1 I	Rochester, MN	263 V
2 I	Punta Gorda, FL	1 I
3 I	Alexandria, LA	2 I
4 I	Wheeling, WV	14 I
5 I	Iowa City, IA	367 V
6 I	Sherman-Denison, TX	42 I
7 I	Pueblo, CO	3 I
8 I	Tyler, TX	95 II
9 I	Chico Paradise, CA	30 I
10 I	Asheville, NC	102 II

Six of these metros that were ranked in the top ten for health services share of employment are ranked in the top quintile (i.e. within the top sixty-two metros) for Medicare-Medicaid payments, two others within the second quintile. What is particularly interesting, however, is that Rochester, home of the Mayo Clinic, and Iowa City, home of the University of Iowa Medical Center, rank only in the fifth quintile for Medicare-Medicaid payments. The explanation, apparently, is that the health services sectors in these latter two metros treat a somewhat different cross-section of patients, with a larger percentage of more difficult cases. Among those patients requiring specialized care will be younger patients, not on Medicare, and more affluent patients, not on Medicaid.

The Economic Importance of Health Services in the Metropolitan Economy

In the above discussion we have seen that health services have grown rapidly and that for a large number of metros scattered across the country health services have come to play a significant role as part of the export base. Both the analysis of health services as a share of metro employment and of Medicare-Medicaid expenditures at the metro level indicate a hierarchical pattern of health care delivery in which the health care systems of some metros employ relatively more people and receive relatively more dollars in payment as they provide a wider range of services and reach out to a broader market.

But the economic importance of the health service sector at the metro level is not limited to those places in which the more specialized and higher value-added services are provided. Unlike retailing, which is a purely local sector service paid for entirely out of the earned income of residents, health services, as we have seen, are remunerated to a considerable extent by Medicare and Medicaid payments made by federal and state government, and are thus received from outside the metropolitan economy.

Moreover, although health services, taken as a whole, stand somewhere in the middle as regards average annual wages for paid employment (1997)—$27,855 as compared to $16,917 for retail trade, $33,770 for manufacturing, $45,650 for finance and insurance—incomes of doctors and other professionals are substantially higher, and for many specialists may run into hundreds of thousands of dollars annually.

In addition, modern medical practice increasingly involves the use of highly sophisticated and expensive equipment for which charges must be included along with professional fees, wages, and salaries.

Paradoxically, in modern medicine, increased utilization of such equipment does not involve a substitution of capital for labor. Rather, the new technology requires new levels of specialization of labor—and new levels of training and of remuneration. Thus it is that the health sector of a metropolitan area has become, increasingly, a high value-added sector.

This characteristic is true to some extent in all metropolitan economies, but it is especially applicable where the metro functions as a regional or sub-regional center, offering higher levels of specialization and making use of higher levels of technology and equipment.

Highlights of This Post-War Development of Health Services

This final section highlights some of the developments in the U.S. health care sector which help to explain how these services have grown at the metro level.

Modern American medicine is in many ways a product of the post-war era. In 1945 the country had inherited a pre-war structure focused mainly on a handful of major urban medical centers with the daily practice of medicine carried on largely outside the hospital—in the patient's home or in the office of the practitioner.

Yet by the end of the war a new era of modern medical technology was already underway. Penicillin had been introduced along with a number of war-borne techniques. Moreover, some 16 million servicemen and women had observed a level of medical practice that many had not known before. A new demand for access to better health care had begun to develop.

Nor was this all. During the war years a new emphasis was given to specialization as the military organized medical services in order to provide for the sick and wounded and to prepare for the medical needs of returning veterans. With the passage of the GI Bill of Rights (1946) many young doctors, recognizing that better opportunities lay in specialization, took advantage of the new provisions to seek resident training. The numbers of doctors reporting themselves as full-time specialists rose from 24 percent in 1940 to 44 percent in 1955 and to 69 percent in 1966.[8]

It is difficult to overemphasize the importance of the role of government during the early post-war years. Generous funding was provided on three fronts: provision for modernization and construction of hospital facilities, for training of doctors and other health professionals, and for medical research.

Immediately after the war two federal hospital construction programs were adopted—one to expand the Veterans Administration hospitals and the other, the Hill-Burton program, to aid the nation's community hospitals.

Regarding Hill-Burton, Paul Starr has written:[9]

> Between 1947 and 1971, the $3.7 billion disbursed under the program contributed to 30 percent of all hospital projects and provided an average of about 10 percent of the annual cost of construction. The program also generated an estimated $9.1 billion for hospital construction in local and state matching funds. Hill-Burton was modified in 1954 to permit grants to long-term care and ambulatory care facilities, but as of 1971, more than three quarters of the money had gone to hospitals.

In addition to hospital expansion, there was extensive investment by government in research and training. Medical schools grew rapidly with full-time faculty increasing by half from 1940-41 to 1949-50 and doubling during the following decade.[10] From 1963 to 1980 the number of students graduating from medical schools doubled, rising from about 8,000 per year to 16,000.

During these early post-war years and the decades that followed there was rapid growth of suburban areas and major shifts of industry and population to the southern and western states. A continuous process was taking place in which existing hospitals were being modernized or expanded, new hospitals were being built, and new demands upon the health care system were being created throughout the country.

While this expansion provided opportunities for large numbers of young specialists to find lucrative practices in the suburbs of the older cities and the burgeoning industrial communities of the South and West, this source of supply of doctors was far from adequate. The shortage was met in part from foreign shores. In 1965, after forty years of heavy restrictions, immigration laws were liberalized, making it possible for large numbers of foreigners with a medical education to immigrate and apply for residency training. Some 70 percent of these doctors opted to remain after completing their training. They often took jobs that others did not want, and many found their way to practices located in rural areas of the country. By 1997 just under 32 percent of practicing physicians in the United States were foreign medical graduates.

Another important source of supply of young doctors was women. As late as 1970 only about 9 percent of medical students were women; by the end of the decade, the proportion was greater than 25 percent.[11]

The passage of legislation creating Medicare and Medicaid in 1966 introduced a whole new source of funding and support for expansion of the American health care system. On the one hand, these programs covered in large measure the medical bills of the elderly and the poor and disabled. On the other, the Medicare program provided financial assistance to hospitals by allowing costs covered to include depreciation charges on existing capital assets. These payments created an additional flow of funds to the hospitals which were not only beneficial in their own right but had the enormous advantage of providing a basis for financing additional borrowing for expansion and modernization of plant and equipment. In addition, hospital costs for training residents were reimbursed.

Thus it was that by 1975, the beginning year covered by the data analysis, the health care system had already grown sharply and the forces of supply and demand that would propel continued growth during the remainder of the century were in place. Not only did the Medicare and Medicaid programs contribute an increased flow of dollars for the payment of health services, but health insurance (much in the form of HMOs), supported in part by employers, also came to play a larger role. By 2000, shares of personal health care expenditures provided for by government had increased substantially as had the share provided by health insurance:

Shares of Personal Health Care Expenditures (%)

	1950	1975	2000*
Federal and State	23.3	39.5	44.8
Health Insurance	8.9	25.8	33.2
Other private funds	2.9	1.4	3.6
Consumer out-of-pocket	64.8	33.4	18.4

*projected

Source: Statistical Abstract of the United States: 1968, Table 84; 1984, Table 148; 1999, Table 171.

Summary and Conclusions

The objective of this paper has been to examine the rise of health services over the period 1974-1997 in terms of the role played by the sector in the economies of metropolitan areas. No effort has been made to delve into questions relating to how efficiently health services are delivered or how adequately all groups of the public are being served.

An initial finding was that as people everywhere have demanded greater access to doctors and other medical services, shares of employment accounted for by health services have increased across the entire spectrum of metro type-size groups. A second is that, in spite of this broadly dispersed expansion, health services development has proceeded differently in some metros than in others in terms of levels of specialization of services performed and of the extent to which the area served by the metro's health care system extends beyond its borders. Metropolitan economies with relatively large concentrations of health services may be regarded as playing a role within the system as exporters of specialized services.

Still a third finding is that the categories of non-earned income (DIR and transfer payments) have increased sharply as shares of personal income. Combined Medicare and Medicaid, a major category of transfer payments, have contributed importantly to the growth of health services since 1966. For at least a fifth of metros, these direct payments for medical services that are rendered to the elderly, disabled, and poor have contributed substantial "export type" income, with levels of payments ranging from a tenth to a fourth of the levels of metro wage and salary earnings. For the remaining places, the non-earned income flows have ranged downward to about two and a half percent of the level of wages and salaries—in any event, a significant contribution.

A brief highlighting of the factors contributing to the post-war growth of health services in terms of capital expansion, scientific advance, and the training of professional personnel reveals a very large and strategic role played by government sponsorship and financing. The net result of a complex interplay of forces of both supply and demand has been the development of an industry that accounts for a major share of the gross domestic product of the nation today and contributes importantly to the economic health of large numbers of cities and the metropolitan areas centered on them.

Notes

1. This paper draws upon material presented in a larger study prepared by me as a member of the research staff of the Eisenhower Center for the Conservation of Human Resources: Stanback, Jr., T.M., *The Transforming Metropolitan Economy, 1974-1997*, New Brunswick, NJ: Center for Urban Policy Research, in press.
2. Job increases were determined by calculating the *net* change in U.S. employment for each of the industry categories *in which there was an employment increase*. Total job increases were then distributed.
3. Metropolitan areas were classified according to economic specialization and further broken down by size. The several classifications fall into two categories: *diversified service metros* and more specialized metros. Those classified as diversified service metros, which accounted for well over half of U.S. employment, are places with relatively high concentrations in several service categories (principally commercial and/or financial). Among the more narrowly specialized places, three groups are oriented principally to manufacturing: *functional nodal metros*—those with a strong headquarters presence as well as a strong industrial specialization; *manufacturing/ service metros*—manufacturing economies with a significant specialization in services; and *manufacturing metros*—places characterized by heavy specialization in manufacturing with relatively few services. The remaining types are *government/ service metros*—metros that tend to be specialized as state capitals and/or sites of state operated universities and medical centers; *government/military metros*—sites of military or other government installations; and *resort/retirement metros*—metros heavily specialized as resorts or as meccas for retired persons.
4. Here percentage shares are based on aggregate health services employment related to aggregate total employment in each type-size group.
5. See, for example, Mills, Edwin S. and McDonald, John F., *Sources of Metropolitan Growth*, New Brunswick, NJ: Center for Urban Policy Research, 1992, p. xvi. Estimates of the export multiplier have been prepared by the Bureau of Economic Analysis. See Bureau of Economic Analysis, "Regional Multipliers: A User Handbook for the Regional Input-Output Modeling System (RIMSII)," Washington, DC: U.S. Government Printing Office, May 1992.
6. Seven of the eleven larger and twenty-six of the forty-three smaller manufacturing/ service metros lost manufacturing jobs from 1990 to 1997. Nine of the thirteen larger and sixteen of the twenty-one smaller government/military centers lost military employment from 1990 to 1997.
7. Source: Statistical Abstract of the United States, 1984, Table 144, 1999, Table 170.
8. Starr, Paul, *The Social Transformation of American Medicine*, New York: Basic Books, 1992, p. 358.
9. Ibid., p. 350.
10. Ibid., p. 352.
11. Ibid., p. 391.

13

The Economic and Political Costs of Britain's National Health Service

Rudolf Klein

In 1939, Eli Ginzberg, future author of many books and articles on health care, first met Aneurin Bevan, future architect of Britain's National Health Service. At the time neither man could have predicted an involvement in health care. Ginzberg was researching a book on labor mobility in the mining valleys of Wales, an area of high unemployment. The book which emerged, A World Without Work,[1] still reads with amazing freshness: it is a reminder of how, in those days, an aspiring young economist could write a compelling analysis of labor market policies without loading it down with technical jargon or mathematical models. Bevan was a rebellious, radical Labour Member of Parliament. The prospect of a Labour Government, let alone the prospect of Bevan himself becoming Minister of Health, seemed remote. The occasion of the meeting was a visit by Bevan to the valleys—where his parliamentary constituency was—to discuss some issues of the day with his constituents.

The acquaintance was renewed, over a series of dinners, after the war. By now Minister of Health, Bevan discussed his plans for the NHS with his American friend who, given his wartime experience as the Chief Logistical Adviser to the Army's Surgeon General, probably knew rather more about organising hospital services than the politician. Ginzberg was strongly supportive of Bevan's ideas and

Rudolf Klein, an emeritus professor of social policy, is a senior associate of the King's Fund, London, and a visiting professor at the London School of Economics and the London School of Hygiene and Tropical Medicine.

encouraged him to go ahead with his plans. However, the conversations came to an abrupt end when Ginzberg pointed out that it was not unlikely that a poor New Yorker would receive more medicine and better care at a municipal hospital than the future enrollee of the NHS—simply because the United States was a much richer country and could afford larger outlays for health care than could Britain. Bevan, as Ginzberg recalls, "took tremendous umbrage" at this statement. And the two men were never again to renew their dialogue.

The exchange is, however, worth recalling for one very simple reason. Ginzberg's remark, which so offended Bevan, challenged one of the foundation myths of the NHS: that Britain could have a "national health scheme which is the admiration of the post-war world" (as Labour's 1951 election manifesto put it) irrespective of the performance of the country's economy. Funded out of the government's general exchequer revenue, the NHS was in fact particularly vulnerable to the vagaries of the economy. When the economy caught a cold, the NHS came down with pneumonia as the government (whether Labour or Conservative) sought to restrain or reverse the growth of public expenditure. And the history of the NHS in the decades following its launch in 1948 is largely the history of fiscal stringency as Britain lurched from one economic crisis to another. Bevan's aim in creating the NHS was "to generalise the best," i.e. to ensure that everyone—irrespective of income and where they lived—would have access to the highest quality medical treatment. In the outcome, the NHS was indeed successful in achieving social equity in access, but it was access to adequate services, with great geographical variations in quality and availability.

The link between health care and economic status (Ginzberg's point) can be simply illustrated. In 1948 Britain, while still recovering from its battering during the war, was a rich country relative to the rest of Europe if not the United States. But over the following decades Britain's economic performance limped behind that of the rest of Western Europe (not to mention Japan). As income per head rose more slowly than in other countries, such as France and Germany, awareness grew that Britain was becoming relatively poorer. And spending on health care mirrored economic trends. Already by 1960 spending on health care in Britain lagged behind that of other prosperous industrialised countries: 3.9 percent of the Gross Domestic Product as against 4.3 percent in France, 4.8 percent in Germany and 5.3 percent in the United States. Over the next decades the gap was to widen and become more dramatic still when translated into per capita spending on health care. By the end of the 1980s, France and Germany were both spending about $1100 a year per capita (calculated at GDP purchasing power parities) as against Britain's $760.

These figures are, of course, capable of very different interpretations. On the one hand, Britain's low spending can be seen as evidence of the special, unique virtues of the NHS. Here was a model that offered universal coverage but, because it operated within a single, fixed budget and offered no incentives to doctors and other providers to increase their incomes by expanding activity, could do so at a remarkably low price. In short, the NHS could be regarded as an example of virtuous parsimony. On the other hand, the NHS could be seen as a system that, over the decades, forced clinicians and others to restrict the services they make available to consumers. In short, the strength of the NHS from the first perspective—that it works within a capped budget set by central government—can be seen as its fundamental weakness from the second perspective, leading to the systematic under-funding of health care in Britain.

On January 16, 2000, the Prime Minister, Tony Blair, announced a large infusion of extra money for the NHS.[2] The aim was to bring the level of spending on health care in Britain—as measured by the percentage of GDP devoted to it—up to the average of the European Union countries. It appeared to be an acknowledgment of the thesis—argued by the official historian of the NHS,[3] among others—that the service had been starved of money throughout its existence: a contention that, of course, calls into question the whole design of the NHS since it suggests a fatal flaw in the way health care has been financed in the United Kingdom. New Labour, so anxious to distinguish itself from Old Labour in most respects, was dedicating itself to reviving Bevan's ambition to "generalise the best." In what follows, I shall examine the reasons for this conversion and conclude by asking whether the ambition is realistic. Ginzberg's insight remains valid: medical technologies are international, but national incomes are just that—national. If the success of Blair's Government is to be measured in terms of comparisons with richer countries than Britain, there may be problems ahead.

The Lean Decades

The NHS was born in a state of fiscal innocence. Going through the voluminous Ministry of Health files that record the years of argument and debate that preceded the launch of the NHS in 1948, one topic is remarkable by its almost complete absence. There is virtually no discussion of money and no awareness of the dynamics of health care expenditure. Estimates of the likely cost of the NHS seem to have been based on a simple-minded extrapolation of pre-war expenditure on health care. Once launched, however, the NHS fell victim to the original sin of all health care systems: an apparently unlimited capacity for soaking up ever more resources. The NHS's financial troubles began almost as soon as it was born. Year after year the service overshot its budget. Year after year Bevan engaged in fierce argument with his Cabinet colleagues about the spending total (although ironically a subsequent analysis showed that much of the NHS's increased expenditure was more apparent than real since the budget figures did not allow for inflation).

In a 1950 Cabinet memorandum, Bevan—having stressed the need to improve the building fabric of hospitals, to develop specialist services, and to keep pace with research progress in the development of new drugs—summed up the situation as follows: "Allowing for all sensible administrative measures to prevent waste, the plain fact is that the cost of the health service not only will, but ought to, increase... The position cannot be evaded that a nationally owned and administered hospital service will always involve a very considerable and expanding Exchequer outlay. If that position cannot, for financial reasons, be faced, then the only alternatives (to my mind thoroughly undesirable) are either to give up—in whole or in part—the idea of national responsibility for the hospitals or else to import into the scheme some regular source of revenue such as the recovery of charges from those who use it. I am afraid that it is clear that we cannot have it both ways."

The Cabinet proved unsympathetic. Tight spending limits on the NHS were set, and legislation introduced for patient charges on prescriptions, spectacles, and dental treatment. Bevan (though by now in a different Ministry) resigned in protest over the charges. Soon afterwards, the Conservatives replaced Labour in office and remained there for the next thirteen years. The issue of charges continued to haunt Labour: not until the late 1980s did the party abandon its commitment to abolishing charges. The Conservatives, in contrast, positively embraced them. Even so, charges remained a peripheral issue, financially if not politically. They have never accounted for more than 5.5 percent of total NHS expenditure—a low proportion by international comparative standards—largely because both parties endorsed a generous system of automatic exemptions. So, for example, children and retired people pay nothing towards the cost of their drug prescriptions (and neither do the unemployed and those on welfare benefits).

So the NHS's fiscal fate essentially hinges on two linked annual decisions. The first is about the level of taxation. The second is about the distribution of the tax revenue: i.e. the collective decision taken by ministers in the annual public expenditure review about how to allocate resources between the competing claims of different government departments and services. The NHS thus has to compete with education, social security, defence and so on. These decisions inevitably reflect both political priorities and economic imperatives. Crucial to an understanding of the NHS's fiscal history, therefore, is the fact that the five decades following its launch were marked by periodic economic crises.

It is therefore not surprising that the pattern of spending on the NHS followed a somewhat erratic path.[4] In seven years, the NHS budget was actually cut in real terms. In seven years, too, it rose by more than six percent in real terms. The annual increment ranged from 0.02 percent (in the fiscal year 1993-94) to 10.73 percent (1971-72). Both extremes were recorded under a Conservative Government, a reminder that ideology tended to be overridden by economic considerations. A comparison of the records of Labour and Conservative Governments between 1951 and 1997 shows, contrary to what one might expect from the former's dedication to the NHS, no clear ideological pattern. If the Thatcher years were an exceptionally hard time for the NHS, this could be put down as much to the economic turbulence of the period as to the Prime Minister's wish to roll back the frontiers of the Welfare State (which was never translated into practice).

The manic-depressive pattern of spending on the NHS tells us something about the difficulties faced by those running and working in the service. It tells us nothing, of course, about the adequacy of the level of funding. And that, in a sense, is the root problem of the NHS. Those working in the NHS have, almost since the beginning, protested about the inadequacy of the funding: roughly every three years throughout its history the medical and nursing professions have proclaimed the NHS to be in a state of crisis, on the edge of collapse. Most commentators (myself included) tended over the years to dismiss such claims as reflecting self-interest, a political ploy designed to force the government of the day to find more money for higher salaries. However, there was no way of resolving the dispute. The Department of Health, in its negotiations with the Treasury, devised a formula that suggested that an annual increase of two percent was needed to accommodate demographic change and technological advance. But that took no account of the adequacy, or otherwise, of the base line. As the 1979 Royal Commission on the NHS concluded: "There is no objective or universally acceptable method of establishing what the 'right' level of expenditure on the NHS should be."

Which is why, to reiterate the argument of this paper, setting the NHS budget is a political decision taken by ministers acting under economic constraints. That follows ineluctably from Bevan's original design (though it must be stressed that governments in other countries, with different methods of funding health care, are also concerned about the level of spending). Tony Blair's announcement on January 16, 2000, and its seeming acknowledgment of the under-funding thesis, must therefore be explained in terms of the changing politics of health care in the UK: the theme of the next and concluding section of this paper.

The Changing Politics of the NHS

The NHS imposes two different kinds of costs on governments: economic costs and political costs. The economic costs are summed up in the spending figures. The political costs are impossible to quantify, but can be identified: the blame (or credit) that governments earn by their stewardship of the NHS. All governments want, if at all possible, to minimize both economic and political costs. But what has happened over the last decade or so is that the political price of minimizing costs has risen sharply. In other words, while governments have successfully managed to keep NHS spending low by international standards, the political costs of so doing have risen sharply. Hence the Prime Minister's announcement.

There are a number of reasons why this has happened. First, attitudes towards the NHS have changed. Support for the concept of the NHS remains overwhelmingly strong, as survey after survey testifies. It is the most popular institution in the UK. But these same surveys also show increasing criticism of the actual performance of the NHS. This could be taken as a sign of a decline in performance. But a more plausible interpretation, in my view, is that public expectations have changed at a faster rate than the performance of the NHS. The consumerism of the supermarket society is now at odds with the provider paternalism that was the hallmark of the original NHS model. Hence, the political salience of waiting lists, with the parties competing in their promises to reduce them. Waiting lists have been a feature of the NHS since its birth. But what in the past was accepted as inevitable (queues and shortages were, after all, a normal part of life when the NHS was born) is now resented. The passive patient is turning into the active consumer.

Second, the professionals working in the NHS have become increasingly, and publicly, critical of the service. Again, it must be stressed, there has been no loss of faith in the principle of the NHS: the British Medical Association, which fiercely fought the introduction of the NHS, has become its staunchest defender. But the efforts of successive governments to wring more productivity out of the NHS—to compensate for the parsimony of inputs by squeezing out more outputs—has put increasing pressure on the professions. And resentment has been compounded by the fact that, starting in the 1980s, the emphasis of public policy has been to strengthen management in the NHS. Although doctors have on the whole successfully fought off perceived threats to medical autonomy, there is a lingering sense that they have lost status and power. And, in political terms, a discontented profession tends to translate into a critical public. Ministers may reel off statistics of the increase in the number of patients treated or operations performed, but it is doctors and nurses who carry conviction when they appear on television to lament the conditions under which they have to treat patients.

Third, the activities of the NHS have become increasingly exposed. On the one hand, there has been an explosion of media interest in health care over the past decade or so. On the other hand, one of the unexpected by-products of Mrs. Thatcher's 1991 reforms of the NHS—which introduced the so-called "internal market" and separated the roles of providers and purchasers—was to reveal buried skeletons. New sets of statistics stripped the veils of deference and ignorance from the NHS; geographical variations in provision and what came to be known as "postcode rationing" became ever more visible. At the same time there has been an explosion of news stories about medical failures, incompetent clinicians and overcrowded emergency departments.

Fourth, the NHS has become increasingly centralised. From the start, the NHS was a "command and control" model. The fact that all funds flowed from the centre meant, in turn, that the centre was responsible for the way in which the money was spent. The Minister of Health (subsequently Secretary of State for Health) was accountable to parliament for the operations of the NHS: "If bedpan is dropped in a hospital ward, I want the noise to reverberate in the corridors of Westminster," as Bevan put it. Initially, the ability of the centre to either command or control was limited by managerial capacity and lack of information. Over time, however, as managerial capacity was strengthened and information improved, the trend was always to greater centralisation.

Enter the 1997 Labour Government. Its plans for the NHS[5] involved the rhetorical repudiation of the changes introduced by the Conservatives in 1991, while in practice largely building on them. The details are of no concern here. Crucial for our analysis are two aspects of Labour's plans. On the one hand, it represented a reversion to Bevan's original vision. "National standards of care will be guaranteed. For the first time the need to ensure that high quality care is spread throughout the service will be taken seriously," the Prime Minister proclaimed in his foreword to the document. On the other hand, the service was to become more responsive to consumers: "The NHS needs to modernise in order to meet the demands of today's public." To achieve these aims, the power of the centre was strengthened: the managerial hierarchy of accountability was made stronger, a battery of performance indicators was introduced, and an inspectorate of health services was created.

One thing, however, was missing: money. As part of its overall economic strategy, the government maintained a tight grip on public expenditure. The NHS was drip-fed with some extra funds but overall its budget remained tightly constrained. And the noise of dropped bedpans in television studios assumed epidemic proportions. An outbreak of flu in the autumn of 1999 brought chaos to some emergency departments. Waiting lists (which Labour had promised to reduce) remained stubbornly high. A variety of studies suggested that Britain's cancer and coronary care services were less effective than in many European countries. A prominent clinician, known as a Labour supporter, denounced the inadequacies of the NHS.

So, we come to the Prime Minister's announcement of a large increase in funding for the NHS—part of a more general, pre-election relaxation of public expenditure stringency. The announcement was followed up by *The NHS Plan*[6] specifying the improvements that were to be made. The plan acknowledged that "The NHS is too much the product of the era in which it was born. In its buildings, its ways of working, its very culture, the NHS bears too many of the hallmarks of the 1940s." So the emphasis again was on creating a consumer-friendly service designed "to meet modern patient expectations." It promised 7,000 extra NHS beds, 20,000 extra nurses, 6,500 extra therapists, 7,500 hospital specialists, and 2000 extra general practitioners by 2004. It pledged itself to cut waiting lists, to ensure that all patients would have GP appointments within 48 hours and a television set by every bed, among a host of other targets.

There was general welcome for *The NHS Plan*. At last, it seemed, resources would match the vision of a modernized service capable both of achieving the original ambitions of its founders and of responding to raised consumer expectations. But doubt remains. First, the relaxation of public expenditure stringency was made possible by a large budget surplus, reflecting an economic boom. But what would happen if a worsening global economic situation forced the government to reconsider its spending strategy—as had happened so often before in the history of the NHS? Second, the *Plan* represented a race against time. Could the government deliver the promised improvements fast enough to satisfy rising public expectations? If it did not, the political costs for the government would be heavy. For the centralization of control meant, in turn, the concentration of blame on ministers. In the exposed NHS—exposed both to the searchlight of publicity and (as Ginzberg had warned all those years ago) to a stream of comparisons with other, often much richer, countries—there would be no escape for them.

Notes

1.   Ginzberg, Eli, *A World Without Work: The Story of the Welsh Miners,* New Brunswick (USA) and London: Transaction Publishers (Revised edition), 1990.
2.   Klein, Rudolf, *The New Politics of the NHS*, Harlow, Essex: Prentice Hall (4ᵗʰ edition, revised), 2000.
3.   Webster, Charles, *The Health Services Since the War*, Vol. 1, London: Her Majesty's Stationery Office, 1988.
4.   Appleby, John, "Government funding of the UK National Health Service: what does the historical record reveal?" *Journal of Health Services Research*, Vol. 4, No. 2, April 1999, 79-89.
5.   Secretary of State for Health, *The New NHS: Modern-Dependable*, London: The Stationery Office, 1997, Cm. 3807.
6.   Secretary of State for Health, *The NHS Plan*, London: The Stationery Office, 2000, Cm. 4818.

14

The Theory of Policy:
Eli Ginzberg as Social Scientist

Irving Louis Horowitz

In the more than 1,500 books, articles, review essays, and comments authored by Eli Ginzberg, one of the least employed words that would be found is *theory*. Ginzberg lives in a world of service to presidents, fulfilling terms of a wide variety of grants, and targeting presentations to decision-making bodies of all sizes and shapes. In such a busy schedule, *theory* may not exactly be a dirty word, but it cannot readily be celebrated in the context of the empirical tradition in economics, even an older qualitative version of that tradition.

That said, it is my contention—one I have firmly held since 1975, when I invited Ginzberg to address a course on policy I was teaching at the Woodrow Wilson School in Princeton University—that he not only has a theory of policy, but an effective one at that. I am not making this statement as the sort of tautological claim one hears that pragmatic thinking is based on an epistemology. Rather I am basing it squarely on Ginzberg's appreciation of critical figures in the history of economic thought that helped shape our contemporary vision of the social world.

The reasons that *theory* has acquired a bad reputation in policy circles are not hard to identify. To start with, those who do parade about their commitment to *theory* often have a disdainful, if not outright dismissive attitude to policy as a function of social research. If one believes that Providence dictates all of our moves, and that on

Irving Louis Horowitz is Hanna Arendt Distinguished Professor Emeritus at Rutgers, the State University of New Jersey, and serves as Chairman of the Board at Transaction Publishers.

judgment day the world as we know it will be destroyed and or dissolved, and hence purged of its cumulative sins, then the rationale for policy is clearly superfluous. Policy in a purely theological universe becomes a display of human vanity, hubris exhibited best by leaders and policymakers.

By the same metaphysical token, those who believe in the determinist character of social and economic systems—as the theory goes, from primitive communism, to slavery, to feudalism, to capitalism, to socialism and then a return to communism at an advanced level— also have little need for policy as a standard of human betterment. To be sure, such historical materialist doctrines see policy as an adjunct to State planning, but not as a standard of measurement of changes and advances in its own right. In the classical Marxist-Leninist vision, the sins of policy are variously described as reformism and at times, the outright betrayal of class interests.

In other words, policy advocacy ultimately presumes a meliorative condition of society. For if real changes cannot be brought about in the social order, then policy is indeed to be judged akin to vanity in the heavens and betrayal on the ground. But the amelioration of ills is not only what policy is about, it is what most political postures and ideologies are about. Beneath the claims on behalf of policy is, I submit, a metaphysical supposition that improvements can be made, directions can be changed, and human life can be made to square the circle of self-interest and social interests.

Eli Ginzberg's work is the perfect embodiment of policymaking as part and parcel of the liberal imagination. It is a selective liberalism, one predicated on the utilitarian line that extends from Adam Smith's *Wealth of Nations* in the eighteenth century to John Stuart Mill's *Political Economy* in the nineteenth century, to Wesley Mitchell's papers on *Business Cycles* in the twentieth century. It is a line that lays great emphasis on a variety of premises: That self-interest correctly perceived and the interests of society also properly perceived are harmonious in nature. That political economy embraces the policy imperative, that is to say, if the city of London needs a sewage system, the costs must be determined, the options weighed, and the time and labor gauged—but the sewage system must be put in place. That economics is as much an art as a science, as much a function of experience and experiment as of manipulating data, and finally, as much a function of personal proclivities as systemic requirements.

Ginzberg's academic life spans so many decades that it is easy to forget that his doctoral dissertation was on Adam Smith. For Ginzberg, Smith, and in particular *The Wealth of Nations*, was an essential primer in the liberal project of the eighteenth century—a project he endorsed. In particular, one finds a great sympathy shared by the two for the "laboring poor." Unlike many of Smith's compatriots, who thought that the ticket to success was low wages and high productivity, Smith himself saw the need for complementarity. Listen to Ginzberg extol the virtues of utilitarian ethics:

> "Workingmen are more active, diligent, and expeditious in countries where they received large rather than small rewards. The contention that high wages make for riotous living is without foundation; men do not work four days a week in order to spend the remaining three days in the pub. It is the strain of their work which forces them to take prolonged and frequent rest. Masters might well listen to the dictates of reason and humanity, and moderate rather than intensify the application of their workmen" (1).

This vision of the moral basis of labor and the laborer registered well with Eli Ginzberg, whose earliest work concerned the fate of the Welsh miners during the early stages of the depression. One can see here the breach with Marx, for whom the drive to deplete wages and increase profits is an inexorable part of history itself. Ginzberg sees "the dictates of reason" as working its way through the State, or as Smith would say, "civil government."

While recognizing that in the past, government simply sided with the rich, Smith foresaw a period in which "the government would eventually exert itself in behalf of the poor, and make it unnecessary in the future for them to pray daily to the Gracious Lord God...to pour down thy blessings on this whole parish." In one fell swoop, Smith captured Ginzberg's faith in rational government—read policy—and a "better world for all" promised by the Judeo-Christian faith. These linkages of political economy and social justice became a part of Ginzberg's life arsenal.

We shall leave for others to explore Ginzberg's remarkable interest—bordering on fervent exploration—in the Roman Catholic Church. This at a time again, when radical social scientists and socialists could hardly get beyond formulaic thinking of religion as the opium of the people. Indeed, Ginzberg early on sensed that communism was the opium of the intellectuals. In this he was solidly aligned with people like Arthur Schlesinger, Jr. But unlike other academics of his background, the importance of being Jewish was uniformly factored into his social science thinking. This appreciation of religion in the affairs of ordinary people, the vital center, was where Ginzberg felt most comfortable, and assuredly where he wanted to be. Family religious tradition and faculty impulses alike conspired to move him to the political middle.

By a decade later, in *The Illusion of Economic Stability,* the sense of economic history was displaced by a sense of public policy. The New Deal conspired to preserve capitalism, but not without a huge cost—the near infinite expansion of government. He wrote, "in a rapidly changing world, the moral of history and the logic of theory are always limited. Yet they are indispensable, for the critical evaluation of the past offers the sole approach to an intelligent anticipation of the future" (77). Ginzberg becomes a flintier fellow. The project that he envisions Smith believing, becomes a reality for him. More important than fluctuations in the private sector "is the enlargement of the state's direct entrepreneurial activity" (220-221). Even if the banking community was unhappy, the larger public was squarely behind such changes. Indeed, it accurately reflected what the New Deal was about—reform without reaction, policymaking without radicalization.

Wesley Mitchell was both mentor and friend to Ginzberg, and he clearly set the tone for the theoretical framework Ginzberg was to follow. In his relatively recent introduction to Mitchell's *The Backward Art of Spending Money,* Ginzberg gets to the heart and soul of his own theoretical points of reference, no less than Mitchell does. He pointed out that "Mitchell's disavowal of social movements that derive their principal strength from the emotional involvement of the participating members is significant in evaluating his approach to economics." Ginzberg adds, almost reflexively: "Where is one to look for the dynamics of change if rejection of authority is banned?" Having rejected "reform through agitation," and no less rejecting the status quo, Mitchell was thrown back to the "religion of facts," to statistical analysis. But the end was more than facts, it was an "appeal to history," but without the lower classes as active participants. With the rejection of "non-rationalistic elements," he was left with few "weapons" for change.

And here a certain tension between master and pupil become apparent. For Ginzberg, people who took things into their own hands were a part of the process of policymaking. It also opened up the prospect that social change was non-rational, whilst economic change was presumptively rational. The break between them superficially was over "statistics"—Ginzberg saw Mitchell's appeal to the empirical and statistical as "an escape from reality." Ginzberg saw economic systems in qualitative terms. But it is interesting that he breaks off his introduction to the Mitchell's classic precisely at that point, and rests with a "tragedy of paradox." The police force of the state was needed for social order, yet the violence of the masses was needed for social change. Ginzberg recognizes the problem, but remains uncomfortable with the solution he proffered.

Ginzberg instinctively moved to middle range theorizing. If it prevented him from the types of statistical reductionism that came to dominate economics at mid-century, it was also a tradition that excluded Continental styles of abstract thought, of universal system building, and a variety of determinisms and predeterminisms. As a result, Ginzberg was "saved," if that is the right word, from the Hegelian-Marxian axis to which so many young budding economists of the 1920s and 1930s fell easy prey. While others saw Soviet red stars in the economic future, Ginzberg saw—more accurately—the Stars and Stripes of America. He shared with his mentor a core feeling of animosity for dogma passing as science.

That does not mean Ginzberg was uncritical of capitalism and its byproducts. Indeed, he has a lifetime of service to underdogs and outsiders, and opposition to top dogs and insiders. So even when preparing agendas and policies for corporate activities in the human resources field, we find him reiterating this long-standing critical New Dealism if you will. "We have advanced two major arguments. The first contends that the modern corporation has evolved structures that are dysfunctional for utilizing the abilities of its managerial personnel. The second stresses that these structures impede the chief executive officer from effectively discharging his multiple duties, which include oversight of the corporation's human resources" (4). In some elliptical way, Ginzberg's theory shines through his observations. In one fell swoop he claims that gigantism in industry is dysfunctional (although never quite explaining what is optimal size in Paretan terms) and yet, provides succor to chief operating officers to reform administrative and hiring practices. The way of the Lord turns out to be as dead center as can be reached.

Dead center was not only the way of Ginzberg's Lord, but also of his intellectual master, Adam Smith. In describing "the broadening of option" in one of his most famous books, *The Human Economy*, he seeks to clarify one predicate: "The progress of men and nations depends in the first instance on the development and utilization of their potential and skill. As they success in this undertaking they will be more likely to accomplish the goals they have set" (223). Ginzberg could hardly have struck a more Smithian note. Here in his summary of a longstanding interest in manpower allocation, skill acquisition, opportunity structures, and employment imbalances, we come again face to face with the liberal ethos that drives Ginzberg from his early beginnings to the present.

In one of his infrequent excursions into the theory of policy, Ginzberg again strikes a middle position: between historicism and determinism on one side and pure anarchy of the marketplace. Indeed, he speaks of the need to be "masters of their fate...[and] control the future as much as possible." This comes down to shape and reshape manpower policy. "This mandate derives from the fact that the institutions which determine the skills that people acquire and the institutions which govern the use of these skills will inevitably lose their alignment because of the forces unleashed by change." He offers a concise statement of policy "as the actions that a society can take to increase the opportunities available to its members to develop and utilize their skills" (234-35). Again, that unerring sense of balance, of a middle way: policy is the concrete manifestation of registering options. However that does not mean that every policy can be successfully implemented.

When the notion of implementation and execution is introduced, it becomes apparent that Ginzberg may have been a policy advisor to seven presidents and countless other agents of state and local government. However, he was by no means a policymaker in the sense in which lawmakers participate in decisions about economic change. Indeed, he has always been a part-time policymaker and a full-time academic. Even if he has had a lifelong interest in bottom-up analysis of basic stratification categories—African-Americans, Jewish Americans, working women, welfare poor, children in the workforce, etc.—these concerns translated more readily into symposia and conferences of experts than into actual changes in policy. Ginzberg, in a self-deprecating mode, sometimes calls himself the

consummate kibitzer. And in so far as that Yiddish expression de-
notes the outsider goading the insider to action, he well expresses in
personal rhetoric a larger reality of his long years of public service.

The admixture of exhortation and explanation is a perfectly honorable role in American academic life—perhaps the most honorable.
But such concerns have their pitfalls. The outsider as advocate must
constantly appeal to the better instinct of the people in power while
holding up a mirror of needs and wants of the much larger group of
people out of power. In the case of Ginzberg, this led to a certain
practical tension that was glossed over by careful modulation. The
issues he ceaselessly addressed—income inequality, unemployment,
minority exploitation, educational achievement—stamped him a "liberal" in the broad meaning of the term, but by seeking remedies
piece by piece, protest by protest, issue by issue, Ginzberg avoided
the fate of those who shared his values but not his methods.

In theoretical terms, one might say that he has had a lifelong commitment to the idea of progress, but no corresponding faith in the
idea of planning. The quintessential faith in the marketplace as arbi-
ter of social goods—that tradition extending from Smith through
Mill to Mitchell—spared him an exaggerated faith in top down planning and political rule characteristic of authoritarian regimes such as
the Soviet Union. Ginzberg was clearly at home in "The New Deal"
of Franklin Roosevelt or a "Great Society" of Lyndon Johnson, but
was suspicious of Stalinist planning techniques that opened the door
to repression and corruption on a gigantic scale. Needless to add,
the Nazi version of planning that entailed the total mobilization and
militarization of German society along racist lines was totally unac-
ceptable to Ginzberg on ethical, no less than economic grounds. In
such a context, targeted policy rather than total planning became the
order of the day for Ginzberg. The temper of the country, the United
States, fit well with the theoretical framework in which he was most
comfortable. How much this is by accident or design is a purely
speculative consideration. Suffice it to say that Eli Ginzberg became
for a liberal epoch what Bernard Baruch was for the conservative
epoch that preceded the New Deal—an advisor to secular and transitional princes.

What gave a certain seamless quality to Ginzberg's thinking is his
rare ability to integrate such disparate entities as economy and religion. True enough, in earlier period great European scholars like

Max Weber and R.H. Tawney saw the relationship of the rise of capitalism and new forms of Christian faith. But once again, Ginzberg's metier was not given over to such grandiose expressions of linkage of the "big picture." It was rather the Rousseauian contract that seemed to intrigue him more. Specifically, it was the covenant between Man and God that characterized a civil society. The covenant tradition linked the Judaic tradition to the democratic imagination. Within that covenant, one could find, and he in fact found, connections of the individual person to the impersonal State, and prospects for social justice that did not violate the respect that people owe to one another, whatever be their background or authority. It is all too easy to see scholars in their literary parts—as if one person who writes on religion is a somehow a different person than the one who writes on the society. It is rather the whole, the fusion of person and society into a symbolic network of beliefs and policies, which makes possible a good society.

The good society is one in which the common purpose is served. Such a society does not require dictatorial edicts or state terror to impose its will. It does not require total planning for goals unconnected to economic maturity. In this, a certain neo-utilitarianism pervades the work of Ginzberg. The perceived self-interests of individuals are linked to the larger social interests of the society through a delicately laced series of symbols of democratic order: racial comity, sexual equality, economic justice. What John Rawls of Harvard stitches together in philosophy, Ginzberg performed in economics in an earlier phase of the liberal American consensus. The heavy emphasis of Ginzberg on health and hospital care in this sense is simply the last stage of a series of proposals to insinuate the common good into the fabric of the social order as such. One might say all of his manifold policy proposals are wrapped up in a theory of fairness— what is best for all members of a society to move in concert.

That his work in health, as with his earlier efforts connected to manpower allocation and work potentials, received such a broad hearing is less a function of the broad theoretical concerns that Ginzberg brought to the table than the practical realization that such proposals carried with them a strong likelihood of reducing social tensions and strife. It would be naive to think that Ginzberg was unaware of this dichotomy between his own broad vision of the American nation and the far narrower impulses motivating those who responded to his various recommendations over time. Then again, it should be realized that liberalism as a theoretical construct must always carry this duality within its model. For liberalism is a less a doctrine than a mechanism for walking a thin line between public needs and private gains. This sense of tailoring policy to reach what is achievable, rather than to stand on principle and fight for that which is not achievable, at least not without deep fissures to the social fabric, separates the liberal ethos from both the conservative and radical options.

While there are multiple sources for Ginzberg's carefully crafted approach to policy, one element that is sometimes overlooked is his strong ethnographic sense. When he wanted to study the early stages of the New Deal he traveled from one end of the nation to the other talking to people and seeing results. When he studied the impact of technological change and unemployment, he spent a year in Wales talking with coal miners on the dole. When urban race riots became a virtual norm in the mid-1960s, he traveled to Watts talking with a wide array of people in that Los Angeles community about their needs. I know of few economists who have even a remote sense of the ethnographic requirements in making realistic policy recommendations. Ginzberg got into the auto, the train, the airplane—whatever it took to *observe* that which he *recommended.*

The unique element in Ginzberg is his ability to raise what for most others is a tactic of survival and policymaking into a principle unto itself. I think it fair to say that for him it is to maximize the gains of the mass without destroying the sources of class. While this is hardly the sort of standpoint that makes for revolutionary struggles at barricades, neither is it the sort of approach that encourages the slaughter of innocents in the name of the abstract slogans or principles of the moment. The craft of policy itself is inherently meliorative. The very notion implies the potential of human beings instigating a series of measures directed to secure a cluster of results as a result of such effort.

Policymaking in this sense stands removed from fire eating notions of determinism and world history. Ultimately, the genius of humanity is precisely in the meliorative potentials of an economic system. But there is a dark side to policy that Ginzberg understood better than most. In speaking of education for example, he noted that "education is a set of social institutions and structures that opens opportunities for some people and closes them for others." In this sense policy is not a general melioration, but specific to some groups only. This is the theoretical foundation of not only Ginzberg's contribution to economics, but to how the economy is part and parcel an instrument to the higher goals and purposes to which a society aspires. Even if the rest of us are uncertain of Ginzberg's vision or version of the good society, that a figure among us can still see the linkage of means and ends, of instruments of production and mechanisms of consumption, of material conditions and moral consequences, it should be plain that we have had a protean figure of the age with us through the last century and into the new one.

At the end of the day, for Ginzberg (and I daresay for most empirically oriented social scientists) theory is a term used to denote a collection of facts that permits explanation and predictability. The outcome of theory is less the search for a unified field of probability and more the acceptance of diversified fields of possibility. And that is what policymaking is about—exploring possibilities. The democratic credo of the public intellectual is one that opens wide the prospects of the art of the possible, with the proviso that in so doing basic human liberties are advanced or at least not retarded. This then is the sum and substance of Ginzberg's contribution to theory construction. Like the man himself, the attempt to generalize, to provide a sense of the whole, is modest. It is limited by the operational, but unlimited in the imaginable.

References

Ginzberg, Eli, *The House of Adam Smith.* New York: Columbia University Press, 1934, pp. 66-67, 219-229.

Ginzberg, Eli, *The Illusion of Economic Stability.* New York and London: Harper & Brothers, Publishers, 1939, pp. 77, 220-21.

Ginzberg, Eli, Introduction to *The Backward Art of Spending Money.* New Brunswick and London: Transaction Publishers, 1999, pp. xxiv-xxxiii.

Ginzberg, Eli, and George Vojta, *Beyond Human Scale: The Large Corporation at Risk.* New York: Basic Books, 1985, pp.188, et passim.

Ginzberg, Eli, *The Human Economy.* New York: McGraw-Hill Book Company, 1976, pp. 223-233, 234.

Ginzberg, Eli, "Planning Full Employment" in *Constructing Policy*, edited by Irving Louis Horowitz. New York and London: Praeger Publishers, 1979, pp. 28-43.

Part III

The Scholarship of Eli Ginzberg

15

Health, Medicine and Public Policy

Eli Ginzberg

"The Reform of Medical Education: An Outsider's Reflections"*

Abstract—After reviewing some of the major structural changes that have altered American medical education over the last 80 years, the author depicts the recent climate that has fostered a number of proposals for educational reform to better prepare physicians for the next century. He lists the five major types of reform that have been suggested (for example, the integration of basic sciences and clinical knowledge) and then reflects on each type, asking questions about implementation such as: Who will accomplish the reform? How will it be carried out? What and where are the financial, knowledge, and other resources that will be needed? What must be overcome to accomplish the reform? He then discusses the forms of instruction that should accompany the proposed reforms in educational content (such as decreasing lectures and increasing small-group discussions). He observes that there is often a serious conflict between the need to provide students some free hours and departments' perceptions of the time needed to educate students properly. He closes with a review of some aspects of reform that have been neglected or minimized, such as the length of time and the costs that medical students must face to complete their education, and the economics of educational innovations. *Acad. Med.* 68 (1993):518-521.

While the Flexner reforms, introduced at the beginning of the second decade of this century, have shaped American medical education over the past eight decades, there have been several major structural changes that have altered the nature of the profession during that time. One has been the elongation of professional training from

* This article originally appeared in *Academic Medicine*, Volume 68, Number 7, July 1993.

Eli Ginzberg is A. Barton Hepburn Professor Emeritus at the Graduate School of Business and director of the Eisenhower Center for the Conservation of Human Resources at Columbia University. His work in social policy, health care, human resources, and the special needs of the poor, young and aged place Ginzberg in a special category: activist scholar rather than academic-turned-activist.

four years of medical school and one year of internship to a minimum of seven years of training, with many residents, especially in the surgical subspecialties, continuing for another seven years, if we include their fellowship training.

Another has been the designation of biomedical research as the critical mission of the leading medical schools, which began with the inauguration of large-scale federal financing of research at the end of World War II. Currently, annual federal appropriations for biomedical research are over $10 billion, up from $3 million (or $30 million in constant dollars) in 1940.

The explosive growth of the professoriate, which today numbers more than 70,000, or more than one faculty member per medical student, reflects still another striking structural change. An important contribution to this explosive growth in faculty has been the fact that patient care income has come to be the leading source of revenue for the nation's medical schools; it accounts for 45%, considerably in excess of the combined contributions from all levels of government, which account for around 38%.

At least brief attention should be paid as well to the preoccupation of most faculties with the training of residents and fellows, which has led to the production of many more specialists and subspecialists than generalists, with a current ratio of approximately 80:20.

The other changed boundary conditions that continue to have pronounced effects on faculty, medical students, and residents are the almost 80% increase in the physician-population ratio during the past three decades without a negative impact on physicians' earnings; the steep rise in the indebtedness of medical students; and the continuing large differentials in earnings between generalists and subspecialists, of an order of two or three to one in favor of the latter.

Finally, in accounting for the principal structural changes that have affected medical education particularly since World War II, attention must be paid to the rapid growth of medical knowledge and technology and the potentials that this growth has had for the practice of medicine and for the care and cure of patients.

Pressures for Reform

Although there were a number of innovations and reforms of medical school education between the end of World War II and the

GPEP report issued by the Association of American Medical Colleges in 1983, the last decade has witnessed a marked acceleration in new efforts to make medical education more responsive to the needs of physicians who will be practicing in the twenty-first century. The pressures for reform come from a number of sources. First, from the complaints of students, who object to being stuffed like turkeys during their first two years of medical school: they are taught about the most recent advances in the basic sciences, which they cannot possibly absorb and much of which they will forget after they enter clinical training. A growing current of criticism is also being voiced by members of the public, who complain that the physicians they need to care for them are not available or, if they are, they cannot communicate effectively and thus cannot provide the counsel and help that their patients need. In addition to that, the payers for health care—both government and employers—are making the point that the out-of-control trend in medical care expenditures appears to be closely related to the faulty preparation that medical students (and residents) have received during their long periods of training.

Proposed Reforms

Because of the disgruntled students and the disenchanted public, a growing number of medical educators have begun to make their voices heard, endorsed and supported by sizable grants from the major health care foundations, which have encouraged them to undertake in-depth reassessments of what is right and what is wrong about medical education.

There are five main substantive components to the conventional wisdom that the reformers are disseminating:

1. *Integrate basic sciences and clinical instruction.* The reformers maintain that the sharp separation between instruction in the basic sciences during the first two years and the clinical training in the third and fourth years is faulty and needs early correction by a radically revised curriculum in which instruction in the basic and clinical sciences is effectively integrated throughout the entire four-year sequence.

2. *Look to developmental biology to serve as the integrator.* There is a widespread assumption, or presumption, that developmental bi-

ology and genetics offer the intellectual basis for an effective integration of the four years of medical school instruction.

3. *Recognize the importance of population-based medicine.* To synthesize basic sciences and clinical knowledge is only the beginning of the reforms being pursued. A number of reformers are convinced that a paradigmatic shift from deterministic prognosis to clinical epidemiology is called for, with attention shifting from the presenting patient to population-based probabilistic evaluations and treatment modalities. In this view, when genes, cells, or organs malfunction, they often can point the directions for therapeutic interventions, but the life history of the patient and the socioeconomic factors that condition his or her life can be overlooked in diagnostic and treatment decision making only at great cost to patient, family, and society.

4. *Make room in the curriculum for considerations of ethical principles at every stage of decision making.* Some reformers go so far as to insist that whatever the "scientific" pretensions of medicine, the role of the physician and physician-patient interactions must be guided by ethical considerations, and that any medical school curriculum that is unresponsive to this reality is malfunctioning and requires urgent attention.

5. *Inform all clinical decision making with an awareness that dollars are scarce and will become scarcer.* In order not to extend the list of priorities for reform unduly, let me mention just one more that has attracted the attention of some thoughtful medical educators, namely, the need to introduce medical students and residents to using cost-benefit criteria in selecting from among diagnostic and therapeutic modalities. The practice of medicine without regard to economic considerations that dominated the U.S. scene between 1965 and 1983 is definitely not the wave of the future, and the oncoming generation of physicians needs instruction at every stage of their education about the role of economics in patient care.

Implementation Issues

How do these five reforms strike an outsider? From my vantage point as a political economist who has had and continues to have an ongoing involvement in health sciences research, let me briefly share my thoughts on each proposition.

Since no medical educator has challenged the desirability of a closer coordination of the basic and clinical sciences, the difficulties of accomplishing this objective must lie not with intent but rather with execution. How is it to be accomplished, and by whom? Since only a small proportion of the basic science faculty are physicians, they are ill suited to take the lead, and while some professors of clinical medicine have an in-depth knowledge of one or another of the basic sciences, that is not their central interest and concern; frequently their knowledge is not deep enough for them to carry out a successful integration even in the area of their specialization. In short, we may be dealing on the integration front with an idea whose time has not yet come or conceivably may already be past.

Most of those who favor integration have gone further and identified the integrating principle that should be used. They maintain that developmental biology and genetics provide the ideas and linkages that can bring the biomedical and the clinical sciences together. Again the outsider asks—if matters are so simple and straightforward, what is holding up the action? Once again, execution may be lagging behind consensus. The hard work that would be required to develop and implement a four-year curriculum for medical education based on genetics and developmental biology would require a significant investment of the talents and time of competent and interested physician-scientist-educators, the old triple threats who, in most informed persons' judgment, are an extinct species. If they are extinct or almost so, they cannot be looked to as the builders of the new curriculum.

What about the third priority, making room in the new curriculum for clinical epidemiology and population-based approaches to the study of medicine? The number of enthusiasts for such an innovation is still relatively low and there are few new resources being invested to transform what many believe to be a good idea into a reality. In the absence of a substantial and sustained investment of new resources, both for research and for teaching, not much progress is likely to occur on this front in the near or mid-term.

Over a quarter of a century has passed since I recommended to Margaret Mahoney, who at the time was senior staffer at the Carnegie Corporation, that the United States establish departments of social medicine at ten or 20 of the leading medical schools in the United States, with sufficient funding to launch and carry through substantial and sustained programs of health policy research. Without such a substantial investment, I saw little prospect for clinical epidemiology to have a place in the medical school curriculum. My view has not changed; it has been reinforced from that day to this.

How does one inculcate ethical perspectives in all aspects of medical education? Many medical schools have introduced lectures and small-group discussions focusing on ethical issues in medical decision making. These innovations are of sufficiently recent date that in-depth evaluations would be premature. From the scattered evidence there is no reason to believe that either faculty or students have been greatly affected by this innovation. But it would be premature to write it off at this early point in time. I think we can say that so far it has had only marginal influence on the reshaping of the medical school curriculum.

This brings us to the last of the substantive recommendations, which is focused on the desirability of introducing economic considerations at every stage of medical decision making. A few observations: In the first place, the physicians who were trained when the dominant view was "money doesn't count" have not bought into the new doctrine of constrained resources. And it is doubtful that they will do so before the total dollars flowing into the health care sector in general, and into medical education in particular, force the issue. The forcing may be long delayed, but if past is prologue it will be some years before the teaching of medical students will be framed by a curriculum that is resource-sensitive. We must first await the emergence or conversion of the faculty to such an ideology—and that will not come easily.

If the foregoing observations by an outsider on the substantive recommendations for the reform of medical education have pertinence and relevance, then it behooves the protagonists of the reform to look again carefully at their agenda items and consider what needs to be done, by whom, with what kinds of resource commitments, to speed the arrival of the brave new world. For without such a serious and continuing effort at implementation, it appears questionable, at least to me, that the reforms can make their own way.

So much for the substantive aspects of the reformers' recommendations. But the proposals they have advanced also include a number of far-reaching parallel suggestions predicated on opportunities opened up by advances in pedagogical technique or a critical reassessment of the pre-existent techniques. For instance, most of the reformers recommend that the heavy reliance on lectures during the first two years of the medical school curriculum be radically reduced in favor of more small discussion groups.

Next, many are enamored of what they call "problem-based" instruction, in which the attention of the student is redirected from the accumulation of discrete pieces of new knowledge in favor of asking and answering, "What kinds of knowledge do I need to make a diagnosis and suggest a mode of treatment?"

Closely related to the foregoing is the enthusiasm of many reformers for directing more time and other resources to instructing students in accessing and retrieving information from large computerized data sets. Once students have acquired these skills, they are on the way to taking control of their future education through "self-study."

The only way to enable students to engage in self-study, however, is to cut back the conventional program with its many corresponding requirements so that every medical student will have significant blocks of uncommitted time to use according to his or her own lights. Finally, the examination and evaluation issue comes to the fore, for the ways that medical students, like all other students, will invest their time and energy will be heavily influenced by the evaluation hurdles that they must surmount to demonstrate competence and to position themselves to move into the next stage of their professional training. As one might anticipate, the reformers are by no means agreed about the directions and specifications that the new evaluation procedures should take. But the more committed they are to deep and far-reaching substantive reforms involving the introduction of new educational techniques, the more likely they are to recognize that pre-existing evaluation approaches need to be reassessed and redesigned, even to the point of eliminating externally-set examinations.

Instruction Issues

What can an outsider—who started teaching at a major research university in 1935 and has continued to the present time to instruct graduate students—offer concerning the forms of instruction that should accompany the proposed reforms in content? On the basis of a two-year stint of lecturing to the second-year class at a distinguished medical school in the early 1980s, I am reasonably certain that any and all actions that are taken to reduce the number of lecture courses that students are forced to attend in the first two years of medical school constitute a move in the right direction. However, if small discussion groups are to be used as a substitute, a word of warning must be added: the instructional costs cannot be ignored when one shifts from one class for 150 students to ten discussion groups!

The emphasis on problem-based instruction and the interest in data retrieval are sufficiently closely linked to be commented on simultaneously. It is difficult for a student with little basic-science or clinical knowledge to make much progress in a problem-solving mode unless and until he or she masters the art and science of data retrieval, and even then the student will be handicapped by an insufficient knowledge base. We know that there are many enthusiasts for a problem-based approach, and it may turn out that the misgivings outlined above are out of proportion and that the problem-based approach is definitely the way to go.

No one is likely to object in theory to remitting some time, even considerable blocks of time, to medical students. The difficulties arise when one asks the different departments and divisions to voluntarily reduce the numbers of hours they require students to devote to the curriculum. At that point, free time for students runs headlong into a conflict with what the several departments consider to be the minimum hours needed to communicate to the students what they need to know to advance to the next stages in their education and training. This struggle over time between the perceptions of the faculty and the preferences of the students is easier to recognize and appreciate than to resolve.

On the question relating to examinations and evaluations, I have little to contribute other than to point out that one of the strengths of American medical education has been the role of external examinations in helping to set and maintain a minimum national standard of professional qualifications while responsibility for licensing continues to reside with 50 sovereign states. This has been no small achievement, and it should not be jeopardized unless the putative gains loom large.

Neglected Aspects of Reform

I will conclude with a few observations about the reforms of medical education that are gaining strength among the medical leadership and will identify selected aspects of reform that I think have been neglected or minimized.

First and foremost is the substantial disregard of the commitment of time and the costs that medical students face in acquiring an MD degree and particularly in completing their residency and fellowship training before they are ready to practice their profession. This neglect is the more striking because of the oft-expressed conviction of many if not all of the reformers that U.S. medical schools should make a contribution to regulating the current imbalance between specialists and generalists by producing larger numbers of generalists.

Robert Ebert and I proposed in the late 1980s how the minimum seven-year cycle of professional preparation from entrance into medical school to first certification could be reduced by two years: 28%. While a few schools picked up on our suggestion, for the most part it has been ignored despite the fact that conservatives and reformers alike agree that the current fourth year of medical school must be restructured. But the majority of the reformers appear to favor using the fourth year to revisit the basic sciences after the third-year clerkship. One does not need to argue against this view to make the point that it may prove more efficient and effective to combine the two years of clerkship and the first three years of residency training into an integrated four-year clinical training program.

The preoccupation of the reformers with altering the four-year curriculum of the medical school is understandable but can nonetheless be challenged. There is no possible way of making room within a four-year program for all of the important new departures—including probabilistic decision making; clinical epidemiology; cost-benefit analysis; ethics; health education; genetics; and much more—without considering the entire span of physicians' training, from their preparation as future medical students during their four years in college to their extended years of residency training. Reformers' primary focus on the medical school curriculum makes sense, but not their exclusive preoccupation with this restricted four-year period, which represents a minor part of a post-secondary school experience that at a minimum exceeds one decade and often approaches two decades.

The reformers appear to pay little attention to the economics of medical educational innovation. There is a pronounced enthusiasm for small-group discussions; for more training in ambulatory care settings; for students' having the opportunity of following a panel of patients for an extended period of months and years; and for exposing them to different types of treatment environments, from nursing homes to home care. Each of these innovations involves additional costs, the payment for which is usually ignored. Clearly, recourse to ever higher tuition is not the answer. Moreover, ever greater reliance of the medical school on revenues from patient care can only worsen the existing dilemma that many faculty members confront of spending so much time supporting themselves through patient care activities and contributing to their departments and the medical school that they have little or no time left to interact with medical students.

Conclusion

Medical school reform is long overdue. But an effective reform program that is not anchored in sound economics can result in making things worse, not better. Improving the preparation of medical students for the more effective practice of medicine involves more than rebalancing medical school disciplines, important as such a rebalancing may be. It requires much closer attention than has yet been focused on such issues as the core size of the medical school faculty, the economics of alternative instructional modes, and to the total cost of training that must be anticipated by the undergraduate student who is preparing to embark on a medical career.

References

Muller, S. (Chair). Physicians for the Twenty-first Century: Report of the Project Panel on the General Professional Education of the Physician and College Preparation for Medicine. *J. Med. Educ.* 59, Part 2 (November 1984).

Future Directions for Medical Education: A Report of the Council on Medical Education. Chicago, Illinois: American Medical Association, 1982.

Friedman, C.P., and Purcell, E.F., eds. *The New Biology and Medical Education: Merging the Biological, Information and Cognitive Sciences.* New York: Josiah H. Macy, Jr. Foundation, 1983.

Adapting Clinical Medical Education to the Needs of Today and Tomorrow. New York: Josiah H. Macy, Jr. Foundation, 1988.

Healthy America: Practitioners for 2005. The Pew Charitable Trusts, 1991.

Marston, R.Q., and Jones, R.M., eds. *Medical Education in Transition.* Princeton, New Jersey: The Robert Wood Johnson Foundation, 1992.

"Managed Care—A Look Back and a Look Ahead"[*]

(co-authored with Miriam Ostow, M.S.W.)

Americans are not inclined to spend much time or effort assessing the past; directing their energies to shaping the future, they believe, will result in much larger benefits. But it can be argued that underinvestment in assessing the past is likely to lead to faulty estimates and erroneous prescriptions for future action.

Consider the history of managed care. Initial legislation by Congress in late 1973 to provide federal funding for the expansion of health maintenance organizations (HMOs) and HMO enrollment failed to achieve its goal for a variety of reasons, not least among them the inhibitory effects of excessive administrative regulations. Only in the early 1980s did corporate America move aggressively to shift its work force from indemnity insurance to one or another variant of managed care. The growth of managed care became rapid only after large corporations decided that they had to bring their steeply rising costs for health benefits under control. Nevertheless, it was not until the early 1990s that corporate payments for health insurance benefits decelerated appreciably.[1] The surplus capacity of hospitals and the weakening of the labor market for physicians enabled managed-care companies to secure lower prices from providers in exchange for increases in referrals of patients. The companies were thus able both to meet the corporate purchasers' objective of slowing increases in their premium costs and to retain for themselves and their stockholders a substantial margin (20 to 30 percent of total revenues) for profit and expansion.[2]

Currently, two thirds of all Americans working for medium-sized and large firms, who only a few years ago were enrolled overwhelmingly in traditional insurance plans and were free to select the physicians who would treat them and the hospitals where they would be admitted, belong to a managed-care plan, usually to one of several plans offered by their employers. The plans determine most of the kinds of treatment available—ambulatory services, consultations with specialists, and inpatient care. One important corollary has been the much reduced power of physicians and hospitals to protect their

[*] This article originally appeared in *The New England Journal of Medicine*, Volume 336, Number 14, 1997.

interests, professional and economic, and to act independently in the interest of their patients. These and related effects of the managed-care revolution are explored here.

A Look Ahead

Shifting one's perspective from the recent past to the near future necessitates caveats: even the soundest projections are likely to be confounded by unexpected developments, and much of the information needed to assess the longer-term implications of recent developments may become available only gradually. For example, it took a decade before the increasing enrollment in managed-care plans in the 1980s was reflected in the substantial slowing of the growth of national health expenditures that became evident in the early 1990s.[3]

A related question on which the experts differ is whether the slower growth in expenditures is a one-time phenomenon or, in fact, a harbinger of the future. The conservative interpretation is that it reflects the one-time 10 to 15 percent savings that accrues to managed-care plans as large numbers of new enrollees are recruited from higher-cost fee-for-service arrangements. Once the enrollees have shifted to a less costly plan, this savings is not likely to be replicated.

The opposing view, in support of the continuing cost-saving potential of managed care, maintains that there are various approaches by which well-operated HMOs and other managed-care organizations can keep price increases under control. These approaches include greater reliance on capitation to pay physicians; intensified use of selected preventive services and better education of patients, especially if enrollee turnover can be moderated; and the development of clinical guidelines aimed at reducing and eliminating costly procedures with little or no potential for improving health. As of the beginning of 1997, the prevailing view among close observers of trends in cost was that premiums are likely to increase. Furthermore, market competition notwithstanding, technological innovation is a powerful contributor to higher costs. We have no reason to assume that the recent deceleration in costs will continue.

Consider further the uncertainties relating to the future growth rate of enrollment in managed care. The dominant view anticipates a steady increase in enrollment, led by the shift of Medicare and Medicaid beneficiaries, voluntarily or under government compulsion, into managed care.[4] This forecast is reinforced by recent trends in the Medicare program, as well as by state legislative initiatives requiring all or many of the population eligible for Medicaid to join managed-care plans.

Despite the high probability of continuing increases in enrollment, caution is in order when it comes to equating larger enrollments with larger potential profits, such as have recently been realized by many managed-care plans. Although younger Medicare beneficiaries are likely to enroll (and remain) in managed-care plans, there is little evidence that the older (over 75) and often less healthy Medicare beneficiaries will opt in large numbers to shift to HMOs, even if doing so were to bring them a personal savings of up to $1,000 by eliminating the need for a supplementary Medigap policy. Moreover, with regard to the future profitability of the managed-care plans, one cannot ignore the repeated warnings by the Department of Health and Human Services that it plans to reduce its Medicare HMO-reimbursement formula by 7 percent—a correction for the "overpayment" that results from the fact that the Medicare beneficiaries who have thus far chosen HMOs have disproportionately represented the healthier segment of the eligible population.

Furthermore, there is little hard evidence that the states will have their Medicaid costs substantially reduced as they encourage or force their Medicaid-eligible population into managed care. Many states will not easily find managed-care plans that are able to ensure ready access to primary care physicians for large concentrations of mothers and children on welfare in low-income urban areas. Even more problematic is the fact that one third of the Medicaid population consists of the elderly, the chronically ill, the disabled, and the blind, who together account for about two thirds of all Medicaid outlays. Whether HMOs can treat these groups effectively at a cost that will be profitable to the plans and save the states money is questionable. This is not to say that such an outcome is impossible, only that there is no precedent.

A related development that calls for caution in projecting recent trends into the near future is the indication by a few large purchasing groups of employers that they intend to bypass managed-care plans and contract directly with large provider units, such as major teaching hospitals and multispecialty groups of physicians. With potential savings of about 20 percent to be divided between purchasers and providers, it is likely that once the purchasers start on this course—if the initiative succeeds—such direct contracting will spread, particularly because of the desire of hospitals and physicians to regain at least some of the market power they lost earlier. At the same time, hospitals and physicians both face major challenges in this effort: hospitals because they must learn to assume risks safely, and physician-directed networks because they must overcome the serious barriers of capital financing and limited management skills.

Still other signs on the horizon challenge the prospect of uninterrupted growth in enrollment in managed care, and particularly the continuing ability of managed-care plans to protect their 20 percent margin. Numerous large teaching hospitals, many of them the principal affiliates of major academic health centers, are located within or near large concentrations of the urban poor. Several of these centers are establishing their own HMOs or entering into partnership with existing HMOs in order to enroll the Medicaid population in the neighborhood as well as people with private insurance coverage.

There are also signs that although physicians are still in shock from their greatly reduced control over the health care delivery system, a growing number of them are taking steps in smaller and larger groups to reestablish their influence. In New York City, discussions are under way between the physician staffs of two of the city's largest academic health centers, Columbia and Cornell. The goal is closer cooperation among the hundreds (and even thousands) of staff members to improve their bargaining position with managed-care companies, which need these physicians' services to treat their more affluent, better-educated enrollees, who seek access to the city's most sophisticated and skilled health professionals. Such arrangements point to strengthened bargaining power in the future for physicians, whose influence was seriously undermined by the recent rapid changes in the health care sector. Especially notable is the success that the giant merged groups of physicians, such as Mullikin, MedPartners, and Caremark in California, have had in competing with managed-care plans.

One of the more tantalizing questions is whether the multiple early efforts to integrate hospitals and their physician staffs more closely (through the establishment of physician-hospital organizations or by means of extensive functional integration) will spread or remain limited. Nevertheless, it is hard to expect that the for-profit managed-care companies, many of which have grown phenomenally during the past 15 years, will not meet with intensified competition in the decade ahead, as providers, particularly physicians and hospitals, seek to reassert their bargaining power and purchasers explore ways to avoid paying a 20 percent surcharge for services they can negotiate directly.

There is another potential barrier to the continuing growth of managed care. The recent expansion of managed-care plans has depended to a large extent on their high level of profitability and their concomitant ability to borrow capital. However, as their profit margins decrease in the face of intensified competition and the long stock-market boom approaches its probable end, the capital needed to sustain further rapid increases in managed-care enrollment may not be forthcoming.

Various other forces, demographic, economic, and political, that affect the evolving U.S. health care system also make one wonder whether the projected continuing expansion in managed-care enrollment will be sustained in the face of an array of imminent challenges. We will explore briefly a few of the most critical of these.

Beyond Managed Care

Whether or not this cautionary view of managed care enrollment proves correct, health care analysts agree broadly that the number of uninsured and underinsured Americans will increase in the years ahead. And no analyst believes that the continuing growth of managed-care companies and enrollments holds the answer to this challenge.

Two related issues are the prospective closure of hospitals in low-income neighborhoods and the uncertain financing for the "public goods" that are the function of urban academic health centers—education, research, and the provision of a large volume of charity care. Thus far, not only have most managed care companies escaped contributing to the financing of such public goods, but some plans have also gained a distinct competitive advantage by contracting with hospitals that do not incur these additional costs.

It is questionable whether local and state governments will remain passive if and when academic health centers no longer find it feasible to use their conventional sources of revenue to provide the critical public goods that contribute so greatly to the future capabilities of the health care sector. Nor will all state and local governments remain inactive if the imminent closure of a community hospital in a low-income area will leave the local population without access to care, and they will not fail to act as the residents of the area lose potential employment and income. The odds are that many governments will be forced to act, a further reminder of critical policy issues that lie beyond the domain of managed care.

Anticipating that the Medicare trust fund will be exhausted by 2001 and that the first baby boomers will reach the age of 65 in 2011, both Democrats and Republicans acknowledge that Medicare requires far more extensive fixing than is accomplished by enrolling its beneficiaries in managed care. The true extent of the repairs needed is suggested by President Bill Clinton's often-repeated statement that balancing the federal budget is contingent on the reform of Medicare. And although priority must be given to Medicare, neither can the prospective, continuing, large-scale federal outlays for Medicaid be ignored. The easy answer is to recommend that Congress force all Medicare beneficiaries into managed-care arrangements, but that appears highly unlikely in the near term, since it would mean radically diminishing the choices that the elderly now enjoy.

The experience of the past year or two has alerted an increasing number of managed-care enrollees, as well as the larger society, to the risks that the rapid evolution of prepayment as the dominant mode of health care funding at the delivery level presents to those enrolled, as well as to government agencies. When managed-care plans sought to limit to one day the hospital stay after a normal vaginal delivery, enrollees were outraged and sought protection from state legislatures and Congress. Both responded with alacrity. And more legislative interventions can be expected. Public concern, discontent, and distrust have grown as enrollees have become increasingly aware of the more egregious profit-oriented practices of their managed-care plans—providing bonuses to physicians who cut back on referrals to specialists, arbitrarily discharging physicians thought to use too many resources, and deliberately delaying the authorization of costly treatments without which the patient's health, and in some cases survival, may be compromised.[5]

Leaders of the managed-care companies maintain that they can continue to deliver effective care to the American people at a sustainable cost only by closely controlling the practice patterns of hospitals and physicians and by limiting the choices available to their enrollees. But increasing numbers of plan members have begun demanding that the federal and state governments use their regulatory powers to ensure that the plans do not engage in policies and practices detrimental to enrollees' health. Finding the balance between the degree of control the managed-care plans need in order to give their members cost-effective care and the degree of assistance the members seek from regulatory authorities to be sure that they are not being exploited, and their health endangered, is a challenge that, once it has surfaced, will not be readily resolved or set aside.

Moreover, the rapid expansion of enrollment in managed care has not prevented the estimated overall spending for health care in 1995 from increasing by 5.4 percent to a level just short of $1 trillion ($988 billion).[6] If one considers the period from 1980 to 1995, a decade and a half in which managed care grew very rapidly, overall health care outlays quadrupled, from $250 billion to $1 trillion (in current dollars).

There is no need to consider further developments, current and emerging, that argue against simple extrapolation based on the recent rapid growth of managed-care enrollment. Even if this trend is sustained into the future, the critical forces identified here are likely to ensure that managed care, of and by itself, will be unable to answer the needs of the American people for universal coverage, sustainable financing, and better care. Unfortunately, the solution to these problems lies beyond the inherent capabilities of the managed-care system.

References

1.   Cowan CA, Braden BR, McDonnell PA, Sivarajan L. Business, households, and government: health spending, 1994. Health Care Financ. Rev. 1996;17(4):157-78.
2.   Eckholm E. While Congress remains silent, health care transforms itself. New York Times. December 18, 1994:1.
3.   Levit KR, Lazenby HC, Sivarajan L, et al. National health expenditures, 1994. Health Care Financ. Rev. 1996;17(3):205 42.
4.   Etheredge L, Jones SB, Lewin L. What is driving health system change? Health Aff. (Millwood) 1996;15(4):93 101.
5.   Bodenheimer T. The HMO backlash—righteous or reactionary? N. Engl. J. Med. 1996;335:1601-4.
6.   Congressional Budget Office. The economic and budget outlook, 1998-2007. Washington, D.C.: Government Printing Office, 1997:126.

"The Noncompetitive Health-Care Market"*

The U.S. health-care sector cannot be meaningfully analyzed in terms of competitive market theory. The simple notion of relying on the competitive market to direct the U.S. health-care sector arose from frustration after the collapse of the Clinton health reform efforts in 1994. The phrase had a nice ring to it.

Consider first that the more than 100,000 students and residents in training to become physicians and specialists do not fit the competitive market model. These men and women, almost all of whom are engaged in a postcollegiate medical educational and training experience of a minimum of seven years, with a minority remaining in some form of training for up to thirteen years or even longer, have as one of their goals making a good living, but very few of them are business-oriented and set their sights singularly on optimizing their income and accumulating a fortune.

The competitive market model likewise does not adequately describe the behavior of the key institution of contemporary U.S. medicine—the acute care hospital. Two out of every three such hospitals operate as nonprofit institutions, and another 20 percent operate under governmental auspices. No more than 14 percent function as for-profit enterprises.

Most of the basic research on which the dynamism of U.S. medical care depends is financed by public moneys. Continuing advances in new knowledge and interventions are made possible by the large public and private investment of close to $35 billion in basic and applied biomedical research. The federal government's share of this large-scale effort is approximately 40 percent. Moreover, U.S. policies allow—in fact encourage—for-profit pharmaceutical and medical supply companies to exploit the results of the publicly financed research for new knowledge.

Yet another reason that competitive market theory cannot be meaningfully applied to the health-care sector is, as Kenneth Arrow recognized, the inability of average consumers to judge among the alternative sources of care to which they have access.[1] It is no accident that Congress recently instructed the president to create a commission to advise the federal government on how to establish a system of governmental rules and regulations to help protect consum-

* This article originally appeared in *Challenge*, Volume 41, Number 4, July/August 1998.

ers enrolled in federal health-care programs who are unable to protect themselves.

Also consider that a high proportion of the more than 40 million persons who at any point in time lack health insurance coverage are able nonetheless to gain access to essential care. This is possible because of "cross-subsidization," reflecting the overcharging of the privately insured to help cover the charity and partially paid bills of those without any or adequate insurance coverage. Moreover, cross-subsidization plays a prominent role in the continuing financing of essential "public goods," such as education and clinical research provided by the nation's academic health centers.

It is therefore inappropriate, for all these reasons, to resort to competitive market theory to assess how our health system operates. As a corollary it follows that it is equally inappropriate to seek guidance from this theory as to how the system should be restructured to operate more efficiently and more equitably.

Kenneth Arrow published his path-breaking analysis of the limitations of competitive market theory in the health-care sector in 1963, two years before the passage of Medicare and Medicaid. The challenge that we now face is to look more closely at how the financing and delivery of health-care services have been transformed in the intervening decades and at the relevance of Arrow's assessment for the functioning of the much-expanded U.S. health-care system in 1998.

Total national health expenditures (NHE) increased from $41 billion in 1965 to more than $600 billion in 1985. By 1996 expenditures exceeded $1 trillion. During the first twenty-year period (1965-85), and even somewhat longer, the demand for and the price of medical services to the American people had been seriously disconnected. The two principal parties who paid the bills—employers and government—did so generally without reviewing what they paid for. In 1965 Americans paid out-of-pocket for half their medical care, while government and employers (private health insurance) each covered a quarter of the bill.

In 1996 the payment structure was noticeably different. The consumer's out-of-pocket share had declined to 18 percent. Private health insurance payments had increased to about 35 percent. Government payments stood at 47 percent, most of this (one-third of total outlays) paid by the federal government. If the special tax benefits, through the use of pretax dollars, that the federal government allows payers and recipients of corporate health insurance plans are taken into consideration, the government's annual share, as recently estimated by Uwe Reinhardt, is about $100 billion.[2] This brings the combined federal, state, and local government outlays to 50 percent, if not a little more.

Responding to the deep disappointment of the American Medical Association in losing its battle to defeat Medicare, President Lyndon B. Johnson sought to placate the leadership by assuring it that nothing would change in the relation of patients to physicians, except that the government would henceforth pick up the bill! Further, to win favor with the hospital sector, it was agreed that Medicare would reimburse hospitals on a cost-plus basis. This system of reimbursement remained in effect until the mid-1980s, when Congress shifted to a prospective payment system (PPS) for in-patient Medicare reimbursement based on diagnostic related groups (DRGs).

A key point generally overlooked by both legislators and heathcare analysts was the spectacular upgrading after 1966 of the quality of the nation's hospital infrastructure as a result of the federal government's new cost-plus reimbursement system, which coincided with the training of more and more specialists and subspecialists by the nation's academic health centers and teaching hospitals. This training was financed largely by the new flow of graduate medical educational funds under Medicare currently in the annual range of $6.5 billion.

In 1963, shortly before the creation of Medicare and Medicaid, the AMA withdrew its long-term opposition to having Congress appropriate funds directly for the expansion of the nation's medical schools. Over the next two decades this policy change led to an increase of about 50 percent in the number of U.S. medical schools, from around 80 to 125. Correspondingly, the number of annual graduates increased from about 8,000 to 16,000.

In 1965 Congress made a major change in its highly restrictive immigration and naturalization statutes. The consequence was a large and continuing inflow of graduates of foreign medical schools, international medical graduates (IMGs). Most of these graduates entered residency training in the United States—subsidized by Medicare—with the vast majority remaining to practice here. Currently, IMGs account for approximately one out of four physicians in practice, many filling positions in unattractive locations, serving disadvantaged populations, thereby reducing the pressure on the AMA to find U.S. medical graduates to fill these assignments.

Realizing that the additions to the physician supply alone would not adequately or quickly enough improve the access of many underserved populations to medical care, Congress established the National Health Service Corps in 1970, with subsidies for those accepting positions in underserved locations. Congress also made special federal funding available for residency training in family medicine in 1971, looking to these innovations to improve access for many of those who had earlier been underserved.

In 1976, Congress declared the physician shortage to have been resolved and terminated most special federal funding. Reporting in 1980, the congressional Graduate Medical Educational National Advisory Committee issued a four-year assessment of future physician demand and supply, warning that the nation faced a surplus of 75,000 physicians in 1990 and 150,000 by the century's end. Congress and the medical leadership ignored this warning.

By 1980, NHE had reached $250 billion (in current dollars) up from $41 billion a decade and a half earlier. The nation's hospital capacity had been expanded and greatly upgraded; the nation's physician supply had likewise been greatly expanded, with a corresponding increase in the proportion of those trained in the specialties and commanding much higher fees. The academic health centers and their principal teaching hospitals were becoming aware of a new source of self-funding via "practice Ian income," by which the centers appointed large numbers of clinical professors to their staffs who in turn would not only earn their own salaries and benefits but also contribute to the dean's fund and to financing the research and educational programs of their respective departments.

The early 1980s saw the first signs of a reaction to the largely uncontrolled flow of dollars into the health-care sector from the principal payers—government and employers. This began in selected localities such as southern California, the Twin Cities, Boston, and a few other metropolitan areas, where enrollments in managed care plans, old and new, were rapidly expanding.

The precipitating factor leading to the early expansion of managed care companies was the unexpected reversal in 1980-81 of the long-term trend toward more hospital admissions, which created increasing amounts of surplus hospital capacity. Moreover, increasing numbers of physicians had the "free time" to accept additional patients. Aggressive entrepreneurs recognized the opportunity of extracting large discounts from the overexpanded hospital sector and the underemployed physicians.

Most important, an increasing number of large corporations developed a belated interest in bringing their steeply rising health-care benefit costs under control. The managed care plans were able to quote lower insurance costs to employers who were anxious to move their employees into these plans where savings could be made by more tightly controlling the costs of patient care.

Further, aggressive entrepreneurs, particularly in California, took the initiative to establish for-profit managed care companies that could act as successful middlemen by securing substantial discounts from providers (physicians and hospitals), part of which they used to reduce the costs for employers. Enrolling workers in the new managed care plans would also help to reduce unnecessary admissions and procedures and excessive lengths of stay. Managed care plans could then, at least in theory, pay more attention to further cost savings from expanded reliance on preventive measures.

During the 1980s large numbers of employers made efforts to rein in their steeply rising health-care benefit costs by persuading or forcing their workers to join managed care plans. As previously noted, the federal government introduced a PPS in 1983 to replace its previous cost-plus reimbursement system for in-patient care. In the early 1990s Medicare also moved to introduce a new system for reimbursing physicians who treated Medicare patients on a resources-based relative value scale. But despite these not inconsiderable innovations, the decade nonetheless showed rapid annual increases in national health expenditure of around 10 percent, more than twice the rate of inflation and the growth of the gross domestic product.

California, with its early involvement in and expansion of managed care enrollments, had a considerably lower rate of health-care expenditures in the 1980s—about 25 percent below the average for the nation. However, in Minnesota (the Twin Cities) and Massachusetts, which were also among the leaders in the proportion of their populations enrolled in managed care plans, rates of health-care expenditures during the 1980s were above the national average and considerably above the rate of increase in California. Clearly "market forces" differed from one market to the next.

The limitations of the competitive market to explain adequately what was occurring in the health-care sector is further reinforced by events on the hospital front. The approximately 20 percent decline in admissions to inpatient hospital facilities registered early in the 1980s, during a period of severe recession, was not reversed when the economy strengthened. As the average length of a hospital stay declined substantially during the remainder of the decade, there should have been a marked falloff in the net profit margins of hospitals. However, the data show that hospital net margins remained about 5 to 6 percent. The explanation for this anomalous result is not all that obscure. While the new PPS system for Medicare reimbursement covered inpatient care, the 1980s saw a striking increase in the number and range of services that most hospitals provided patients in ambulatory care and in other locations. These services helped maintain their profitability.

Admittedly, the declining use of inpatient hospital care facilities had an adverse effect on the revenue of many small or heavily indebted hospitals, which led to a considerable number of mergers or closures. Yet much surplus hospital capacity was not eliminated. When the federal government tightened its Medicare reimbursements for inpatient hospital care in the late 1980s, the four leading for-profit hospital chains each encountered varying degrees of difficulties. Humana got out of the hospital business, and American Medical International went into bankruptcy. National Medical Enterprises had to reimburse the federal government for more than $400 million in false billing. Hospital Corporation of America was forced to reorganize to such an extent that its strongest hospitals were later absorbed by Columbia/HCA—which subsequently (1997) ran into serious troubles with the federal government on the grounds of fraud.

We need to identify more specifically the complex forces that contributed to the rapid expansion of the managed care industry after its emergence in the early 1980s in southern California. The emergence of excess capacity in both the hospital and physician supply arenas that occurred in tandem with the growing concerns of the employer community as they sought to moderate the continuing steep increases in their health-care benefit costs have been previously mentioned. However, excess capacity was only the smaller part of the story. The rapidly expanding managed care companies were able to moderate employer outlays by reducing patient referrals to hospitals and specialists and by cutting back on expensive diagnostic and therapeutic interventions of questionable value. All of this helped to bring costs down during the early to mid-1990s, the first significant retardation in the rate of annual premium increases for employee health-care benefits.

After employees were shifted from fee-for-service health insurance coverage into an effective managed care plan, there was a 10 to 15 percent net drop in coverage costs. In rapidly changing market areas, ambitious entrepreneurs could borrow funds from the upbeat financial industry to start or expand a for-profit managed care company that had good prospects for operating at a medical loss ratio (expenditures on patient care) of around 80 percent. This left 20 percent (and sometimes, as in the case of U.S. Healthcare before its purchase by Aetna, as much as 30 percent) for marketing, information systems, and profits.

In a related trend, many of the largest health-care insurance companies, such as Aetna, Prudential, and Cigna, had the capacity to expand from a previously exclusive focus on selling health insurance to providing health-care services to large numbers of enrollees. In a similar effort, many large Blue Cross companies sought approval from their respective states to convert from their previously not-for-profit to a for-profit status. This allowed them to borrow additional funds on the equity markets to finance their expansion. Generally, they received this permission after agreeing to place some of their accumulated surplus profits into a special fund or foundation to support charitable goals.

By the mid-1990s, the growth of managed care companies had had a substantial effect on the provision of health-care services. Enrollments—particularly in health maintenance organizations (HMO), the most tightly controlled of the various managed care arrangements—were greatly changing the economics of the system. Most large- and medium-sized employers were finally able to enjoy much reduced annual increases in their premium rates for their employees' health-care benefits. In fact, selected large corporations saw their annual premium costs drop below the average rate of inflation, about 2 percent.

In 1994 more than 90 percent of for-profit managed care companies listed on the stock exchange reported that they had had a profitable year; however, this upbeat record did not last very long. In 1996 the percentage that reported net annual profits had dropped to about 40 percent. This reflected the increasingly severe competition among the various managed care plans for enrollments in markets where the number of the most attractive customers—those who were still in fee-for-service insurance plans—had dwindled.

True, most Medicare enrollees are not in managed care plans, but there is little reason to believe that Congress will force Medicare enrollees in the near term to make such a switch. And while most states are committed to forcing many or most of their Medicaid eligibles to join HMOs, it remains to be seen whether the states will have much success in developing service contracts for the 30 percent of the elderly, the chronically ill, and the disabled sub-groups who account for almost 70 percent of Medicaid outlays. In short, the easy pickings have been made.

Since the early 1980s the U.S. health-care sector, starting in southern California, but slowly or rapidly spreading to other metropolitan areas, has seen the rapid development of managed care arrangements to a point where about 150 million Americans have become members of one or another such managed care arrangement. However, nothing has happened or appears likely to happen in the health-care marketplace that would challenge the central theme of Arrow's 1963 analysis that health care must be treated as a noncompetitive market.

Most experts agree that 1998 will see a reversal of the recent decline in annual health insurance premiums as the insurance cycle reverses and as consumers resort to successful legislation and the courts to give them more voice in health-care decisions. Moreover, most of the easy savings have been made by moving about 85 percent of those with private health insurance to a managed care arrangement.

Notes

1.   Arrow, Kenneth, "Uncertainty and the Welfare Economics of Medical Care," *American Economic Review* 53, no. 5 (December 1963): 942-973.
2.   Reinhardt, Uwe, "Wanted: A Clearly Articulated Social Ethic for American Health Care," *Journal of the American Medical Association* 278, no. 17 (November 5, 1997): 1446-47.

"Ten Encounters With the US Health Sector, 1930-1999"*

Many US citizens believe that history can teach them very little, but I disagree. Accordingly, in this article, I identify and discuss 10 major encounters that I, a political economist and government consultant, have had with the US health care sector over the last 70 years in the hope that my reactions to these encounters may be of interest and of value to those whose disciplines and experiences differ from mine.

These encounters had nothing to do with any personal need on my part to seek medical or surgical treatment. I have had the good fortune of spending only 1 night in a hospital when my tonsils were extracted at the age of 31—in hindsight, a questionable procedure. Given this good genetic endowment, which enabled my mother to live an active life until 1 day short of her 94th birthday, it might be asked why I have had ongoing relations with the health care sector throughout most of these last 7 decades, especially since World War II. The answer is simple: the 3 years that I spent in the Medical Department of the US Army between late 1943 and mid-1946 had an important influence in shaping my post-World War II career. Although my primary interest continued to be centered on human resources and employment, health policy became a strong secondary focus and after 1980 was my primary area of research.

My assignment in the Surgeon General's Office (SGO) was to plan and oversee the definitive treatment of the tens of thousands of battle casualties that would be returned to the United States for treatment.[1] My Columbia University mentor, the famous economist, Prof Wesley Clair Mitchell, advised that I retain, if possible, my civilian status. I was fortunate enough to do so, which made it much easier for me to discharge my principal assignment successfully, responsible only to the Assistant Surgeon General, Brigadier General R.W. Bliss, while I also worked closely with the SGO's principal consultants Brigadier Generals Hugh Morgan (Medicine), Walter C. Menninger (Psychiatry), and Colonel Michael DeBakey, Deputy Head of Surgery. But if World War II turned me into a part-, if not full-time, researcher in the health policy arena, the first of my 10 major encounters with the health care sector dates back to 1930.

* This article originally appeared in *The Journal of the American Medical Association*, Volume 282, Number 17, November 3, 1999.

Observing Surgery by Harvey Cushing

I observed Harvey Cushing, MD, perform surgery on a patient with a diseased pituitary gland at the Peter Bent Brigham Hospital in Boston in April 1930, while I was serving as guide-interpreter to my mother's cousin, a physician from Frankfurt. Seeing Cushing operate was at the very top of my mother's cousin's wish list and with the help of another cousin, a member of the Medical School faculty at Harvard, we were able to gain admission to view the operation, although we were not able to see the details of Cushing's operating technique.

The following day I saw a fellow visitor who also had been at the operation and inquired how the patient was doing. His reply: "Don't you know that all neurosurgery is experimental? Of course, the patient died." A half century later I asked the senior resident in neurosurgery at Presbyterian Hospital in New York City about pituitary gland surgery and received the following answer: patients are usually hospitalized for 3 or 4 days, and in most cases, are discharged cured. No small change and a potent reminder that medical research can certainly pay off, not a little but a lot.

A Pattern for Hospital Care

In August 1948 the state of New York entered into a contract with Columbia University to have me undertake a study of its general and long-term hospitals, an alternative to my working directly for New York State, a move that I hesitated to make because of the probable victory of Governor Dewey in the forthcoming presidential election. Several members of his staff were exploring the purchase of houses in Washington, DC, so assured were they of Dewey's forthcoming victory.

My final report contained, in the light of later events, both good and bad recommendations; however, by getting Governor Dewey out of an earlier commitment to use state funds to subsidize several Catholic hospitals in Brooklyn that were in the red because of a failure of Blue Cross to increase its reimbursement rates to match the recent advances in hospital costs, it paid for itself many times over. The shortfall in Blue Cross payments was real, but the payments were in the process of being corrected, and I saw only dangers to the state's future financing if the governor was held to his earlier commitment.

I called on the senior bishop and after talking around the issue emphasized that if he accepted state funding, state control would inevitably follow. He understood and told me to inform the governor's staff that the earlier commitment was no longer operative. With this narrow escape for the State of New York, I was not surprised to see in later years the explosive growth of governmental funding for the health care sector, especially after the passage of Medicare and Medicaid, to a point where combined state and federal funding for health care expanded from 25% of $41 billion in 1965 to about 50% of $1.2 trillion in 1999 and is heading for over $2 trillion by 2008.[2]

No One Wants to Operate on a President Who Might Not Survive Surgery

President Eisenhower had a serious heart attack during the summer of 1955 while vacationing in Colorado. I first realized the seriousness of the president's condition when I started to receive detailed daily letters from his personal physician and friend, Major General Howard Snyder, MD, a close friend of mine since World War II and who, I concluded, was sending me these daily accounts as insurance in the event that the president failed to recover. However, Eisenhower recovered and returned to the White House, only to experience a severe attack of ileitis some months later, for which General Snyder had him transported by ambulance early one morning to Walter Reed Hospital. Tests were performed while urgent telephone calls were made to I.V. Ravdin, MD, at the University of Pennsylvania who had served under General Eisenhower in Europe and Dudley White, MD, of Harvard University, the president's cardiologist, to come as quickly as possible to Walter Reed Hospital where the president was a patient in need of urgent diagnosis and treatment.

As General Snyder told the story, the out-of-town experts arrived shortly before noon and spent the next 12 hours in constant consultations and some testing, but took no definitive action because no one wanted to operate on the president, who might not survive. Finally, shortly after midnight, Snyder told the consultant group that although he had not performed an operation during the last 2 decades, he would wheel the president in to surgery and operate on him if they failed to act within 15 minutes.[3] That did the trick. The operation for ileitis went smoothly and a few months later the president, with Mamie, son John, and me present in the Oval Office, informed the American people in a short broadcast that he would run for reelection in November 1956. At the conclusion of his brief remarks, he asked me to accompany him back to his living quarters while the broadcasters and the photographers took additional photos of Mamie and John.

During our brief stroll, the president said that he hoped that the physicians who had assured him that he was physically fit to run for reelection knew what they were talking about since the job of being president could not be performed by anyone who was not in good condition. Fortunately, the physicians guessed right, but the story is indicative of the uncertainties that existed and always will exist in medicine.

Planning for Better Hospital Care

In a report undertaken at the request of the Federation of Jewish Philanthropies in New York City, Rogatz and I[4] concluded in 1961 that the Federation's 10 hospitals would face a serious financial challenge in 3 to 5 years. Our analysis pointed to a continuing steep rise in hospital costs on the order of more than one third, a conclusion that the lay president of the Federation, a highly successful businessman, Lawrence Wien, refused to accept.

Our report also included a casual aside. We pointed out that a hospital like Mount Sinai, which wanted to retain its position as a leader in clinical care, required a close relationship with a leading academic health center, a connection that Mount Sinai had been exploring but had not yet been able to achieve. Once our report was published this effort took a new turn. Members of the staff proposed that Mount Sinai start its own medical school, a proposition that we had not made and to which we were opposed, given the number of medical schools in Manhattan and the costs involved in starting a new school. We were later told by Gustav Levy, the head of the Mount Sinai Board of Trustees, that the proponents told him that the medical school could be established for around $20 million, a figure that turned out to be a ludicrous underestimate. But Mount Sinai got its medical school, and the authors learned a lesson about the quality of long-range planning in the US health care sector.

The Civil Rights Act of 1964

In 1963, President Kennedy sent a weak bill to the Congress, at least as far as stopping discrimination in employment was concerned, but his assassination stopped even that bill from being enacted. The much strengthened bill drafted in early 1964 was being effectively derailed by the head of the Rules Committee of the House, Judge Howard Smith. At one point, I suggested to Sen Joseph Clark of Pennsylvania that he might consider adding discrimination based on gender to discrimination based on race, thereby enlisting the support of a second large pressure group. He accepted the suggestion, and Judge Smith was convinced that his troubles were now at an end since no Congress would be so offbeat as to outlaw discrimination against both blacks and women. But that is what Congress did.

Four years later, I published a book of essays that included a chapter on "The Female Physician,"[5] which emphasized that the United States had the lowest percentage of women physicians in any advanced country, Spain alone excepted.

Shortly thereafter, I participated in a session arranged by the American Association of Medical Colleges and explained that recent legislation had made the subject of women physicians more or less moot. US medical schools would admit more well-qualified white women than moderately prepared black men. I did not foresee that the proportion of women in US residency programs would increase in 35 years to around 40% of the total class.[6] However, that is what happened. The remaining issue is the need for an expanded role for women physicians among physicians in leadership positions.

Nothing Will Change Because of Medicare Except That the Government Will Pick Up the Bills

Such was the reassurance that President Johnson offered the leaders of the American Medical Association (AMA) after Congress passed the Medicare Act early in 1965. The leadership of the AMA had bet all of its chips on defeating Medicare, and they were distraught and angry when their effort failed.[7] Federal actuaries answered the president's question as to the potential budgetary impact in 1990 of passing Medicare by estimating a $10 billion outlay for that year, about one tenth of what it actually was. But in one respect President Johnson could not have been more right in his forecast.

Little changed during the 3 decades after the enactment of Medicare except that the federal government paid most of the health care bills of the elderly, while employers paid the bills for their insured workers younger than age 65.

Dollars Empower the Academic Health Centers

One by-product of the passage of Medicare was setting the nation's leading research-oriented academic health centers (AHCS) free to finance their own agendas now that they had access to the considerable graduate medical educational funding made available by Medicare. The AHCs no longer had to admit charity patients to meet their teaching needs and learned to become even more self-sufficient financially by appointing large numbers of new clinical professors who earned their own salaries and benefits, as well as contributing to the dean's fund and to their departmental budgets. In learning how to finance themselves, the AHCs were able to devote still more of their efforts and energies to high-tech medicine and pay little attention to the needs of the chronically ill and the shortfalls in health care services to the low-income populations in their communities.[8]

Expanding the Physician Supply

In 1963, the AMA dropped its lobbying efforts against the expansion of medical schools and in the following 13 years Congress enacted measures that doubled the number of US medical school graduates. In 1976, Congress revisited the issue of a physician shortage and decided that the earlier shortage had been eliminated. At that point, Congress established the Graduate Medical Education National Advisory Committee (GMENAC) to reassess the issue of the prospective physician supply for 1990 and 2000. In reports at the beginning of the 1980s, the committee concluded, even before the start of the explosive growth of managed care, that the nation would have a surplus of more than 150,000 physicians out of a total of 685,000 by century's end.[9]

However, the GMENAC's forecast of a substantial surplus in the physician supply by century's end was undermined by a 5-fold increase in total spending for health care that occurred during the last 2 decades of the 20th century and that enabled most physicians to continue to make a good living.

The Clinton Health Care Debacle

In 1994, Ostow and I[10] sought to inform the American public of the health reform measures that were likely to emerge from the passage of the Clinton Health Plan, then under congressional deliberation. When 1 of our collaborators suggested in the spring of 1994 that the Clinton Plan might never emerge from congressional committees, I dismissed his forecast as beyond the realm of probability because I knew that the president still had many large corporations in his corner together with a great many voters who recognized the desirability of the nation providing health insurance coverage for the many millions who lacked it. But the length and complexity of the plan that the president forwarded to the Congress helped its opponents, led by small employers, to derail it. It was apparent that persons out of the loop, like myself, should not try to call close shots.

A Trillion Dollars More a Year for Health Care

In 1980, national health expenditures of the United States totaled just under $250 billion.[2] By the end of 1999, national health expenditures will have increased by $1 trillion,[2] a figure that has not yet caught the public's attention, partly because both the citizenry and its legislators have been so preoccupied with the rights and wrongs of managed care. When one realizes that the trillion dollars of additional health care spending per year has been accompanied by a sizable increase in the number of uninsured persons, from approximately 30 million to approximately 44 million, and that the recent increase in healthy years of life has been in the 1% to 2% range, the mystery deepens as to who got the extra trillion dollars that was spent. I think I know but I am not sure. Every one of the 12 million Americans who is employed in the health care sector and the many others who do business with the health care sector has been able to take a smaller or larger piece of the additional trillion dollars per year that is being spent. An additional trillion dollars will become available by 2008.[2] The challenge that the nation faces is to make sure that the public obtains commensurate benefits.

Conclusion

What is the most important lesson that I derived from these 10 encounters over the span of 70 years? Americans think of illness and disability as a condition that can be fixed by an expert, in this case a physician. Accordingly, they want more medicine, more research, and more physicians—all with a lower cost and equitable distribution. This was the case in 1930 and it is still the case today at century's end. However, the fact that each individual is ultimately responsible for the maintenance of his or her own health is a lesson that most Americans still need to learn.

Acknowledgment: I would like to thank Panos Minogiannis, MPH, MPhil, for his help in assembling the references for this article.

References

1. Ginzberg E. The shift to specialism in medicine: the U.S. Army in WWII. *Acad-Med.* 1999;74:522-525.
2. Smith S, Freeland M, Heffler S, McKusick D. The next ten years of health spending: what does the future hold? *Health Aff (Millwood).* 1998; 17:128-140.
3. Ginzberg E. *The Eye of Illusion.* New Brunswick, NJ: Transaction Publishers, 1993:186-190.
4. Ginzberg E, Rogatz P. *Planning for Better Hospital Care.* New York, NY: King's Crown Press; 1961.
5. University Press; 1969.
6. Graduate medical education [Appendix II, Table 1]. *JAMA.* 1999;282:893-895.
7. Campion FD. *The AMA and U.S. Health Policy Since 1940.* Chicago, III: Chicago Review Press, 1984.
8. Ginzberg E, Berliner H, Minogiannis P, Ostow M. *Academic Health Centers and the Urban Poor.* New Haven, Conn: Yale University Press. In press.
9. Department of Health and Human Services. *Graduate Medical Education National Advisory Committee Summary Report.* Vol 1. Washington, DC: Government Printing Office; 1980.
10. Ginzberg E, Ostow M. *The Road to Reform.* New York, NY: Free Press; 1994.

"US Health Care: A Look Ahead to 2025"*

Abstract—The chapter begins with a reminder that forecasting changes in the health care sector a quarter to a third of a century in the future is likely to be a losing effort, based on past experience. It next considers changing organization and financing and questions that managed care and market competition will be the key forces introducing change. The author looks forward to the passage of universal health insurance coverage for essential care by early in the new century, with patients having to pay for more choice and more quality. The analysis next focuses on the physician supply and points to three challenges: how to moderate the numbers being trained; whether to reconsider the conventional wisdom of training more generalists; and how to support more resources for the National Health Service Corps to improve coverage in underserved areas. The author predicts the restructuring of acute care hospitals, with a marked reduction of in-patient beds, and that leading-edge research-oriented academic health centers should be able to remain out in front. There are also potential gains in health status from prevention and molecular medicine in a nation where chronic disease will dominate.

A Cautionary Note

This article has been written in response to a request. Otherwise, I would never have set out my views about prospective changes in the US health care sector more than a quarter of a century into the future. The reasons for my hesitancy can be easily explained. Just consider how far off our recent presidents, medical leaders, and professors have been in foretelling changes in the US health care sector during the past quarter to third of a century.

President Johnson sought to reassure the leaders of the American Medical Association (AMA), shortly after the passage of Medicare legislation, that nothing would change in patient-physician relations except that the government would pick up the bills. The federal actuaries forecast a $10 billion outlay for Medicare in 1990; when the data came in, the total outlay stood at close to $100 billion (14).

In the first year of his first administration, President Nixon warned the nation that the acceleration of medical expenditures threatened to undermine both our health care system and even the national economy (21). It was close to a quarter century later that the United States began serious efforts to moderate its rate of health expenditures. Presidents Ford and Carter favored the introduction of national health insurance, but nothing happened. Ronald Reagan and his staff promised to reform the US health care system by relying on market incentives but settled with Congress in 1981 on a three-year reduc-

* This article originally appeared in *Annual Review of Public Health*, 1999, 20:55-66.

tion in federal contributions to Medicaid (14). And whereas President Bush passed when it came to health care reform, the Clinton administration's miscalculations are still very much with us.

Consider next the inaccurate foresight of the leaders of the medical community. The AMA bet all of its chips on the defeat of Medicare and lost (5). However, physicians entered a new boom period. Paul Ellwood sought to persuade Nixon and the Congress to pass special legislation, which they did in 1973, to stimulate the growth of health maintenance organizations (HMOs), legislation that had such little effect that it was permitted to lapse some years later. After four years of hard work, the Graduate Medical Education National Advisory Committee (GMENAC), in 1980, warned the nation that the United States faced forthcoming overages in the number of physicians of 75,000 in 1990 and close to 140,000 by century's end (12), a worry ignored by both the medical profession and the Congress and with little validation up to the present from the marketplace.

Finally, what about the professors of health policy? In 1977, Alain Enthoven of Stanford forwarded the first version of his managed competition plan (16) to Secretary of Health, Education, and Welfare Joseph Califano, who found it impractical and put it aside. Despite later improved versions, Enthoven's managed competition remains a promise, little more. Himmelfarb and others (27) sought to persuade the Clinton administration to adopt a Canadian-type single-payer plan, but their effort failed as did all the other proposals that the White House staff put forward in its 1300-plus pages of proposed reform legislation.

For the record, I do not want to omit my name from the professors who stumbled along the way. For many months after President Clinton's September 1993 presentation to the Congress on his Health Security bill, I anticipated that he had the votes to move towards universal health insurance coverage (cf 21).

The Changing Organization and Financing of the Health Care Sector

The conventional wisdom as of the end of this century is that the US health care industry is being restructured in response to two dominant forces: the growth of managed care and the cost controls that flow from intensified market competition. I have serious questions about each of the foregoing premises, and I look forward to much more radical changes on both fronts—organization and financing—by 2025.

The first phase of the managed care revolution appears to be nearing its end. Witness that most enrollees in fee-for-service insurance plans have been moved into managed care arrangements, with a 10-15% "savings" resulting from reductions in their access to care, including hospital admissions, hospital stays, consultations with specialists, and still other choices once available to them which are now "managed" (19).

I also seriously question whether states will save any significant amounts of money by forcibly enrolling their Medicaid-eligibles in managed care plans, with 70% of their current Medicaid expenditures reflecting outlays for the disabled, the blind, and the elderly, who more frequently than not require a range of housing, social welfare, home care, and other supports in addition to medical care (30). There are diverse reports that managed care companies initially enrolled Medicare and Medicaid patients only to later decide to no longer do so because the profits were not forthcoming (1). Although I expect the number of Medicare patients in HMOs to increase, probably substantially, it is not clear that Congress will remove the option that Medicare enrollees currently enjoy of shifting from HMOs to fee-for-service arrangements when they confront serious health challenges that many HMOs may fail to respond to satisfactorily.

There are additional reasons for my belief that the present versions of managed care arrangements have almost run their course. Consider the following signs: the consumer revolt via legislation and administrative initiatives to restrict the uninhibited decision-making of managed care management. The consumer outrage with the practices of managed care organizations led to the passing of regulatory legislation in most states that among other things stipulates that women who have given birth must remain at least two days in the hospital, thus eliminating what had been termed drive-through deliveries (8). It also led to the exploration by some employer groups of opportunities to establish direct contracts with select providers—large teaching hospitals and multispecialty groups—without relying on the intermediary services of a managed care plan, with its 15% overhead charge (22).

I have little doubt that the organization of health care delivery in 2025 will be within the framework of a cost control mechanism, but I anticipate that the members of the physician community, not the managers of managed care companies, will have primary responsibility for determining, in consultation with their patients, the treatment modalities to be selected and followed.

Even more radical changes loom ahead on the financing front. I anticipate that, relatively early in the next century, the United States, after having experimented with still more ad hoc arrangements, will move to a system of universal health insurance coverage for all that will offer access to "essential care," with the emphasis on "essential." For instance, I anticipate that Medicare beneficiaries will be offered a defined contribution plan by the federal government that will provide them access to basic services but not to high-cost hospitals and other procedures involving outlays of $150,000 or more. Patients who want access to a broader range of services will have to pay for such access via supplemental insurance, which they will either buy with their own money or obtain as a fringe benefit from their employer.

In a capitalistic economy, dollars have always been the preferred mechanism to determine who gets what and how much they get. True, governments provide access for the entire population to designated levels of public safety, education, housing, health care, and other "essentials," but no nation has ever found it possible to assure all of the public equal and prompt access to high-cost services such as health and education. In 1965, when Medicare and Medicaid were first enacted, payments for medical care were distributed as follows: 25%, private insurance; 25%, government outlays; and 50% out-of-pocket disbursements. At this century's end, the distribution approximates the following: private insurance, 35%; government outlays, 47%; and out-of-pocket, 18% (14). By 2025, I expect the out-of-pocket share to be considerably higher, with corresponding declines in employer-provided private insurance coverage.

The Congressional Budget Office has estimated that total national health expenditures are likely to reach $2 trillion by 2008, up from $1 trillion in 1996 (10). A conservative projection would see total expenditures reach $4 trillion annually by 2025, which could turn out to be a serious underestimate given the steep increase in the number of the elderly, who make much greater use of health care services than the below-65 population.

The Future of the Physician Supply

In 1960 the ratio of physicians per 100,000 population stood at about 140. In the following decades, with a strong boost from enlarged federal (and state) support, the ratio almost doubled to approximating 270 per 100,000 at century's end (3). Although the federal government has begun initiatives recently to moderate the flow of new physicians, by placing some modest restrictions on the inflow and residency support for international medical graduates and by paying teaching hospitals not to train as many residents as previously (15), the projections point to continuing increases in the number of physicians per 100,000 population (24).

Aside from the gross numbers being trained in US medical schools and residency training programs, there are other high-priority physician supply issues that warrant at least brief inspection: what types of physicians should be trained; how physicians can be encouraged to practice, at least for a time, in underserved areas; and the prospects of cooperative arrangements being worked out among the current sponsors of medical schools (state governments, not-for-profit universities, and free-standing schools), together with the federal government, which would result in constraining the numbers of future entrants into the medical profession.

There is little prospect that, in the face of the aforementioned potential increases in annual spending for health care, market forces will result in a significant decline in the number of applicants to medical school. So far, the average earnings of physicians have declined in only one year, 1994 (28), and the number of applicants has recently reached a new high (3). If more dollars continue to flow into the health care sector as appears highly probable, it will become that much more difficult to restrict the numbers of medical school students and residents. It is hard to see from where support will come to implement the Pew Health Professions Commission's recommendation that, by 2005, US medical schools reduce their graduating class size by 25% (31).

With respect to the types of physicians that should be trained, the conventional wisdom is that the United States needs more generalists, not more specialists. I have long questioned this prescription based on the following counter-arguments. With 80% of the US population living in metropolitan areas, most Americans with health insurance coverage could have easy access to specialists, who are often better equipped than generalists to treat them effectively. Moreover, many generalists find it difficult to remain in the general practice of medicine for multiple decades. Many specialists serve as the preferred physicians for patients suffering from one or more chronic diseases (17).

A more important challenge than optimizing the ratio of generalists to specialists is restructuring the training of physicians and other health care providers so that they are able to direct a diversified health care team, consisting of nurse practitioners, health care technicians, social workers, psychologists, outreach workers, and still others. The combined skills of such a team will be required to meet the challenges of patients increasingly treated outside the acute care hospital, afflicted with one or more chronic diseases, and requiring close monitoring.

To improve the distribution of physicians and provide broadened access to care for underserved populations, urban and rural, the National Health Service Corps (NHSC) needs to be broadened and improved, with much enlarged financial resources placed at its disposal. Because the American people have not shown enthusiasm for additional governmental controls, such as legislation that would require recent medical school graduates to spend two years in an underserved area, and because increasing the number of medical school graduates to force larger numbers to practice in locations that they would otherwise eschew will be too expensive and would not work, the only possible alternative is to enlarge and improve the NHSC with sufficient attractions, monetary and otherwise, to increase the physician supply in underserved areas.

But the critical role that the future supply of physicians will continue to play in the provision of quality care to all groups of Americans, including the tens of millions now living in underserved areas, warrants the exploration and establishment of an ongoing commission with broad representation. The aim of the commission would be to bring about a better alignment between the educational and training systems and the rapidly changing health care delivery system.

The Restructuring of the Acute Care Hospital

About two decades have passed since the first indications that the acute care hospital was about to undergo major changes. Early warning signals included a decline in in-patient admissions; the shifting of many diagnostic, therapeutic, and rehabilitative services from in-patient to ambulatory care settings; prospective steep declines in in-patient census; and a significant decline in hospital occupancy ra-tios. All of these early indicators of change came to pass in the 1980s and 1990s (18), and among the questions that we need to explore is the likely role of the acute care hospital in 2025, our target date for assessing changes that lie ahead.

Despite the phenomenal growth of the for-profit Columbia/HCA chain of hospitals in the 1990s—at least up to the point of the fed-eral investigation of 1997—the acute care hospital sector has con-tinued to be dominated by community hospitals under nonprofit auspices, with public hospitals composing the second largest sub-group and for-profit hospitals continuing to lag far behind, account-ing for no more than about 1 out of every seven acute care hospitals (18). The first questions that we need to explore are the following: How much did the acute care hospital sector change once its in-patient admissions not only stopped growing but declined by about 20%, and, more importantly, what are some of the possible/probable trends that may impact the hospital sector in the quarter century that lies ahead?

Different students emphasize different aspects of the developments of the last two decades. I am impressed with the ability of most hos-pitals to have maintained their net profit margins despite the rela-tively steep declines in admissions and total days of care. The net profit margin over the past decade has remained around 5% (2), which reflects the ability of most hospitals to build up their revenues from ambulatory care. Somewhat belatedly but nonetheless aggres-sively, many hospitals that find themselves under increasing finan-cial pressure are looking carefully at their organization and staffing patterns and finding ways to bring their cost structures into balance with their more constrained revenues.

A sizable number of hospitals that recognized that their future held more threats to their survival and continued effective function-ing sought to work out agreements with former competitors, became members of larger networks, or sold out to for-profit buyers (E Ginzberg, submitted for publication). Many small hospitals, prima-rily those under 100 beds and located principally in rural areas, of-ten had no option, after they had exhausted their modest reserve funds, but to close their doors. Clearly the last two decades have witnessed a great many changes in the hospital arena, particularly in regions of the country where managed care companies came to dominate the regional marketplace, usually accompanied by significant declines in in-patient admissions and in days of care (18).

Despite the many closures, mergers, and realignments just noted, the striking phenomenon is the relatively modest number of changes that occurred in the organization, management, and operation of the nation's hospital plants in the face of such radical declines in hospital admissions and days of care, together with the expansion of ambulatory care, and the sizable growth in the use of home care and fewer acute care beds to care for increasing numbers of patients, particularly those with chronic illnesses or diseases.

Although the number of admissions per 1,000 population below and above 65 years of age has been declining in all areas of the country, the gap in the rates between the most advanced areas and those in the rear remains very wide, with the laggards often reporting rates of in-patient utilization two- or threefold greater than the leaders, such as California or the Twin Cities (11). In the face of these wide and persisting differentials, the question that arises is whether the capacity-occupancy norms of a decade or two out will be set by the present leaders or by the larger numbers of lagging followers. But no matter who is and who becomes the norm setter, the odds are strongly in favor of a continuing and growing oversupply of hospital capacity with no clear indication of whether, when, and how the excess capacity will be converted to alternative uses or eliminated. Part of the uncertainty derives from the fact that, in a great number of metropolitan communities and especially in low-income neighborhoods, the local hospital and its clinics have long served as the basic health resource to many in the community and the absence of comprehensive community health centers would leave the population at substantial risk for obtaining essential care. To make matters still more difficult, the closure of the local hospital would deprive many in the community of their jobs and income, as well as their effective health care benefits, losses that responsible governmental and community leadership will seek to avoid.

Still, by 2025, the odds strongly favor a large shrinkage in the number of in-patient beds of the nation's acute care hospitals, to a point at which only patients undergoing the most complex surgical interventions are likely to be admitted and treated in in-patient fa- cilities; and for most, their stay is likely to be limited to only a few days. But with hospitals still accounting for about 35% of the nation's annual health care outlays and with physicians' earnings from treat- ing hospitalized patients accounting for another 10-12%, the pro- spective declines resulting from the future peripheralization of hos- pital care are easier to forecast than to delineate and assess (19).

The Academic Health Centers

The nation's academic health centers (AHCs), more particularly the 25 or so that have set the pace for biomedical research over the past several decades, have entered or are about to enter a period of increasing difficulty. The federal government, together with a se- lected number of state governments, has taken early steps to reduce the number of residents that they will be willing to support in the years ahead, given the widespread agreement that the nation has an excess supply of specialists (15). But the present and prospective declines in the future financing of residency training are only one of several challenges and threats that face the nation's leading research- oriented AHCS.

Over the past several decades, the nation's leading research-ori- ented AHCs have helped to finance themselves by vastly expanding their clinical staffs, the members of which have directed all or most of their time to patient practice, resulting in an explosive growth in practice plan revenue, a considerable part of which has been used to cross-subsidize underfunded activities in the AHCs' educational, research, and charity care missions (4). Further, most AHCs were able to attract insured patients whose fee-for-service plans were will- ing to pay the 30% or so surcharge that most AHCs levied on their privately insured patients (29). Increasingly, many managed care plans, in addition to moderating the number of patients whom they authorize to seek in-patient care, especially in high-cost AHCS, are also balking at paying the 30% AHC surcharge, thereby further threat- ening the financial viability of many of the nation's leading teaching hospitals.

The leading research-oriented AHCs will probably be able to as- sure themselves of some additional revenue through new arrange- ments with for-profit companies that will pay their licensing and other fees for the use of patented knowledge and know-how. But this upbeat assessment does not offer a solution to the future scale and scope of the number of undergraduates and residents that they should accept for training. As noted earlier, the federal and state governments have recently initiated actions to moderate the number of residency slots that they will subsidize in the future. But the challenge that remains unaddressed and unanswered is any form of prospective collective activity among the nation's 125 allopathic and 17 osteopathic medical schools to agree on a prospective limitation and reduction in the number of medical students accepted for training. With the Council on Graduate Medical Education (COGME) and leading health workforce analysts such as Wiener at Johns Hopkins (32) and Kindig at Wisconsin (25) pointing to excesses in the range of 150,000 physicians out of a 750,000 total and with a reminder that physicians have been responsible for generating about 75% of all patient care costs, the issue of a national policy focused on the future supply of physicians should not be kept on the back burner, no matter how difficult it will prove to shape an effective national policy.

As a further reminder, efforts to put in place a sound and sensible set of policies governing the future supply of physicians must also focus attention on the following considerations: What principles are to govern the cutback in admissions to medical schools, as well as the selection of schools for closure, taking into consideration the variation among states as to the relative opportunities of their residents to gain admission; what new mechanisms are required to restrict the numbers and rationalize the structure of residency training opportunities, recognizing the influence of the location of the residency or later choice of practice location; and what changes are required in the scale and scope of the NHSC to address more effectively the future needs of seriously underserved areas.

Prevention, Molecular Medicine, and Chronic Disease

There remain at least three more trends and tendencies on the health care horizon that need to be addressed, at least in a preliminary fashion, because of their individual and collective influence on the future restructuring of our nation's health care system. The key categories are prevention, molecular medicine, and chronic disease. It is appropriate that we consider at least briefly the potential of greater emphasis on prevention to alter health care initiatives and outcomes.

Improved prevention can reduce morbidity, delay mortality, and extend the years of healthy life. But improved prevention faces many difficulties, the most important being the role that the individual's behavior plays in the genesis of disease and poor health status and the difficulties of altering such personal behavior. Granted that easier access to selected preventive interventions, from more on-time immunizations to mammography for women in their fifties, would be cost-efficient, even much expanded use of medical preventive interventions would have only a marginal effect on reducing the death rate of the more than 50% of the population that dies because of chronic disease (23). Many people who are born into, reared in, and forced to live on the margins of society with inadequate prenatal support, limited educational and career opportunities, and an inability to shape their future, will be unable to protect their future health or uninterested in doing so.

The above cautionary views about the potential of prevention, based on changes in the life styles of individuals and families, do not deny that we may be on the verge of significant breakthroughs in molecular biology that will have decisive life-lengthening consequences in the early decades of the next century and that will lead to important new developments in diagnostic and therapeutic interventions by 2025. The ability to spot bad genes early and to eliminate or neutralize them is no longer problematic. What remains uncertain is the rate at which knowledge of the bad genes will become available, and, equally important, the rate at which successful interventions to eliminate or control them will advance. The more enthusiastic health policy analysts believe that a prolongation of the average life span to 120 years may be just beyond the horizon (26). But it surely does not follow that such an accomplishment, by 2025 or somewhat later, will enable the populations of the United States and other advanced economies to be large-scale gainers.

This brings us to our third point, the increasing importance of chronic disease or its corollary—the ability of the elderly to continue to function effectively.

Increasing numbers of Americans are instructing their physicians, lawyers, and responsible relatives that they do not want to be attached to life-support systems unless there is a reasonable chance that they will be able to regain effective functioning. As more and more people live into their seventies, eighties, nineties, and even longer, increasing numbers are likely to be afflicted with advanced Alzheimer's disease, which prevents many of them from knowing who they are and recognizing the person to whom they have been married for 40 or 50 years. Optimists believe that the cure for Alzheimer's is not that far off, and one must hope that they turn out to be right. But the broader challenge presented by chronic illnesses facing the early twenty-first century remains. The health care sector must restructure its focus, awareness, and institutions away from its earlier preoccupation with acute care interventions in favor of the prevention, treatment, and care of the elderly (and some not so elderly) who suffer from one or more chronic diseases. The challenge to the society and its caregivers—physicians and others—is to enable the chronically ill to continue functioning effectively within their liabilities and limitations and to reassess the adjustments that need to be made in the decision-making process as the chronically ill lose their ability to function as their end of life draws near.

We have some early clues as to what this radically changed focus implies, such as the explosive growth of home health care (7). But we are at or close to the starting line in preparing to alter the structure and functioning of the US health care system from acute to chronic care, and we need the answers to this shift as early as possible and surely before 2025. No serious health care analyst can pretend to know, at this century's end, how the nation's health care sector will be reorganized and operate in the year 2025, for the simple and compelling reason that the nation has not yet recognized, except for a very few leaders, the basic shift in focus that is required as the care of the chronically ill becomes the new societal imperative.

Acknowledgment: I wish to acknowledge Panos Minogiannis for his considerable assistance in checking the references in this chapter.

Literature Cited

1.   American Health Line. 1998. *Policy issues No. 2. Medicare + Choice: Only 3 Applications Received.* Washington, DC: National Journal Inc., Tuesday, September 8
2.   American Hospital Association. 1997. *Emerging Trends.* Chicago: Am. Hosp. Assoc.
3   Barzewsky B, Jonas HS, Etzel SI. 1997. Educational programs in U.S. medical schools, 1996-1997. *JAMA* 278(9):744-49
4.   Blumenthal D. 1997. Understanding the social missions of academic health centers. *Rep. Commonw. Fund Task Force Acad. Health Centers, New York* Jan:37
5.   Campion FD. 1984. *The AMA and US Health Policy Since 1940.* Chicago: Chicago Rev. 285 pp.

6.   Deleted in proof
7.   Ciszewski P. 1997. Home health care: A growing industry continues to flourish. *Med. Interface* 10(5):70-75
8.   Coleman D. 1996. Here comes the backlash. *Managed Health Care* 6(9):30-34
9.   Deleted in proof
10.   Congressional Budget Office. 1997. *Reducing the Deficit: Spending and Revenue Options*. Washington, DC: US Gov. Print. Off. 298 pp.
11.   Delloitte and Zouche Tohmatsu International. 1994. *US Hospitals and the Future of Health Care: a Changing Survey*. Philadelphia, PA: Delloitte & Touche Tohmatsu Intl. 5th ed.
12.   Department of Health and Human Services. 1980. *Report of the Graduate Medical Education National Advisory Committee*, 1:4-5. Washington, DC: US Gov. Print. Off.
13.   Deleted in proof
14.   Department of Health and Human Services. 1997. *Medicare and Medicaid Statistical Supplement*, 1997, pp. 18-22. Washington, DC: Health Care Financ. Rev.
15.   Department of Health and Human Services. 1997. *New York Teaching Hospitals Participate in Graduate Medical Education Demonstration*. Press Release, Mon., Feb. 17. Washington, DC: Health Care Financ. Rev.
16.   Enthoven A. 1978. Consumer choice health plan. *N. Engl. J. Med.* 298(12):650-58
17.   Ginzberg E. 1996. The future supply of physicians. *Acad. Med.* 71:1147-53
18.   Ginzberg E. 1996. *Tomorrow's Hospital: A Look to the Twenty-First Century*. New Haven/London: Yale Univ. Press
19.   Ginzberg E. 1998. The changing US health care agenda. *JAMA* 279(7):501-4
20.   Deleted in proof
21.   Ginzberg E, Ostow M. 1994. *The Road to Reform: The Future of Health Care in America*. New York: Free Press
22.   Ginzberg E, Ostow M. 1997. Managed care: a look back and a look ahead. *N. Engl. J Med.* 336(14):1018-20
23.   Hoffman C, Rice DP. 1996. *Chronic Care in America: a 21st Century Challenge*. San Francisco: Univ. Calif.
24.   Lahr K, Detner D, Vancklow N. 1996. *The Nation's Physician Workforce*. Washington, DC: Inst. Med.
25.   Rivo M, Kindig DA. 1996. A report card on the physician workforce in the United States. *N. Engl. J. Med.* 334(4):892-96
26.   Rowe JW, Kahn RL. 1998. *Successful Aging*. New York: Pantheon
27.   Simon CJ, Born PH. 1996. Physician earnings in a changing managed care enviroment. *Health Affairs* 15(3):124-33
28.   Skocpol T. 1996. *Boomerang*. New York/London: Norton
29.   The Commonwealth Fund. 1997. Leveling the playing field: financing the missions of academic health centers. *Rep. Commonw. Fund Task Force Acad. Health Centers, New York*, May:ix
30.   The Henry J Kaiser Foundation Policy Brief. 1995. *Medicaid and Managed Care*. Washington, DC: Kaiser Foundation
31.   University of California at San Francisco. 1995. *Critical Challenges: Revitalizing the Health Professions for the Twenty-First Century*. San Francisco: Univ. Calif.
32.   Weiner JP. 1994. Forecasting the effects of health reform on US physician workforce requirements. *JAMA* 272:222-30

Bibliography

This bibliography is organized into three major subdivisions. To assist the reader in using it, I will briefly explain its arrangement:

Part I lists, in chronological order, all the books I have written, edited, and published on human resources and employment, alone or with associates, between 1932 and 2002.

Part II continues the above approach with respect to my books on "health policy," except that I have added a wide selection of my articles (often with associates) on health policy that appeared in *The New England Journal of Medicine* (NEJM) starting in 1966, and in the *Journal of the American Medical Association* (JAMA) in the early 1980s, together with references to additional articles I authored that were published in other health policy journals or elsewhere.

Part III provides references to a large number of additional presentations and publications focused primarily on human resources and employment policy often resulting from my four decades (1940-1980) of active consulting for the United States government, other governmental agencies in the United States and abroad, as well as for selected non-governmental organizations.

I am greatly indebted to Ms. Shoshana Vasheetz, who made time in her busy schedule to prepare this bibliography for the publisher.

Eli Ginzberg

Part I: Human Resources and Employment—Books

Studies in the Economics of the Bible. Philadelphia, PA: Jewish Publication Society, 1932.

The House of Adam Smith. New York: Columbia University Press, 1934.

Preface to Social Economics by John Maurice Clark. New York: Farrar & Rinehart, 1936. Edited with an Introduction by Moses Abramovitz and Eli Ginzberg.

The Illusion of Economic Stability, New York: Harper and Row, 1939.

Report to American Jews: On Overseas Relief, Palestine and Refugees in the US. New York: Harper and Brothers Publishers, 1942.

Grass on the Slag Heaps: The Story of the Welsh Miners. New York: Harper and Brothers Publishers, 1942. Reprinted with a new introduction by the author as *A World Without Work: The Story of the Welsh Miners.* New Brunswick, NJ: Transaction Publishers, 1991

Work Load Studies for Personnel Strength Control. Army Service Forces, 1943.

With Ethel L. Ginsburg, Dorothy L. Lynn, L. Mildred Vickers, and Sol W. Ginsburg, M.D. *The Unemployed I. Interpretation II. Case Studies.* New York: Harper and Brothers Publishers, 1943.

Assisted by Joseph Carwell. *The Labor Leader: An Exploratory Study*, New York: Macmillan Company, 1948.

.Agenda for American Jews. New York: Kings Crown Press, Columbia University, 1950.

With Sol W. Ginsburg, M.D., Sidney Axelrad, and John L. Herma. *Occupational Choice: An Approach to a General Theory.* New York: Columbia University Press, 1951.

With Douglas W. Bray. *The Uneducated.* New York: Columbia University Press, 1953.

With Sol W. Ginsburg, M.D., and John L. Herma. *Psychiatry and Military Manpower Policy—A Reappraisal of the Experience of World War II.* New York: Kings Crown Press, Columbia, 1953.

Eli Ginzberg, chairman. *What Makes an Executive? Report of a Round Table on Executive Potential and Performance.* New York: Columbia University Press, 1955.

With the assistance of James K. Anderson, Douglas W. Bray, and Robert W. Smuts. *The Negro Potential.* New York: Columbia University Press, 1956.

Eli Ginzberg and Ewing W. Reilley, assisted by Douglas W. Bray and John L. Herma. *Effecting Change in Large Organizations.* New York: Columbia University Press, 1957.

Human Resources: The Wealth of a Nation. New York: Simon and Schuster Publishers, 1958.

With James K. Anderson, Sol W. Ginsburg, M.D., and John L. Herma. *The Ineffective Soldier: Lessons for Management and the Nation*, Vol. 1. *The Lost Divisions.* New York: Columbia University Press, 1959.

With John B. Miner, James K. Anderson, Sol W. Ginsburg, M.D., and John L. Herma. *The Ineffective Soldier: Lessons for Management and the Nation*, Vol. II. *Breakdown and Recovery.* New York: Columbia University Press, 1959.

With James K. Anderson, Sol W. Ginsburg, M.D., John L. Herma, Douglas W. Bray, William Jordan, and Major Francis J. Ryan. *The Ineffective Soldier: Lessons for Management and the Nation*, Vol. III. *Patterns of Performance.* New York: Columbia University Press, 1959.

Editor. *The Nation's Children, Vol. I. The Family and Social Change; Vol. II. Development and Education; Vol. III. Problems and Prospects.* New York: Columbia University Press, 1960.

Editor, with Foreword by John W. Gardner. *Values and Ideals of American Youth.* New York: Columbia University Press, 1961.

With James K. Anderson, and John L. Herma. *The Optimistic Tradition and American Youth.* New York: Columbia University Press, 1962.

With Hyman Berman. *The American Worker in the Twentieth Century: A History Through Autobiographies*. New York: Free Press, 1963.

With Ivar E. Berg, with John L. Herma and James K. Anderson. *Democratic Values and the Rights of Management*. New York: Columbia University Press, 1963.

With Alfred S. Eichner. *The Troublesome Presence: American Democracy and the Negro*. New York: Free Press, 1964.

Editor. *The Negro Challenge to the Business Community*, New York: McGraw-Hill Book Company, 1964.

With John L. Herma, Ivar E. Berg, Carol A. Brown, Alice M. Yohalem, James K. Anderson, and Lois Lipper. *Talent and Performance*. New York: Columbia University Press, 1964.

Editor. *Technology and Social Change*. New York: Columbia University Press, 1964.

With Dale L. Hiestand and Beatrice G. Reubens. *The Pluralistic Economy*. New York: McGraw-Hill Book Company, 1965.

With Ivar E. Berg, Carol A. Brown, John L. Herma, Alice M. Yohalem, and Sherry Gorelick. *Life Styles of Educated Women*. New York: Columbia University Press, 1966.

With Alice Yohalem. *Educated American Women: Self Portraits*. New York: Columbia University Press, 1966.

The Development of Human Resources. New York: McGraw-Hill Book Company, 1966.

Keeper of the Law: Louis Ginzberg. Philadelphia: Jewish Publication Society, 1966.

With Herbert A. Smith. *Manpower Strategy for Developing Countries: Lessons from Ethiopia*. New York: Columbia University Press, 1967.

With Vincent Bryan, Grace T. Hamilton, John L. Herma, and Alice Yohalem. *The Middle-Class Negro in the White Man's World*. New York: Columbia University Press, 1967.

With the Conservation of Human Resources Staff. *Manpower Strategy for the Metropolis*. New York: Columbia University Press, 1968.

Manpower Agenda for America. New York: McGraw-Hill Book Company, 1968.

Editor. *Business Leadership and the Negro Crisis*. New York: McGraw-Hill Book Company, 1968.

Career Guidance: Who Needs It, Who Provides It, Who Can Improve It. New York: McGraw-Hill Book Company, 1971.

Manpower for Development: Perspectives on Five Continents. New York: Praeger Publishers, 1971.

Reports: Manpower in Israel. Department of State, Washington, D.C., and Government of Israel, Jerusalem, Israel, 1953, 1956, 1961, 1964, 1967, 1971.

The Job Crisis for Black Youth. The Twentieth Century Task Force on Employment Problems of Black Youth (Eli Ginzberg, chairman). New York: Praeger Publishers, 1971.

With the Conservation of Human Resources Staff. *New York Is Very Much Alive: A Manpower View*. New York: McGraw-Hill Book Company, 1973.

With Alice Yohalem, eds. *Corporate Lib: Women's Challenge to Management*. Baltimore: Johns Hopkins Press, 1973.

Editor. *The Future of the Metropolis: People, Jobs, Income*. Salt Lake City: Olympus Publishing Company, 1974.

With Robert M. Solow, eds. *The Great Society: Lessons for the Future*. New York: Basic Books, 1974.

The Manpower Connection: Education and Work. Cambridge, MA: Harvard University Press, 1975.

With Jerome Schnee, James W. Kuhn, and Boris Yavitz. *The Economic Impact of Large Public Programs: The NASA Story*. Salt Lake City: Olympus Publishing Company, 1976.

Editor. *Jobs for Americans*. Englewood Cliffs, NJ: Prentice Hall, 1976.

The Human Economy. New York: McGraw-Hill Book Company, 1976.

The House of Adam Smith Revisited. Philadelphia: Temple University, School of Business Administration, 1977.

The Corporate Headquarters Complex in New York City. In cooperation with an Advisory Committee of Corporate Headquarters Executives and Professionals. New York: Conservation of Human Resources, Columbia University, 1977.

The Economic Impact of the Japanese Business Community in New York. New York: Japan Society, Inc., 1978.

Good Jobs, Bad Jobs, No Jobs. Cambridge, MA: Harvard University Press, 1979.

American Jews: The Building of a Voluntary Community (in Hebrew). Tel Aviv: Schocken, 1979.

Editor. *Employing the Unemployed*. New York: Basic Books, 1980.

The School/Work Nexus: Transition of Youth from School to Work. Bloomington, IN: Phi Delta Kappa Educational Foundation, 1980.

With George Vojta. *Beyond Human Scale: The Large Corporation at Risk*. New York: Basic Books, 1985.

Understanding Human Resources: Perspectives, People and Policy. Lanham, New York, and London: ABT Books, University Press of America, 1985 (under the sponsorship of Clark Abt).

With Thierry J. Noyelle, and Thomas M. Stanback, Jr. *Technology and Employment: Concepts and Clarifications*. Boulder, CO: Westview Press, 1986.

The Skeptical Economist. Boulder, CO: Westview Press, 1987.

With Howard S. Berliner, and Miriam Ostow. *Young People at Risk: Is Prevention Possible?* Boulder, CO: Westview Press, 1988.

With Terry Williams, and Anna Dutka. *Does Job Training Work? The Clients Speak Out.* Boulder, CO: Westview Press, 1989.

My Brother's Keeper. New Brunswick, NJ: Transaction Publishers, 1989.

Editor, with an introduction. *Science and Academic Life in Transition: Emanuel Piore.* New Brunswick, NJ: Transaction Publishers, 1990.

The Eye of Illusion. New Brunswick, NJ: Transaction Publishers, 1993.

Editor. *The Changing U.S. Labor Market*. Boulder, CO: Westview Press, 1994.

Editor. *Executive Talent: Developing and Keeping the Best People*. John Wiley and Sons, 1988. With a new introduction by the Editor. New Brunswick, NJ: Transaction Publishers, 1995.

New Deal Days: 1933-1934. New Brunswick, NJ: Transaction Publishers, 1997.

With a new preface, introduction and afterword. *The Backward Art of Spending Money*, by Wesley Clair Mitchell. New Brunswick, NJ: Transaction Publishers, 1999.

Addendum

In the period 1952-1959, I also served as director of research and director of staff studies and contributed to the first seven publications of the National Manpower Council, all published by the Columbia University Press, New York.

Student Deferment and National Manpower Policy, 1952.
A Policy for Scientific and Professional Manpower, 1953.

Proceedings of a Conference on the Utilization of Scientific and Professional Manpower, 1954.

A Policy for Skilled Manpower, 1954.

Improving the Work Skills of the Nation, 1955.

Womanpower, 1957.

Work in the Lives of Married Women, 1958.

Part II: Health Policy

The Committee on the Function of Nursing. Eli Ginzberg, chairman. *A Program for the Nursing Profession*. New York: Macmillan Company, 1948.

A Pattern for Hospital Care. New York: Columbia University Press, 1949.

With Peter Rogatz, M.D. *Planning for Better Hospital Care*. New York: Kings Crown Press, Columbia University, 1961.

With Miriam Ostow. *Men, Money, and Medicine*. New York: Columbia University Press, 1969.

With the Conservation of Human Resources Staff. *Urban Health Services: The Case of New York*. New York: Columbia University Press, 1971.

With Alice Yohalem, eds. *The University Medical Center and the Metropolis*. New York: Josiah Macy, Jr. Foundation, 1974.

The Limits of Health Reform. New York: Basic Books, 1977.

Editor. *Regionalization and Health Policy*. Washington, D.C.: U.S. Government Printing Office, 1977.

Health, Manpower and Health Policy. Montclair, NJ: Allanheld Osmun, 1978.

With Warren Balinsky and Miriam Ostow. *Home Health Care: Its Role in the Changing Health Services Market*. Totowa, NJ: Allanheld Osmun, 1984.

With Miriam Ostow, eds. *The Coming Physician Surplus: In Search of a Public Policy*. Totowa, NJ: Allanheld Osmun, 1984.

American Medicine: The Power Shift. Totowa, NJ: Rowman and Allanheld, 1985.

Editor. *The U.S. Health Care System: A Look to the 1990s*. Totowa, NJ: Rowman and Allanheld, 1985.

With Edith M. Davis and Miriam Ostow. *Local Health Policy in Action: The Municipal Health Services Program*. Totowa, NJ: Rowman and Allanheld, 1986.

With the Conservation of Human Resources Staff. *From Health Dollars to Health Services: New York City, 1965-1985*. Totowa, NJ: Rowman and Allanheld, 1986.

Editor. *From Physician Shortage to Patient Shortage*. Boulder, CO: Westview Press, 1986.

Editor. *Medicine and Society: Clinical Decisions and Societal Values*. Boulder, CO: Westview Press, 1987.

With David E. Rogers, eds. *The AIDS Patient: An Action Agenda*. Boulder, CO: Westview Press, 1988.

With David E. Rogers, eds. *Public and Professional Attitudes Towards AIDS Patients*. Boulder, CO: Westview Press, 1989.

With Anna B. Dutka. *The Financing of Biomedical Research*. Baltimore, MD: The Johns Hopkins University Press, 1989.

With David E. Rogers, eds. *Improving the Life Chances of Children at Risk*. Boulder, CO: Westview Press, 1990.

The Medical Triangle: Physicians, Politicians and the Public. Cambridge, MA: Harvard University Press, 1990.

Editor. *Health Services Research: Key to Health Policy*. Cambridge, MA: Harvard University Press, 1991.

With David E. Rogers, eds. *Adolescents at Risk: Medical and Social Perspectives*. Boulder, CO: Westview Press, 1992.

With Howard S. Berliner, Miriam Ostow, and others. *Changing U.S. Health Care: A Study of Four Metropolitan Areas*. Boulder, CO: Westview Press, 1993.

With Miriam Ostow and Anna B. Dutka. *The Economics of Medical Education*. New York: Josiah Macy, Jr. Foundation, 1993.

With David E. Rogers, eds. *Medical Care and the Health of the Poor. Boulder*, CO: Westview Press, 1993.

Editor. *Critical Issues in U.S. Health Reform*. Boulder, CO: Westview Press, 1994.

Medical Gridlock and Health Reform. Boulder, CO: Westview Press, 1994.

With Miriam Ostow. *The Road to Reform: The Future of Health Care in America*. New York: The Free Press, 1994.

With David E. Rogers, eds. *The Metropolitan Academic Medical Center*. Boulder, CO: Westview Press, 1995.

Chair. Proceedings of a Conference. *The Financing of Medical Schools in an Era of Health Care Reform*. New York: Josiah Macy, Jr. Foundation, 1995.

Editor. *Urban Medical Centers: Balancing Academia and Patient Care Function*. Boulder, CO: Westview Press, 1996.

Tomorrow's Hospital: A Look to the Twenty First Century. New Haven, CT: Yale University Press, 1996.

With Howard Berliner and Miriam Ostow. *Improving Health Care of the Poor: The New York City Experience*. New Brunswick, NJ: Transaction Publishers, 1997.

With Associates. *Teaching Hospitals and the Urban Poor*. New Haven, CT: Yale University Press, 2000.

With Associates. *The Health Marketplace: New York City 1990-2010*. New Brunswick, NJ: Transaction Publishers, 2000.

With Panos Minogiannis. *U.S. Health Care and the Supply of Physicians* (forthcoming 2001).

Health Policy Articles

For over half a century I have been concerned with problems of health policy, and have often published articles in the following journals:

Journal of the American Medical Association
New England Journal of Medicine
Health Affairs
Inquiry
Bulletin of the New York Academy of Medicine and related publications
The Modern Hospital
Hospitals
The Journal of Medical Practice Management
Milbank Memorial Fund Quarterly
Health Management Quarterly (The Baxter Foundation)
Academic Medicine

The following are illustrations of these efforts:

"Army Hospitalization." In *Bulletin of the U.S. Army Medical Department,* January 1948, Government Printing Office, pp. 38ff.
"The Nature and Interrelationships of the Private and Public Sectors in Health Services." The 1983 Michael M. Davis Lecture, Graduate School of Business, University of Chicago.
"American Medicine: The Power Shift." The Master Memorial Lecture. *Bulletin,* American College of Surgeons 70 (4), April 1985.
"A Century of Health Reform," *Society,* November-December 1992, p. 19ff.

I am listing below in reverse chronological order my fourteen contributions to the *New England Journal of Medicine* starting in 1966; and eighteen citations from the *Journal of the American Medical Association* (JAMA) dating from 1983.

New England Journal of Medicine

"The uncertain future of managed care" [see comments]. 340 (2): 144-6, Jan 14, 1999.
With Miriam Ostow. "Managed care—a look back and a look ahead" [see comments]. 336 (14): 1018-20, April 3, 1997.
"Health care reform—where are we and where should we be going?" [see comments]. 327 (18): 1310-2, Oct. 29, 1992.
"Health care reform—why so slow?" 322 (20): 1464-6, May 17, 1990.
"For-profit medicine. A reassessment" [published erratum appears in N Engl J Med 1989 Jan. 19 320 (3): 188]. 319 (12): 757-61, Sept. 22, 1988.
"A hard look at cost containment." 316 (18): 1151-4, April 30, 1987.
"The destabilization of health care." 315 (12): 757-61, Sept. 18, 1986.
"The monetarization of medical care." 310 (18): 1162-5, May 3, 1984.
"Sounding Boards. Cost containment—imaginary and real." 308 (20): 1220-4, May 19, 1983.
"The competitive solution: two views. Competition and Cost containment." 303 (19): 1112-5, Nov. 6, 1980.
"The National Academy of Sciences Report on the VA: how not to offer Congress advice on health policy." 298 (11): 623-5, March 16, 1978.
"Paradoxes and trends: an economist looks at health care." 296 (14): 814-6, Apr. 7, 1977.
Sounding Board. "Notes on evaluating the quality of medical care." 292 (7): 366-8, Feb. 13, 1975.
"Physician shortage reconsidered." 275 (2): 85-7, July 14, 1966.

JAMA

"Ten encounters with the US health sector, 1930-1999." 282 (17): 1665-9. Nov 3, 1999.
"US health system reform in the early 21st century." 280 (17): 1539, Nov. 4, 1998.
"The changing US health care agenda" [see comments]. 279 (7): 501-4, Feb. 18, 1998.
"Managed care and the competitive market in health care. What they can and cannot do" [comment]. 277 (22): 1812-3, June 11, 1997.
"The health care market. Theory and reality" [see comments]. 276 (10): 777-8, Sept. 11, 1996.

"A cautionary note on market reforms in health care" [see comments]. 274 (20): 1633-4, Nov. 22-29, 1995.
"Improving health care for the poor. Lessons from the 1980s" [see comments]. 271 (6): 464-7, Feb. 9, 1994.
"Physician supply policies and health reform" [see comments]. 268 (21): 3115-8, Dec. 2, 1992.
With Miriam Ostow. "Beyond universal health insurance to effective health care." 265 (19): 2559-62, 1991.
"Access to health care for Hispanics" [see comments]. 265 (2): 238-41, Jan. 9, 1991.
""High-tech medicine and rising health care costs" [see comments]. 263 (13): 1820-2, Apr. 4, 1990.
"US health policy—expectations and realities." 260 (24): 3647-50, Dec. 23-30, 1988.
"Medical care for the poor: no magic bullets." 259 (22): 3309-11, June 10, 1988.
"Academic health centers—can they afford to relax?" 258 (14): 1936-7, Oct. 9, 1987.
"Is cost containment for real? [editorial]. 256 (2): 254-5, July 11, 1986.
"What lies ahead for American physicians: one economist's views" [editorial]. 253 (19): 2878- 9, May 17, 1985.
"A new physician supply policy is needed." 250 (19): 2621-2, Nov. 18, 1983.
"The grand illusion of competition in health care." 249 (14): 1857-9, April 8, 1983.

Part III: Selected Reports to the U.S. Government, other Organizations, and Human Resources Journals

In the latter 1930s I wrote frequent book reviews for the *Saturday Review of Literature*, and focused on publications by British and American social scientists, including John Strachey, Thorstein Veblen, Frank H. Knight, and others.

Between the late 1930s and early 1950s, I was a frequent contributor to the annual symposia of the Conference on Science, Philosophy, and Religion in their Relation to the Democratic Way of Life, edited by Lyman Bryson, Louis Finkelstein, and R.M. MacIver, distributed by Harper and Brothers, New York and London.

Between 1962 and 1981 I was the chair of the National Commission of Employment Policy, which reported to the President and the Congress. The following three reports list most of the publications prepared under the auspices of the three governmental agencies I chaired between those years.

Manpower Advice for Government. National Manpower Advisory Committee Letters, 1962-1971. U.S. Department of Labor, Manpower Administration (1972).
National Commission for Manpower Policy. The First Five Years 1974-1979. A Report by Eli Ginzberg, Chair.
National Commission for Employment Policy. The Sixth Annual Report to the President and the Congress, December 1980.

In the years between 1950 and 1963 I testified, according to Congressional Hearing volumes in my library, seven times before the following Committees:

Committee on Expenditures in the Executive Departments—House of Representatives, June 14, 1950, pp. 107ff; also pp. 211-213 letter dated June 24, 1950 addressed to Hon. William Dawson, Chair of Committee.
Joint Economic Committee, November 18-23, 1957, on "Federal Expenditure Policy for Economic Growth and Stability," p. 539ff.
Committee on Labor and Public Welfare, U.S. Senate, June 16, 17, and 18, 1959 on "The Aged and the Aging in the United States," p. 211ff.
Joint Economic Committee, Sept. 28 to Oct. 2, 1959, "Employment, Growth, and Price Trends," p. 2661ff.
Committee on Labor and Public Welare, U.S. Senate on Manpower Problems of the Sixties, June 14 and 15, 1960, pp. 94-107.
Committee on Education and Labor, House of Representatives, hearings of Subcommittee on Labor, "Hours of Work," June 11, 1961, pp. 217-232.
Committee on Labor and Public Welfare, U.S. Senate, May 20, 1963, pp. 257-272.

Governmental and Other

"The Economics of British Neutrality During the American Civil War." Agricultural History 10 (4), October 1936.
Report to James F. Byrnes, Secretary of State, Washington, DC, from Eli Ginzberg, U.S. Representative to Five-Power Conference on Repatriation for Non-Repatriable Victims of German action, Part I, Accomplishments of the Conference, 1946.
"Symposium on Psychological Test Screening for the Armed Forces." March 6-7, 1952, Department of Defense, Research and Development Board.
"Criteria for a Military Manpower Policy," pp. 49-68 in America's Manpower Crisis, edited by Robert H. Walker, Public Administration Service, Chicago, Ill., 1952.
"The Skilled Work Force of the United States." U.S. Department of Labor. USGPO, 1955.
With James K. Anderson. *Manpower for Government: A Decade's Forecast*. Chicago: Public Personnel Association, 1958.
Nation's Manpower Revolution. Hearings before the Subcommittee on Employment and Manpower of the Committee on Labor and Public Welfare. United States Senate. 88th Congress. First Session. November-December 1963.
"Report of Field Trip to Puerto Rico, Virgin islands, and Dade County, Florida, January 23 to Februray 5, 1964." Memorandum for the Manpower Administrator, U.S. Department of Labor, Washington, DC. February 13, 1964. From Eli Ginzberg, Chairman, Naitonal Manpower Advisory Committee.
With Dale L. Hiestand, and Samuel B. Richmond. *Manpower for Aviation: Final Report to the Aviation Human Resources Study Board*. Federal Aviation Agency. New York: Conservation of Human Resources, Columbia University, 1964.
"Jobs, Dropouts and Automation." Consultant paper for White House Conference on Education, Committee on Labor and Public Welfare, U.S. Senate, August 1965, pp. 18-24.
With Ivar E. Berg, Marcia K. Freedman, and John L. Herma. *The Social Order and Delinquency. The Report of the President's Commission on Crime in the District of Columbia*, Appendix Volume, 1966.
With Carol A. Brown. *Manpower for Library Services*. New York: Conservation of Human Resources, Columbia University, 1967.

"The Social and Economic Outlook," *Manpower for the Medical Laboratory*, Proceedings of a Conference of Government and the Professions in Washington, D.C., Oct. 11-13, 1967, U.S. Dept. of Health, Education and Welfare, Public Health Service Publication No. 1833. USGPO.

Perspectives and Policies on Employment Problems of Youth and Juvenile Delinquency. Task Force on Individual Acts of Violence, National Commission on the Causes and Prevention of Violence, Washington, D.C. New York: Conservation of Human Resources, Columbia University, 1968.

"Professional Manpower for an Affluent Society: The Opportunity Gap," *Report of a Conference on Meeting Medical Manpower Needs: The Fuller Utilization of the Woman Physician*, sponsored by American Medical Women's Association, the President's Study Group on Careers for Women, Women's Bureau, U.S. Department of Labor, Washington, D.C., January 12-13, 1968, pp. 3-8.

National Commission on Health Science and Society. Hearings before the Subcommittee on Government Research of the Committee on Government Operations. United States Senate. 90th Congress. Second Session on SJ Res. 145. March-April 1968.

With Dale L. Hiestand, "Mobility in the Negro Community: Guidelines for Research on Social and Economic Progress," U.S. Commission on Civil Rights, Clearinghouse Publication No. 11, June 1968, Government Printing Office.

"An American Economist in Eastern Europe." *International Educational and Cultural Exchange*. A Publication of the U.S. Advisory Commission on International Educational and Cultural Affairs, Vol. IV, No. 1, Summer 1968.

People and Progress in East Asia. New York: Columbia University, 1968.

One-Fifth of the World: Manpower Reports on Iran and South Asia. New York: Conservation of Human Resources, Columbia University, 1969.

"Black Power and Student Unrest: Reflections on Columbia University and Harlem." *The George Washington Law Review* 37 (4), May 1969.

"Patterns of Career Development, Part I." *The Journal of Navy Civilian Manpower Management* Vol. II, No. 4, Winter 1968; Part II, Spring 1969.

"America's People Resources," in *Perspectives in Defense Management*, International College of the Armed Forces, March 1970, pp. 1-9.

"Swedish Manpower Policies: A Look at the Leader," in *Manpower*, official monthly journal of the Manpower Administration, U.S. Department of Labor. Vol. 2, No. 11, November 1970.

"Professional Manpower for State Government," for *A Planning Workshop on Executive Development—"Improving State Management for the Seventies."* Saratoga, New York, December 1970. Sponsored by New York State Institute for Governmental Executives.

Manpower Research and Management in Large Organizations: A Report of the Task Force on Manpower Research. Defense Science Board (Eli Ginzberg, chairman). U.S. Department of Defense, 1971.

Perspectives on Indian Manpower, Employment and Income. Ford Foundation, New Delhi, and Conservation of Human Resources, Columbia University, 1971.

With James W. Kuhn and Beatrice G. Reubens, *Private and Public Manpower Policies to Stimulate Productivity*. Prepared for the U.S. National Commission on Productivity, 1971.

"The Role of Human Resources and Manpower in Ford Foundation Programming in India." *End of Tour Report*. Delhi, February 10, 1971.

"New York Does Have a Future." Salomon Brothers, May 26, 1971.

"Perspectives on Manpower and Education in the South," pp. 7-15 in *Higher Education for the Future: Reform or More of the Same*. Proceedings of 20th SREB Legislative Work Conference, July 1971.

Reform of Federally Funded Manpower Training Programs. Background Material. Prepared by the Majority Staff Subcommittee on Employment, Manpower, and Poverty of the Committee on Labor and Public Welfare. United States Senate. December 1971.

The Employment and Manpower Act of 1972. Hearings before the Select Subcommittee on Labor of the Committee on Education and Labor. House of Representatives. 92nd Congress. First Session on HR 6181, HR 11167, HR 11688, HR 12845. October 27, 1971-March 2, 1972.

With Charles Brecher. "New York's Future: A Manpower View." *City Almanac*, October 1972.

The Emergency Jobs Act of 1974. Hearings before the Select Subcommittee on Labor of the Committee on Education and Labor. House of Representatives. 93rd Congress. Second Session on HR 16596. October 1974.

Authorization of Appropriations for Fiscal Year 1976 for Carrying Out Title VI of the Comprehensive Employment and Training Act of 1973. Hearings before the Subcommittee on Manpower, Compensation, and Health and Safety of the Committee on Education and Labor. House of Representatives. 94th Congress. First Session on HR 2584. February-June 1975.

An Economic Development Agenda for New York City. New York: Conservation of Human   Resources, Columbia University, 1975.

"Eli Ginzberg: Pioneer in Work Force Research," Gloria Stevenson. *Worklife*, U.S. Department of Labor, Employment and Training Administration, Vol. 1 No. 5, May 1976.

Keynote Address. *Report of National Conference on Health Manpower Distribution.* National Health Council. "Incentives to Distribute Health Personnel to Underserved Areas." June 1976.

"Toward a Concept of Full Employment." Proceedings of 40th Annual Meeting, Interstate Conference of Employment Security Agencies, Miami, Florida, September 20-22, 1976.

Interview in *Challenge*, "Manpower and Economic Policy," September-October 1976, with   periodic other contributions during the past three decades.

"Women and the Work Force: A Candid Conversation with Eli Ginzberg" in *Adherent* 3 (3): 2- 16, Dec. 1976.

"Eli Ginzberg Looks at the Next 100 Years." *Worklife*. U.S. Department of Labor, Employment and Training Administration. Vol. 1 No. 12. December 1976.

"Apprenticeship and Manpower Policy" on "The Future of Apprenticeship." Report of the Symposium, Focus on Apprenticeship, sponsored by the Province of Ontario, Ministry of   Colleges and Universities. September 1977.

Conference Chairman. "Facilitating the Re-entry of Women to the Labor Force." Summary of Proceedings, Co-sponsored by the German Marshall Fund and the Assistant Secretary of Labor for Women's Employment, France, Assemblee Nationale, Paris, Nov. 28-30, 1979. "The Problem and Policy Perspectives," pp. 3-4 and "Summary and Conclusions," pp. 20-23.

Keynote Address, *Women in the Work Force: A Conference on the Economic and Social Impact of Working Women in the 1980s.* Sponsored by American Telephone and Telegraph and Ladies Home Journal, New York City, January 1980.

Tax Rules Governing Private Foundations. Hearings before the Subcommittee on Oversight of the Committee on Ways and Means. House of Representatives. 98th Congress. First Session. June 1983.

Direct Federal Job Creation: Key Issues. Committee on Education and Labor. U.S. House of   Representatives. 99th Congress. First Session, October 1985.

"Is More Money the Answer?" In Financing Mental Health Services and Research:Current Perspectives. *Proceedings of the Second Annual Rosalynn Carter Symposium on Mental Health Policy. Sponsored by Emory University School of Medicine Department of   Psychiatry, November 20, 1986, Washington, DC, National Academy of Sciences.*

"Scientific and Engineering Personnel: Lessons and Policy Directions." *Eli Ginzberg. For the Impact of Defense Spending on Nondefense Engineering Labor Markets: A Report to the National Academy of Engineering.* Panel on Engineering Labor Markets, Office of Scientific and Engineering Personnel, National Research Council. National Academy Press, 1986.

"Technology, Women, and Work: Policy Perspectives." *Computer Chips and Paper Clips: Technology and Women's Employment, Volume II, Case Studies and Policy Perspectives.* Panel on Technology and Women's Employment, National Research Council. National Academy Press, 1987.

In the 1970s and 1980s I was a frequent contributor on human resources and employment issues to *Scientific American.*

For Product Safety Concerns and Information please contact our EU
representative GPSR@taylorandfrancis.com Taylor & Francis Verlag GmbH,
Kaufingerstraße 24, 80331 München, Germany

Batch number: 08153776

Printed by Printforce, the Netherlands